A BIOGRAPHICAL SKETCH OF SARDAR MIR ABDUL ALI

A BIOGRAPHICAL SKETCH OF SARDAR MIR ABDUL ALI

KHAN BAHADUR HEAD OF THE DETECTIVE POLICE, BOMBAY WITH AN ACCOUNT OF INTERESTING CRIMINAL CASES

GYAN

Published by

Gyan Publishing House
5, Ansari Road
Daryaganj, New Delhi-110002
Phone: 011-47034999, 9811692060
E-mail: books@gyanbooks.com

Distribution Network
gyanbooks.com
India, USA, Canada, UK, Australia

ISBN: 978-93-7225-675-8 (PB)

First Published, 1896

2nd Impression 2026

Printed at: Gyan Press, Delhi.

A BIOGRAPHICAL SKETCH OF SARDAR MIR ABDUL ALI

A BIOGRAPHICAL SKETCH

OF

SARDAR MIR ABDUL ALI,

KHAN BAHADUR,

HEAD OF THE DETECTIVE POLICE, BOMBAY.

WITH AN ACCOUNT

OF

INTERESTING CRIMINAL CASES.

Bombay:

PRINTED AT THE

BOMBAY GAZETTE STEAM PRINTING WORKS.

1896.

PREFACE.

Among the many departments into which the administration of a country is divided in these days, there are few, if any, that occupy a position of more moment to the public well-being than that which is charged with the detection of crime. If the officers at the head of this department succeed in the task committed to them, a powerful motive for obedience to the law is created and maintained in the minds of men whose want of moral stamina would otherwise lead them to the commission of felonies and misdemeanours. On the other hand, if these officers repeatedly fail to trace offenders, criminal acts are multiplied in ever-growing volume, until the public confidence and sense of security is shaken. Crime undetected engenders further and more serious crime. Hence the detective officer, whose efforts are generally crowned with success, does an inestimable service, both of a negative and positive kind, to the city or district which is the scene of his labours.

When we consider the vast population of the city of Bombay, the ignorance and poverty of the greater proportion of its inhabitants, and the facility afforded by many of the habits and customs of the people for predatory acts, we cannot fail to be struck with the comparative freedom from serious crime we enjoy. For a city of between 800,000 and 900,000 inhabitants—some of them belonging to hereditary criminal classes—to only have eight or nine prisoners as a rule to be tried at each of the five Criminal Sessions of the High Court annually held, speaks volumes for the manner in which the department above referred to carries out its duties. Sardar Mir Abdul Ali has served under successive Police Commissioners as head of the department for many years, and there can be no doubt that it is to his personal skill, resourcefulness and intuitive perception, conjoined with great organising ability, that we may largely attribute the comparative freedom from serious crime—and indeed from minor crime also—of which Bombay can justly boast.

This being so, some of the friends of the worthy Sardar have felt that, despite the objections a man of his retiring and modest disposition might raise if his opinion was asked, the deeply fascinating details of his brilliant career should no longer remain unrecorded. It is at their request this book has been written. The great interest which the author has felt in the wonderful detective tales it has been his privilege to relate, will, he is confident, be shared more or less by every reader of these sober records of facts, which will seem to them stranger than fiction. He trusts that their interest therein will lead them to overlook the defects in the record of which he is fully conscious, and he will be amply repaid for his labour if the perusal of the book leads the reader to a deeper sense than he may yet have had of the inestimable value of the services of the Sardar to the City in which he has laboured for so many years.

INTRODUCTION.

It is always most difficult, nay, sometimes impossible, to delineate the character of a personal friend in his life-time. The author, being keenly sensible to this difficulty in the present instance, has approached the task of describing the career of the Sardar Mir Abdul Ali with no light heart, and he has only touched on those things that he has felt at liberty to refer to. No apology is needed for publishing the highly interesting biographical sketch of a detective, so long as it is a record of absolute facts, since it gives an incentive and encouragement to other officers to better understand and more faithfully perform their duty. The Sardar, in his capacity as a detective, has to play a diplomatic part; but there is not a single instance in which professional effort has led him to set aside his conscience. It is truly said that "men's lives are not to be judged by the outward show and the visible suggestion, but rather by the inward sentiments and promptings which accept conscience at once as the inspirer of action and arbiter of fate."

The Sardar's genius for following clues, his instinct for discerning guilt, his patient power of subtle analysis, his pureness of motive, and, above all, the entire absence of selfish aims have raised him to the highest post to which a native can aspire in the Police Force of *urbs prima in Indis.* Even in this prosaic age of non-hero worship, the bar of public opinion has pronounced again and again in his favour. His endeavours have invariably resulted in the triumph of justice, to the confusion of law-breakers. More than that, his actions have saved many lives to the great mortification of would-be murderers. Though the courage and devotion of a Police officer is often little recognised at the hands of the public, the Sardar may have his reward in the recollection that his actions have generally benefited each and all of the diversified communities of Bombay. In France and elsewhere, the actions of detectives find a commemoration in the publication of their memoirs. But in India the practice had not hitherto been adopted chiefly because the public were slow to appreciate such things. But now the times are changing, and the growing appreciation of the efforts of the Police on the part of the public will, in the writer's belief, ensure a favourable reception to this book.

As Mr. R. V. Hearn, the late Government Solicitor and Public Prosecutor, testified, the Sardar is a most valuable officer, never exceeding or neglecting his duty. The Sardar has been engaged in a large number of prosecutions, including almost all the important cases of forgery or murder, and he is never known to give the prosecution a fall by any omission or want of tact or temper in the witness-box. Nor is he ever censured by the Court for displaying any animus against a prisoner ; but, on the contrary, he has often been complimented on his fair and impartial attitude towards a man standing his trial. Mr. Henry Cleveland, who was Government Solicitor and Public Prosecutor for nearly eighteen years, was a great admirer of the Sardar's character, and before he retired in April 1884, said that he had so high an opinion of the Sardar and the useful influence which he possessed and exercised over the criminal class that, if he were to leave the Police Force, his loss would be a great one to Bombay. Mr. F. A. Little, the present Government Solicitor and Public Prosecutor, also fully concurred with Mr. Hearn and Mr. Cleveland in the very high opinion they formed of the Sardar, and readily testified that he knew of no officer of Police upon whom he can place more reliance, and from whom he would rather receive instructions, than the Sardar, the record of whose eventful career in life will not fail to make others keenly sensitive to their duty, if they have an ambition to rise in the Service.

Chapter I.

EARLY FAMILY HISTORY AND PARENTAGE.

SARDAR MIR ABDUL ALI, Khan Bahadur, the subject of these memoirs, is a striking example of the law of hereditary predilections and capacities. He is the eldest son of the eminent Bombay Detective Khan Bahadur Mir Akbar Ali, who served Government with conspicuous ability, zeal, and fidelity for more than half a century. The past history of Khan Bahadur Mir Akbar Ali reads more like a romance than a real tale. He achieved great distinction: indeed it is no exaggeration to say that as a detective officer his fame was world-wide. He was a born detective, and if a tithe of the instances of his professional skill were recounted, the story would fill several volumes. It will, therefore, be desirable before saying anything regarding Sardar Mir Abdul Ali to briefly recount the meritorious services of his father, both to the State and the public at large, during a period extending over fifty-two years. Mir Akbar Ali belonged to an ancient and illustrious house of Syads, who were obliged to seek refuge in India against the persecutions of the Abbasaide Caliphs of Bagdad. The time of the flight of the forefathers of Mir Akbar Ali was several centuries back. The animosity that existed between the descendants of Ali and the intolerant and ever-jealous Caliphs of Bagdad is a matter of common knowledge to every student of

Arabian history. In consequence of these terrible persecutions, the founder of the family, Syad Muhammad Jafari-ul-Huseni-ul-Madani, came to India from Arabia and settled here. Various records show he was a man distinguished for his learning even in those days, and was looked upon by his contemporaries as an exceedingly pious and holy man of benevolent nature. By his arrival in India he not only gained the personal safety denied him in Arabia, but was also the recipient of great honours from the Mahomedan ruler who then held sway in India. He was granted an Inam for the maintenance of the dignity of the family, and Sardar Abdul Ali, the subject of this biographical sketch, is the present recognised holder of that Inam in the village of Manchar, in the Khed Taluka of the Poona District. Sardar Mir Abdul Ali is the thirty-sixth descendant, from Hazrat Ali, the son-in-law of the Prophet of Islam.

Mir Akbar Ali, the only ancestor to whose record detailed reference need be made in this biography, was born in the village of Manchar. When he was only a child he had the misfortune to lose his father. At an early age he began to show the traits which led on to his future greatness. His shrewdness in many respects was marked, and his mother took great care to give him a good moral training. He learnt Marathi and Hindustani, and when he was still attending the school his mother, to whom he was indebted for his early training, died, leaving Mir Akbar Ali an orphan. By his marriage he was connected with another branch of the eminent Syads of Narayengaon, about eight miles from Manchar. An Inam was granted to the ancestors of his wife also by the Mahomedan Emperor. As Mir Akbar Ali's family was very large, the income from the Inam village was found to be inadequate for their maintenance, since it was shared by a number of members of the family. Mir Akbar Ali came to Bombay with a view to find some employment. As his elder brother was not in a position to support him, he had to fall back on his own resources and natural genius. He was a man of intrepid spirit, and preferred a life of activity. He made his choice of a career by joining the Bombay Police Force, on the 1st of September 1831. He soon distinguished himself, as a superior policeman, under Captain (afterwards General) Shortt, the then Head of the Police. At that time the Police Force was very meagre. Most of the sepoys were illiterate persons; hence his knowledge of Marathi and Hindustani stood Mir Akbar Ali in good stead.

After he had joined the Force, he was not long in showing that he knew his work well, and that he possessed special qualities to fit him for his duties. Among the chief qualifications of a detective possessed by him may be mentioned the power of observation, knowledge of the people and the locality, promptitude of action, a keen foresight into the workings of the human mind, a gift of good reasoning powers, great judgment, remarkable courage, and exceptional acuteness. In the short space of two years, he was acquainted with every nook and corner of Bombay and its criminals. Not only did he know the Vernacular languages, but he was well acquainted with native customs, feelings, &c. He was very clever at disguises, and could simulate any character. In the year 1840 he was sent to Aden, which had just then come into the British possession, to organise the Police Force there. After discharging this duty and putting matters on a satisfactory basis he returned to Bombay about the end of 1843. In the year 1844 he took a very active part in unravelling the great frauds perpetrated by that notorious Allu Paru, who was convicted of wilfully destroying the ship Belvedere. He served in the Police Force with great credit to himself and his superior officers, until the 28th of August 1846, when he left the force owing to some disagreement with Captain Curties, the then Superintendent of the Police. On the 14th of December 1847, however, he rejoined the Bombay Police, and served in different grades for an uninterrupted period of upwards of thirty-five years. In the year 1852 he was promoted to the rank of a Jamadar, and four years later he became a Subedar. During the dark and gloomy days of the Mutiny he rendered very valuable services to Government, for which he was specially mentioned in eulogistic terms by Mr. Forjett, the then Deputy Commissioner.

The Mutiny is such a landmark in Indian history, that it will not be out of place to describe the state of affairs then prevailing in Bombay. In the autumn of 1857 (a little previous to the Moharram), it was discovered that the house of one Ganga Parsad, a priest and physician at Sonapore, was resorted to by sepoys of the Line. He was found to be the best tool of the sepoys who made his house their rendezvous, and confided in him all their secret plans, which were to murder and pillage every European they could find in Bombay, march to Poona, and proclaim Nana Saheb Peshwa of the Deccan. He became an agent of the Police, and gave valuable assistance to Mr. Forjett. According to his confession, a plot was made among the sepoys of the Marine Battalion and Native Infantry to murder every person they came across during the Moharram, but simply for the sake of monetary gain, the cowardly purpose was postponed to the Dewali festival, as on the night of *Dhunteras* the Hindus bring out all their money and jewels and wash them in milk before depositing them again in the safes. The anticipated heavy loot of the valuables led the sepoys to postpone their attack, and this enabled it to be nipped in the bud by the foresight and boldness of Mr. Forjett, with the assistance of Mr. Edgington (who afterwards rose to the office of the Deputy Commissioner), and the fidelity and vigilance of his men. There was a sudden exodus of Europeans from Malabar Hill and other places, and they found shelter in the ships in the harbour. According to Mr. James Douglas' 'Book of Bombay,' "The Marine Battalion was then where it is at present, and the sepoy lines to the north of the Bori Bunder station, and suspiciously near lay the Jumma Masjid or mosque of the Mussalmans, of which sect there were supposed to be 150,000 men in Bombay. The European force in the island consisted of 400 Infantry and 50 Mounted Police to quell any outbreak. It was intended that the rising should take place on the night of Moharram, but the vigilance of Mr. Forjett's fifty Mounted Police frustrated the design in spite of the fact that the military had broken up the small force at their disposal to guard the entrances to Malabar Hill and Mazagon." Mr. Forjett actually told the people that he was undeterred by the trammels of law, that he would shoot or cut down the first man who committed himself, or hang every guilty man before his own door; and to show that he was in earnest, he erected a gallows in the police yard.

After bringing round Ganga Parsad, Mr. Forjett, accompanied by Major Barrow and Mr. Edgington, proceeded to Ganga Parsad's house by arrangement. The Deputy Commissioner did this because he had reason to believe that unless an officer of the suspected regiments accompanied him, and verified what was to be seen and heard, his work would be almost worthless, there being a very strong conviction among the officers that their sepoys were thoroughly trustworthy. The three officers went one by one, and concealed themselves in the back-room. This was a most daring attempt to go in the midst of men plotting insurrection. Ganga Parsad was warned by Mr. Forjett that he would be put to instantaneous death in case he played them false by word or sign. A whisper, a heavy breathing, a gentle knock against the wall, or any false move would have been fatal to the whole business. Mr. Forjett and his two companions had during the trying moments to take the greatest care to see that they were not betrayed. When Major Barrow descried through a hole in the wall his own havildar plotting treason and murder with the sepoys, he was greatly astonished. The traitorous soldiers were arrested, tried by court-martial, and two of them were blown from the guns on the Esplanade. It is believed that "thirty of them deserved the same fate, but Lord Elphinstone, who acted with great courage and ability during the Mutiny, was a merciful man."

During the meeting Mir Akbar rendered most signal services to the State as well as the public which were appreciated both by his superiors and the Government.

In referring to the valuable services of Mir Akbar Ali during the Mutiny, Mr. Forjett in his report to Government said :—"I would at the same time beg to bring to the notice of Government the merits of another very deserving native officer, the more so, as it enables me to base upon it a suggestion which, if sanctioned by Government, will, I feel assured, be hailed by the whole police force with feelings of gratification. Subedar Mir Akbar Ali has now completed a period of more than twenty-nine years' service in the Bombay Police Force and has always been held in high estimation by his superiors, and all the time I have been in charge his conduct has been exemplary. During the recent troubles, he was of much assistance to me, and was my constant attendant during my visits in disguise to mosques, coffee houses and other places of Mahomedan rendezvous, and as a police detective he has rendered very valuable service." Mr. Forjett then said that every regiment of the line, though not exceeding 750 in strength, had its Subedar Major, and most regiments also their Sardar Bahadurs. And although the Bombay Police Force was more than 1,000 strong, it was without any such post of honour. He strongly urged the Government to create such a post with a salary of Rs. 75 in addition to an honorary allowance of Rs. 25 for the title of Sardar Bahadur. Mr. Forjett gave it as his opinion that it would be a boon as well as an encouragement to the whole force if such a post were created, and he recommended Subedar Mir Akbar Ali as the fittest and most deserving officer to fill it. The Governor-in-Council assured Mr. Forjett that the praises bestowed by him upon the police were well deserved. However, they regretted that it was not a time when any recommendation involving increased expenditure could be submitted to the Government of India.

Mr. Forjett thereupon sent another representation to the Government urging the claims and qualifications which entitled Mir Akbar Ali to advancement, stating that if the proposal was negatived, the beneficial results in increased zeal and devotion to duty, to which such an appointment was calculated to give rise in the police force, would be lost. The Government of Bombay this time forwarded Mr. Forjett's proposal to the Government of India, with a recommendation in favour of Mir Akbar Ali, who accordingly received the title of Subedar Major, and a personal allowance of Rs. 40 per mensem in addition to his salary, "in recognition of his distinguished services" during the eventful period of the outbreak in India. The Government of India were also pleased to sanction the payment of a sum of Rs. 200 to Subedar Mir Akbar Ali "as a mark of recognition by Government of his faithful services" during the crisis in 1857. The title of Subedar Major in the police corps was subsequently abolished, and that of Native Commandant substituted in its stead, as recommended in Sir G. R. Clerk's Police Minute, and the office was held by Mir Akbar Ali. On the 21st May 1861 the title of Khan Bahadur was conferred on Mir Akbar Ali by the Government of India in recognition of his meritorious services, on the recommendation of Mr. Forjett, who described the services of this deserving officer as "eminently useful and praiseworthy."

Khan Bahadur Akbar Ali frequently succeeded in detecting the perpetrators of the most serious crimes committed in Bombay, when other officers of ability had failed to do so, and his zeal was constantly commended both by his superiors and Government. After he had been granted the title of Khan Bahadur, he continued to serve with fidelity and unremitting zeal which never failed to earn for him the favours of his superiors. Mr. Forjett, who was sensible of the good services of Khan Bahadur Akbar Ali, considered that they had not been sufficiently rewarded, and he recommended the Government to confer upon the distinguished officer the title of Sardar Bahadur. But this proposal was not favourably entertained, the title being specially reserved for high military officers only. Upon the reorganisation of the police force in October 1865, Khan Bahadur Akbar Ali was made an Inspector on a salary of Rs. 150, but he lost his personal allowance as the post of the Native Commandant was abolished. In December 1865 Colonel Henderson recommended to Government that the personal allowance of Rs. 40 to Khan Bahadur Mir Akbar Ali be recontinued in view of his valuable services in numerous cases. He enumerated about fifty-five cases of most serious crime, the perpetrators of which were brought to justice by the exertions of the Khan Bahadur alone, when other detectives had been baffled in their endeavours to bring them to book. Colonel Henderson in submitting the proposal to Government for the re-continuance to Khan Bahadur Mir Akbar

Ali of the personal allowance of Rs. 40 during his life-time, expressed a very high opinion of his services in the following terms :—"As the services of this meritorious officer are well known to Government, it would be out of place on my part to enter on any lengthened panegyric here, further than mentioning that since assuming charge of the Bombay Police in May last *his conduct has been in every way exceptional and most satisfactory. In dexterity as a detective I have never in all my experience met his equal European or Native.*"

Owing to some ambiguity in the letter, Government understood that they were solicited to continue the personal allowance to the Khan Bahadur after retirement from service, and accordingly intimated to Colonel Henderson by a Resolution, dated 31st January 1866, that "Government have received with satisfaction his notice of the continued good services of the Inspector, and that when the time for his retirement arrives, Government will be prepared to consider his claims to consideration."

Successive Commissioners urged that the services of the Khan Bahadur were not adequately rewarded, while the Government records showed that less conspicuous services of several other officers in Bombay and the Mofussil were very liberally recompensed during the Mutiny,—some having received Inam land in perpetuity, some handsome pecuniary rewards, while others rose from insignificant posts of Karkoons to the posts of Fouzdar, or even Deputy Collectors.

They submitted that Mir Akbar Ali performed very delicate and responsible duties for more than two years during the Mutiny, and that throughout that period such preventative measures were devised and adopted that nothing very serious happened in Bombay. Besides these services, Sir Frank Souter, Kt., C. S. I., C. I. E., said that Mir Akbar Ali had claims upon Government for the detection of innumerable crimes. Most of them were so serious and important that the detection of each of them entitled Mir Akbar Ali to some kind of distinction and reward by Government. In the words of the Commissioner, "Since the Resolution of Government regarding his personal allowance, he meritoriously distinguished himself by detecting several other serious crimes, in some of which his services were acknowledged by Government." There was a case of forgery of currency notes for Rs. 1,000 each, and for the detection and conviction of the forgers a reward of Rs. 10,000 was proclaimed. Khan Bahadur Akbar Ali and his son Mir Abdul Ali by their skill and industry traced out the forgers, who were sentenced to a long term of imprisonment. He received Rs. 1,250 as his share in the reward. There was another case of forgery of currency notes of the Bombay Circle in which two forgers were skilfully tracked and arrested by Mir Akbar Ali at Surat. One of the forgers was a European, while the other was a very influential citizen of Surat. Both the forgers were convicted and sentenced, and the services of Mir Akbar Ali were warmly acknowledged by Government. There were two more cases of forgery of currency notes in which the utterers only were brought to justice. In 1879, Mr. Vincent was the means of breaking up a nest of clever forgers of currency notes at Ahmedabad. Khan Bahadur Mir Abkar Ali rendered very valuable assistance to Mr. Vincent, whose services were very warmly acknowledged by Government. Mr. Vincent and Khan Bahadur Mir Akbar Ali received their well-merited rewards from Government for working up the case in an admirable manner and bringing it to a successful and satisfactory termination. The forged notes were for Rs. 50 each, and were such clever imitations that they not only deceived the general public but also some of the Banks in Bombay. When the fact was known that forged notes were circulated in markets without being detected, it created a feeling of distrust amongst the people; and Mr. Vincent and the officers who assisted him in the matter received hearty congratulations from the public for removing from their minds the cause of uneasiness. Mr. Vincent was complimented by Sir Frank Souter for the tact, energy, and sound judgment displayed by him in the case, which created a profound sensation at the time, the forger being connected with a highly respectable family at Surat. The forger, one Surajidin, who was arrested by Mr. Vincent at Ahmedabad, was sentenced to seven years' rigorous imprisonment in addition to a fine of Rs. 2,500. Two others, Mya Dadkhan, who was arrested at Hydrabad while uttering forged note, and his accomplice, Gulam Hoosein, were sentenced to ten and five years' rigorous imprisonment respectively. The Government, on the recommendation of the Commissioner, sanctioned a reward of Rs. 5,000, out of which Mr. Vincent received Rs. 3,000 as his share, while Khan Bahadur Mir Akbar Ali received Rs. 1,500; the remaining sum being distributed among subordinates. This was the last and one of the many cases of importance, in which Mir Akbar Ali worked side by side with Mr. Vincent.

Two Sikhs who had been giving a deal of trouble to the police were also run to earth by this able officer. They had committed no less than twenty thefts in the houses of Europeans at Parel, Mahalaxmi and Malabar Hill, and the European residents of those localities were so frightened that they could hardly enjoy sound sleep in their houses. The Commissioner of Police bore willing testimony to the fact that "all the police had failed to trace out these offenders." It was solely owing to Mir Akbar Ali's own personal arrangements and exertions that he one day at 4 o'clock in the morning personally encountered these men with the whole of the stolen property on the Byculla Flats. Having learnt of their plans, he lay in ambush the whole of the night to capture the burglars, and his labours were crowned with success. Both the burglars were convicted and sentenced to a long period of imprisonment in 1871.

About the same time a notorious Chinaman, named John Wynn, was harassing the inhabitants of Bombay in certain localities, and was also a terror to many European families. He had committed a series of thefts, and defied all attempts at arrest. But the redoubtable Khan Bahadur again evinced his detective skill by his success in apprehending the Chinaman, who was sentenced to fourteen years' rigorous imprisonment in the year 1872. This Chinaman subsequently escaped from prison, and during his temporary freedom, he vigorously pursued his old calling. In the short space of four days, that he breathed the free-air once more, he committed at least half a dozen thefts. He was again arrested by the Khan Bahadur, and this time he received the penal servitude for life. In both cases the Commissioner had authorised Mir Akbar Ali to offer a reward to the extent of Rs. 1,000, but as they were detected by Khan Bahadur Mir Akbar Ali himself, no reward was paid. A dangerous character in the person of Caetan Lopes, who committed a series of thefts at the residences of the General Kennedy and other gentlemen, was a source of constant and great anxiety to the police as well as the public. Mir Akbar Ali, however, relieved the public anxiety by apprehending the burglar who was in every respect a desperate man. Most of the stolen property was recovered, and the burglar was sentenced to a long term of imprisonment. In the Ahmedabad conspiracy and Surat conspiracy cases a gang of persons had made it their business to trump up charges against respectable and innocent persons, in consideration of the money which they obtained from their instigators to get the innocent victims of the conspiracy sent to jail. In these instances Mir Akbar Ali and his son Sardar Mir Abdul Ali rendered very valuable assistance to our present deserving and popular Commissioner of Police, Mr. R. H. Vincent, C. I. E. Another noteworthy case in which Mir Akbar Ali and Mir Abdul Ali took a prominent part deserves mention. Pestonji Dinshaw, an Attorney of the High Court, and Saccaram Raghoba instigated one Khakishaw, a fakir, to murder Nicholas DeGa and his wife Rose Mary DeGa. The information of this plot was first received by Mir Akbar Ali who communicated it to Mr. Vincent. Means were at once devised, which resulted in the arrest of Pestonji Dinshaw and Succaram, who were sentenced to seven years' rigorous imprisonment by the Hon'le Mr. Justice Bayley. Numerous other crimes were detected by Khan Bahadur Akbar Ali in a most ingenious and remarkable manner, and the perpetrators were successfully brought to justice. The services of Khan Bahadur Akbar Ali were very trying and arduous during the visits of His Royal Highness the Duke of Edinburgh and His Excellency the Viceroy, when all the Rajas and Chiefs, with their innumerable followers, were staying in Bombay. Mir Akbar Ali, however, made such excellent arrangements that not a single theft was committed during the period these dignitaries honoured Bombay by their presence.

The proof given of Khan Bahadur Akbar Ali's abilities in the Baroda Poisoning case, which resulted in the deposition of Malharrao Gaekwar, may be said to have eclipsed every one of his previous performances. His valuable services in this most important case, which caused profound sensation all over India in 1875, are enumerated in another chapter. During the enquiry by the Commissioner into the charges against Malharrao Gaekwar, the Hon'ble the Advocate General in summing up the evidence, and while alluding in particular to the detective officers, made very eulogistic remarks about Khan Bahadur Mir Akbar Ali who was characterised "as a man of unspotted character, whose services have been recognized by the State, and nothing whatever discreditable to him is on record." Sir Frank Souter also observed, "it is a remarkable fact that though Khan Bahadur Mir Akbar Ali has served Government for upwards of two score years, there does not appear on the records of the office a scratch against his name, while on the other hand his testimonials and official documents containing honourable mention are too voluminous for quotation or comment." On the 3rd of May 1875, Sir Frank Souter in again writing to Government on the Baroda case, spoke about Khan Bahadur Mir Akbar Ali in the following terms :—"It would be impossible to narrate the numerous instances in which this faithful officer has rendered most valuable service, but the appended documents will show some of the principal occasions on which his singularly successful exertions have been acknowledged by Government and the many officers under whom he had served. Mir Akbar Ali is a most eminent detective, and his fame as such has spread far and wide; he is a terror to evil-doers, and his individual presence among them is of more value than a considerable body of police. Such is the moral influence he exercises over the bad characters in this great city." This was no ordinary or formal praise, but it was only his immediate superiors who expressed high opinions of him derived from personal knowledge. As a reward for his most meritorious services in this case the Government of India bestowed upon him a grant of land assessed at Rs. 500, and to be settled on his heirs in perpetuity at permanent quit rent of half the assessment.

Sir Frank Souter considered the reward inadequate when "the past meritorious services" of this brilliant detective were considered. The rewards he admitted were liberal, but not more so, in his respectful opinion, than the nature of the services rendered by the detectives at Baroda entitled them to. The Commissioner, therefore, solicited the local Government to submit to the Government of India such proposals for securing a substantial recognition to them as would embrace their past and present exertions, and might in some measure be commensurate with the faithful and extraordinary services rendered by the detectives to the State. Sir Frank Souter asked the Government to remember that Khan Bahadur Mir Akbar Ali had served Government faithfully for upwards of forty-four years, and had also during the time of mutinies and other occasions rendered very valuable service, often more of a political than of a police character. Under the circumstances he strongly recommended Government to enhance the reward bestowed upon the Khan Bahadur. The Government of India, in addition to the grant of lands, gave Khan Bahadur Akbar Ali a reward of Rs. 1,000 in cash and a gold bracelet, valued at Rs. 333. These were presented to him in open Darbar by H. E. Sir Philip Wodehouse, the then Governor of Bombay, at the Government House, Parel. The Khan Bahadur also received a reward of Rs. 2,500 from the Baroda State as his share for his exertions in recovering forty lacs of rupees which were being made away by the agents of the Maharaja.

Some of the most remarkable cases in the criminal history of Bombay were traced by Mir Akbar Ali in a most ingenious manner, worthy of description by noted writers of detective stories, who have done so much by their novels to gain for European detectives the high reputation for professional skill with which they are credited. It would, however, be a very heavy task to enumerate even a fraction of the intricate cases of crime he brought to light, and therefore only one or two further instances can be given. On the 3rd of March 1856 Major Edward Baynes, the then Commissioner of Police, wrote: "Mir Akbar Ali has been under my immediate supervision since 1847 employed as a detective officer, in which capacity *he is equal to the best in Europe*, as the records of the Mazagon police office will prove. * * * * He is a very steady, just and trustworthy man." Major Baynes enumerated a few instances of clever detection of crimes by Mir Akbar Ali. Amongst them was the Matoonga gang robbery case. There was an actual gang of robbers who at night times, and even in broad daylight, committed burglaries, and gave an unlimited amount of labour to the police, whose exertions were rendered abortive by the ingenuity and careful precautions of the robbers to evade detection. A large amount of treasure was accumulated by the robbers, whose daring was astonishing. No clue whatever could be obtained from the party in charge of the treasure. A townsman was heard to say, "I have received a *hoondie* and a silver bangle, and I am going to my country." An ordinary man hearing this remark would have forgotten it ten minutes afterwards, but to Mir Akbar Ali it was full of significance. In less than six hours the individual who had uttered the words was in police custody. He was arrested by Mir Akbar Ali himself as he was leaving the island. Mir Akbar Ali followed up the clue and apprehended the whole gang present in Bombay, and recovered the greater portion of the stolen property.

Another *cause celebre* was a mysterious case of wholesale poisoning at Kalbadevi. Five females were poisoned and two of them died. There was no clue to the poisoner. The only information that could be gathered was that a Parsee and a Ghatee were seen visiting the place of the women. In a short time both the Parsee and the Ghatee were arrested through the exertions of Mir Akbar Ali. The Parsee was sentenced to be hanged, while the Ghatee was discharged. In the case of the murder of a man at the salt pans near Sion no clue whatever could be obtained of the murderer who had, however, left behind a drum, which was sufficient for Mir Akbar Ali's purposes to trace the culprit. Ten days after the occurrence two Pardeshies were seen looking on at a distance, while the inquest was sitting, and the very next day the men who were at first supposed to have committed the murder were in custody. The clue, however, was a false one, but was worked into the proper channel, and the real culprits were brought to justice. There were beside many other cases of forgers, coiners, robbers and murderers, and they were detected with as slight a clue as those above related from the record left on the subject by Major Baynes.

In March 1873 a robbery was committed in the bungalow of Mr. John K. Bythell. All hopes of the discovery of the theft were abandoned, but the perseverance of Mir Akbar Ali was unflinching, and he succeeded not only in arresting and bringing to justice the criminal, but in recovering the stolen property also. Mr. Bythell was greatly impressed with the way in which the theft was traced and was so much pleased at the recovery of the goods, that he sent Rs. 100 to Sir Frank Souter requesting him to be kind enough to hand it over to Khan Bahadur Mir Akbar Ali as a reward for his diligence in recovering his goods and bringing the thieves to justice.

Another theft, which has been alluded to above, was committed at Walkeshwar in the bungalow of General M. K. Kennedy. Mir Akbar Ali brought the thieves to justice, and got another reward for Rs. 100 from the General who wrote to Sir Frank Souter that old Akbar Ali was indeed a terror to evil-doers, and that the result of the case was perfectly wonderful and reflected the greatest credit on the police.

In a letter to Government in August 1883, Sir Frank Souter said : "Khan Bahadur Mir Akbar Ali has now served Government for no less a period than 52 years.and has attained the age of 75. He is the eminent detective whose fame is such in the important branch of the Police Department as I believe no other Police officer in India has yet acquired."

Mir Akbar Ali retired from the service with full honours and glory in December 1883, and received an enhanced pension for good services. In December 1883, Sir Frank Souter in intimating to Government the fact of his retirement, wrote as follows :—"I have the honour to remind the

Government that at the end of the current month, I shall be deprived of the services of Khan Bahadur Mir Akbar Ali, the eminent detective of the Bombay Police who has now served Government faithfully and with a great distinction for a period of more than 52 years. Khan Bahadur Mir Akbar Ali's retirement will be a serious loss to the Bombay Police Force, for though his health has for some time been declining and he has not had the strength latterly to take the same active part as hitherto in the important detective branch of the Police duties of this city, still his very presence in the Force has given strength to it.

A few days after Mir Akbar Ali had retired from the service, a mass meeting of his friends and admirers was held in the bungalow of Aga Abdul Husein Haji Zannel Abedin Shirazi on the 3rd of February 1884. The chair was taken by His Highness the late Aga Shahbuddin Shah. Several speakers bore testimony to the excellent services rendered by the Khan Bahadur for over half a century with conspicuous ability, zeal and fidelity, and a sum of Rs. 4,000 was subscribed on the spot for the purpose of commemorating his services.

Khan Bahadur Mir Akbar Ali received several testimonials from several leading European and Native gentlemen in Bombay. One of them was signed by Sir Jamsetji Jejeebhoy, Bart., C.S.I., C.I.E., Sir Dinshaw M. Petit, Bart., Mr. Byramji Jijibhoy, Messrs. Faizoolabhoy Hebtoolla, Vandravandas

Purshotamdas, Anandrao Narayen Wasudeo, Rahimtoola Khairaj, the late Sir Mangaldas Nathubhoy, the late Mr. Shantaram Narayen, the late Mr. Jairajbhoy Peerbhoy, the late Mr. Varjivandas, and numerous other prominent citizens. They testified that Khan Bahadur Mir Akbar Ali had discharged " the duties of a detective with great ability, untiring energy and uncommon sagacity, and had given satisfaction alike to the Government and the public who had equal confidence in him."

Mr. Dosabhoy Framji, the then second Presidency Magistrate, said :—" Long before I was appointed a Police Magistrate, I had heard that Khan Bahadur Akbar Ali was a most active and zealous officer in the Bombay Police Force. After my appointment to the Magistracy I had personal and frequent opportunities of seeing how he has discharged his very onerous and responsible duties. As a detective officer he is, I think, invaluable, and his retirement from the public service is to be regretted as it will be difficult to supply his place."

The Khan Bahadur has now gathered among his forefathers. He died on the 8th of March 1894, at the patriarchal age of 92 years.

Chapter II.

SARDAR MIR ABDUL ALI'S CAREER.

GREAT as were the services of Mir Akbar Ali to the State and the public, his son Mir Abdul Ali, whose brilliant career forms the subject of the present memoir, has a still more remarkable record. There is, perhaps, no more notable and prominent figure among the detectives in India, European or Native, than Sardar Mir Abdul Ali, Khan Bahadur, the present able and experienced head of the Criminal Investigation Department in Bombay. The mantle of Mir Akbar Ali could not have fallen on better shoulders than those of his son, Mir Abdul Ali. His detective instinct, acuteness, energy, promptitude and genius, combined with a good knowledge of English and of criminal law and vast experience and knowledge of native character and custom, combine to mark him out as exceptionally suited for the responsible and arduous duties of the Chief Detective of Bombay. Our city being the gate-way for the arrival of foreign adventurers who seek to live by their wits, in other words, by duping all whom they can, the task of the detective service is rendered the more trying, and it often requires no little amount of dexterity to discover the ingenious frauds perpetrated by these foreigners. Khan Bahadur Akbar Ali may be said to have left a double portion of his spirit to his eldest son, whose fame has reached far and wide all over India. He has assiduously cultivated his natural talents and gifts which often stand him in good stead when called upon to discharge duties more of a political than of a police character. Owing to his great tact, diplomacy, talent and shrewdness he has become almost indispensable to the cause of the public peace and safety in Bombay.

A man of remarkble industry, inexhaustible patience, cool nature, and exceeding courage, Sardar Mir Abdul Ali rose to this post of eminence by his own exertions and has distinguished himself in almost all the important and sensational cases that have taken place in and out of Bombay during the last thirty years. His reputation is so great, and his talents so marked and acknowledged, that he is often called upon to do special detective work in different places of the Presidency, and he can rightly be styled the Indian "Sherlock Holmes." It has been admitted on several occasions by his superiors that he will not suffer by comparison with the best Detectives in Europe and elsewhere. Born in August 1840, Sardar Mir Abdul Ali is now in his fifty-seventh year, but he is well preserved and looks much younger. His robust constitution and his intrepid spirit enable him to stand far more severe strains than his younger colleagues, European or native. In energy and vitality he can equal, if not excel, many younger men in whatever walk of life they may be. He has a charming and fascinating manner, and it is a pleasure to converse with him, the more so as he possesses an endless fund of anecdotes, and his wit and humour are of no mean order.

At an early age he began to show signs of great ablity. His diligence in study, his fondness for the Oriental languages and his thirst for a sound knowledge of English were great. His school career was a very brilliant one, and his teachers predicted great success in his future years. His father believing that the boy, if properly educated, would bring great credit to his family, wisely took care to give him a good education. Under the fostering care of his father and his teachers he made good progress, and in 1865 successfully passed the Matriculation Examination of the Bombay University, he being among the first batch of Mahomedan students who passed the examination. On the 15th of December he joined the police, and is said to be the only man in the force who is matriculated.

Only a few months after young Mir Abdul Ali had entered on his career in life he got an opportunity to distinguish himself, and was not slow to embrace it. His first great case was the capture of the notorious swindler Karsondas Purshotamdas Bhansalee, who was transported for seven years. This happened in the year 1866. His next *cause celebre* was the apprehension of a daring Hindu forger and his two associates who had palmed off on the public a large number of forged currency notes, each representing a thousand rupees. In the year 1866 a series of cases of using forged currency notes were tried, and the utterers of the notes were sentenced to various terms of imprisonment. In all the cases Mir Abdul Ali took a very prominent part.

In March 1867, the police were actively engaged in the detection of one of the most ingenious note forgeries ever brought to notice in this part of the world. For several days a number of extremely well got up notes for large amounts had been in circulation, and some of the most experienced persons had been deceived thereby. After a great deal of labour the Sardar got a clue to the forger himself, and at once reported the matter to Mr. Edgington, the then Deputy Commissioner. The forger possessed two plates which were very neatly engraved. From one of these the water-mark was printed on the paper, and from the other the impression of the note was taken. The paper used was rather thicker than in genuine notes, and it was only by a slight scratch of the graver's tool that the valueless character of the notes was detected.

On the 11th of March 1867 Mr. Edgington and Mir Abdul Ali and other officers went to a room on the first floor of a house in Kumbharwada, and concealed themselves behind a *bamboo* partition. In a few minutes Hargowandas, a police agent, entered the room, followed by one Wasudeo Govind, with whom he entered into conversation.

The police agent produced a roll of genuine notes which he said he had brought for the purpose of purchasing forged notes for Rs 1,000 each. Wasudeo in a few minutes left the room and brought Succaram Yoshwant, and a consultation took place between them. The police agent urged that he should treat only with the master and not the servants which the two persons, Wasudeo and Succaram, were represented to be. Accordingly, Bhagwantrao Purshotam was introduced as the principal in the transaction. A long conversation ensued; the police agent asked for ten or twelve pieces, but the men said that they could then give him only five and more afterwards. Bhagwantrao, in answer to the police agent, said in a boastful tone that he could give such good notes that when they were presented he would defy any one to refuse payment of them. As the transaction was being completed, Mr. Edgington and Mir Abdul Ali and his father stepped forward, pounced upon the three men and arrested them. Bhagwantrao was transported for life, while each of the other two were sentenced to rigorous imprisonment for seven years each. The successful result of the case was in a great measure due to the skilful efforts of Mir Abdul Ali, who traced the plates which were engraved by one Balkrishna Babaji, an engraver employed in Her Majesty's Mint, and who was related to the accused. For his valuable services Mir Abdul Ali received Rs. 1,000 as his share of the reward of Rs. 10,000 proclaimed by the Government.

Sardar Mir Abdul Ali by his own merits soon rose to the post of Subedar from his original post of Jamadar, and he began to take an active part in the unravelling of almost all the intricate cases that came up for solution. At the Second Criminal Sessions of the High Court, in the year 1868, a case of robbery was tried by Sir Joseph Arnold, who was much struck with the way in which the case was detected by Mir Abdul Ali, and bestowed high encomiums upon the young officer to whose ability and dexterity was due the successful result of the case. Sir Joseph Arnold wrote a letter, through Mr. John Marriott, the then Clerk of the Court, to Mr. Nana Moroji, the then Third Presidency Magistrate, in which he complimented Mir Abdul Ali, and requested the Magistrate to reward his services in the case by presenting him with Rs. 80 (a part of the proceeds of the stolen property remaining in the hands of the police). The letter was forwarded by the Magistrate to the Commissioner, who in forwarding the reward to Mir Abdul Ali observed :—" The Commissioner has much pleasure in fowarding copies of letters to Subedar Mir Abdul Ali, and also the Rs. 80, which accompanied the original communications. The Commissioner considers that the remarks made by the Hon'ble Sir Joseph Arnold with regard to the getting up of the case of Queen *vs.* Amra Pudma are highly creditable to Subedar Mir Abdul Ali."

Next came the great Aurora case, in which the ship was deliberately and fraudulently burnt, a crime in which the skipper and several brokers of Bombay were concerned. All the persons implicated were convicted and sentenced. The case was of the utmost importance to the mercantile community, and had excited the greatest attention, not only in Bombay, but in London and Liverpool. The services of Mir Abdul Ali were very conspicuous in this case, and were promptly brought to the notice of Government by the Commissioner. In the Ahmedabad Conspiracy case Mr. R. H. Vincent, the then Deputy Commissioner of Police, Khan Bahadur Akbar Ali, and Mir Abdul Ali earned the highest commendation from Mr. Justice Bayley, before whom the case was tried. The presiding Judge brought the valuable services of Mr. Vincent and the officers acting under his instructions to the notice of Government, who complimented them for the skill, ability, and perseverance displayed in this most important case, which in effect was the breaking up of an association of criminals organised in the heart of Bombay for the purpose of trading in the evil dispositions of vindictive persons, to the ruin of their weak and innocent victims.

The Sardar's services in the case of Moulvi Liakat Ali, a notorious outlaw, and an active accomplice of Nana Saheb of Bithoor, who in the dark days of the Mutiny massacred every Christian he came across, gained him not only high encomiums, but high honours as a mark of Government's appreciation of his valuable services in the case. Sir Frank Souter, the Commissioner, in his report to

Government, dated 18th October 1872, said :—"In the case of Moulvi Liakat Ali, Inspector Abdul Ali was, as a confidential officer, engaged for a fortnight with the Oriental Translator to Government in translating all the papers found upon him, and subsequently in getting together evidence and tracing out his associates, and it was in the execution of these very important and delicate duties that he offered so much valuable assistance to Major Parson, who has now brought his services to the notice of the Government of India. As regards the prominent part taken by Inspector Mir Abdul Ali in this important service, and the uniform zeal and ability with which he always conducts his very responsible duties, chiefly in the detective branch, he is deserving of the highest praise. Government are, I believe, aware that Inspector Abdul Ali is the son of Khan Bahadur Mir Akbar Ali, the famous detective officer, who has now served in the Police Department with so much credit and distinction for upwards of forty years. The son has fully inherited his father's intelligence, and his usefulness has been enhanced by a good English education, and by his having acquired an excellent knowledge of Criminal Law. As Khan Bahadur Mir Akbar Ali must from infirmity now soon retire from the service of Government, I would venture strongly to recommend that the valuable and faithful services of Inspector Mir Abdul Ali, in whom I place the greatest trust, be marked by the Government, conferring upon him the title of Khan Bahadur."

The Government of Bombay, thereupon, made a recommendation to the Government of India to carry out Sir Frank Souter's suggestion, which was accepted, and the title of Khan Bahadur was conferred upon Mir Abdul Ali as personal distinction in 1873. In the same year Khan Bahadur Mir Abdul Ali rendered very valuable assistance under Mr. Vincent in the case of Mr. Pestonji Dinshaw, a Solicitor of the Bombay High Court, and his clerk, Sacaram Raghoba, who were charged with attempting to cause the death of one Nicholas DeGa and his wife Rose Mary DeGa. The attempt failed by the timely discovery of the nefarious plot, and great credit was due to Mr. Vincent and Khan Bahadur Mir Abdul Ali and his father for preventing the conspiracy from being put into execution. Pestonji Dinshaw was a man of extraordinary genius and was considered to be one of the ablest Solicitors of his time, but his spendthrit habits seem to have worked his utter ruin. The case would supply material for a most exciting novel. On the result large sums of money were staked, and it is said that thousands of rupees changed hands in payment of bets upon it. The valuable services of the police in detecting and frustrating the diabolical plot were acknowledged by Government, who considered that "great credit was due to the officers of the Bombay Police for the zeal and ability displayed by them in connection with the case." The Sardar's ability to write the English language with fluency and correctness is well known, and even Mr. Justice Bayley complimented him on his acquisition of a sound knowledge of English while summing up the DeGa case to the jury. While commenting upon the evidence of the witnesses in the case his Lordship said, "Mir Abdul Ali gave his evidence as he always does in English, with remarkable precision and a thorough knowledge of our idioms." In the same year the Sardar had the good fortune to receive a pecuniary reward from the Madras Government for the assistance he rendered to Colonel Weldon, of Madras, in the course of his enquiries in connection with forged currency notes of that circle. This "great note forgery case" excited the greatest interest all over India, some of its details being most romantic. A Government resolution was issued from Fort Saint George, Madras, dated 20th March 1873, conveying the thanks of the Government to Sir Frank Souter and Mr. Vincent for the ready and valuable assistance they afforded to Colonel Weldon, and authorising a reward of Rs. 100 to be presented to Mir Abdul Ali on the recommendation of that officer "for his good services." In the same year the Sardar was the means of preventing a beautiful Circasian girl being sold as slave to a Hydrabad Nabab. The dazzling beauty of the girl was for some months the main subject of conversation in European and Native societies, and when the report of her proposed sale got abroad, it created the greatest sensation in Bombay.

Great and valuable as these services were they fall into insignificance as compared with the Sardar's brilliant performance in the famous trial of Malharrao Gaekwar of Baroda. The value of his splendid services in this instance was cordially recognised both by the public and Government. It may be truly said that since the removal of Malharrao Gaekwar, Baroda enjoys a peace absolutely unknown in his day. There was actually a rule of anarchy prevailing in the State, and the services of those who were instrumental in bringing home the guilt of the late Gaekwar cannot be too highly commended. As was officially stated by Sir Richard Meade "upon the vigilance and integrity the credit of the Government of India for some weeks depended." Even Sir Frank Souter admitted that it said a great deal to the credit of the detective officers selected for the work that no one ever accused them of accepting bribes which they might have done to any amount if they had so chosen. "Lakhs of rupees," said Sir Frank Souter, "were available as bribes at the most critical moment of the whole enquiry," but the detectives proved true to their salt. The charge against the Maharaja was that of attempting to poison Colonel Phayre, the British Resident at Baroda.

While the preliminary police investigations were going on, lakhs of rupees belonging to the Baroda State were being made away by the agents of the Gaekwar, but the Sardar was able to ferret out nearly forty lakhs of rupees, and in the words of Sir Frank Souter, the credit of recovering this enormous sum of amount belonged to the subject of this sketch and his father. Besides, according to Mr. Henry Cleveland, the Public Prosecutor, it was owing to Mir Abdul Ali that some most important evidence was forthcoming. The Advocate General in summing up the case remarked that though the junior Khan Bahadur had been for a less period of time in the service of the State than his father, yet he had also gained from the Government of India the honourable title of Khan Bahadur ; and when he was put in the witness-box for cross-examination, not a single question was asked of him. No question was put to him, and they must therefore presume that he, "like his father, has a character untarnished, notwithstanding the *difficulty and delicacy of the services he has to perform.*" Sir Frank Souter in a report to the Government on the Malharrao case said that "Mir Abdul Ali is an officer of comparatively short service, having been appointed to the police in 1865 ; but during this period *he has given proof of his excellent ability and high police qualifications,* which have been most usefully exercised in the service of Government." Sir Richard Meade, the Resident at Baroda, brought the value of his services to the notice of Government, who granted him an annuity of Rs. 400 for his life, with a moiety continuable to his next heir. Besides he got Rs. 3,500 in cash and a gold bracelet, which were presented to him in the open Darbar by His Excellency Sir Phillip Wodehouse, the then Governor of Bombay, at the Government House, Parel.

The forest frauds next received the attention of Mir Abdul Ali in 1876. The contractors perpetrated great frauds on Government by way of stealing timber-woods which were cut without permission or authority. Mir Abdul Ali rendered very valuable assistance in discovering the frauds to Mr. Arthur Crawford, the then Collector of Colaba, in his prolonged enquiries, extending over several months, into the complicated system of frauds in connection with the Forests. His services were brought to the notice of Government, who promptly acknowledged them. Mr. Arthur Crawford in his report to the Commissioner of the Northern Division said :—

"By this time also I was assured that the contractors could have closed their own accounts with their salesmen or brokers in Bombay, to whom the wood was consigned; accordingly I proceeded to Bombay and placed myself in communication with Mr. Edgington, Acting Commissioner of Police, and Khan Bahadur Mir Abdul Ali, the well known detective. With their assistance and the zealous aid of my first informant, the names of the brokers of the different contractors were ascertained, and the persons made little difficulty in placing their books at my disposal.

"Soon, however, I received information from the Khan Bahadur that Hanmanta was only the chief member of a large gang —and of several gangs of Ghattis organized in Bombay—to take contracts in the Concan, and under cover of them to rob the forests, and that the different gangs or firms were known in Bombay, much as the old Bunder gangs were, as 'Harri Bhow's Toli' or the 'Bori Bunder Toli,' and so forth. The gangs had, as their ostensible business in Bombay, porterage contracts on the different wharves, and the partners in the porterage business were usually all partners in the wood trade, though many members might not be working in the forest at all.

" At this moment I took into my confidence Mr. Framjee Cursetjee (now Khan Saheb), the newly appointed Chief Constable of Alibag, and with his valuable and untiring zeal at Alibag, and the assistance of Khan Bahadur Mir Abdul Ali in Bombay, the general inquiry into the forest frauds continued. I retained, however, all the threads of inquiry in my own hands.

" The Khan Bahadur in Bombay speedily unearthed the false books just finished by Hanmanta's karkoons in Bombay and at a village in the Poona Zillah. Further information enabled them to find deposited, in various places of safety, by members of Hanmanta's gang, the real or genuine books of the firm of Saccaram Santojee both the rough set kept in the Roha forests, and those kept by the firm in Bombay, which, item by item, tallied with the broker's books.

" The Bombay Police further discovered several bundles of correspondence, a list of the partners of this firm, and a letter sent from Alibag when Hanmanta was on trial before me, giving a complete code of instructions as to the preparation of the false set of books ; all these papers, and the books themselves, coupled with the false reports of the Forest officials, showed that from Appa downwards all had been aiding and abetting in the frauds and receiving gratifications as rewards for their connivance."

In 1877 the services of Mir Abdul Ali were again conspicuous in a serious case of forgery of Government notes and of counterfeiting coin. Mir Abdul Ali received a reward of Rs. 400 from Government.

The action taken by the Police in this case was so satisfactory that for some time at least it had a most beneficial, deterrent effect.

Yet another heavy case of note forgery, in the tracing of which Sardar Mir Abdul Ali played an important part was discovered at Aurangabad. In this case, the Aurangabad Police having failed to trace out the offenders for more than a year the services of the Sardar were specially applied for by the Resident, Sir Richard Meade. The case is on all fours with many of the popular detective stories of Europe. The forgeries were the work of a clever gang, and not of one individual. They always went in for "big things." The principal offender was a very notorious character, who like many other talented criminals, would surely have risen in the world, had he but turned his ability to proper account. He planned his enterprises with the most consummate skill and worked it to completion, with such a thoroughness as to defy the best efforts of the police to detect the offences. The detective abilities of Mir Abdul Ali were highly spoken of by all the authorities concerned, and nothing could have exceeded the praise lavished upon him. The case was managed in such a thorough and masterly manner by Mir Abdul Ali that he received the highest encomiums from Sir Richard Meade, the Resident at Hyderabad, and Colonel Dawker, the Special Commissioner, who tried the case. Both the officers were struck with his sound acumen and remarkable detective powers. On the warm recommendation of Sir Richard Meade, supported by Sir Frank Souter, a reward of Rs. 2,000 was paid by Government to Mir Abdul Ali for his most faithful and valuable services in the case.

Sardar Mir Abdul Ali rendered very valuable assistance to Major Daniel in collecting intelligence regarding the movements of Wasudeo Balwant Fadke, a notorious outlaw of Poona. The Sardar was apparently deputed by Government to assist Major Daniel in effecting the arrest of the dacoit, but really this was merely a blind to throw off the guard Narayen Davaria, a forger, who had been a source of great anxiety both to the police and the public. His real commission was to arrest the Prince of the Forgers, but the Sardar killed two birds with one stone, and his "efficient services" in the case of Wasudeo Balwant Fadke were recognized in the same Government resolution in which the services of Major Daniel and Sardar Diler-ul-Mulk. more commonly known as Syed Abdul Hak, were acknowledged. Wasudeo Fadke had enlisted the services of a few rebels, and having attempted to wage war against the British Government of India, had been hiding in the villages. He had made arrangements to enlist 500 Rohillas and Arabs and other mercinaries residing at Ganur in his service, and moreover had advanced Rs. 2,000. He promised also to purchase horses for them and to pay them Rs. 3,000 more, but before he could put his plans into execution he was arrested. In the year 1880, Khan Bahadur Mir Abdul Ali was thanked in a Government Resolution for acting with promptitude and judgment in the case of a man who was trying to palm off a forged currency note for Rs. 100.

In the year 1880 an Arabic book was written and published in Bombay by Sharaf Ali, a Bohra priest, and dedicated to the chief Mulla of that community. The language of the book was calculated to give offence to the Mahomedan population generally, but more especially to the Sunnis. Khan Bahadur Mir Abdul Ali prudently took prompt steps, and succeeded in suppressing the publication, and thus avoided very serious results. His valuable services were promptly aknowledged by Government.

In 1881 Sir Frank Souter recommended Mir Abdul Ali on the ground of his usefulness and ability for a special personal allowance, stating that often times Mir Abdul Ali performed public duties of a secret and delicate nature that were over and above his ordinary duties. The Accountant-General replied that instead of establishing an inconvenient precedent "by granting a special allowance for his meritorious and useful services, perhaps the proper course would be to promote that officer to a high grade when opportunity occurred, and to reward him by some departmental arrangement." Sir Frank Souter, thereupon, submitted that this officer was already a first grade Inspector, and that the next step in rank and employment was that of Superintendent, of which there were six in the Bombay Police; but from the fact of Khan Bahadur Mir Abdul Ali being a native, he was debarred from such position in which he would necessarily be placed in command of European police officers, and for other reasons, too, he would be out of place as a Superintendent in charge of a division, though his own most important duties were none the less onerous, and were such as could not possibly be performed by any one of the six Superintendents of the Bombay Police. Sir Frank also submitted that important political service, often of a most delicate nature was being daily and constantly rendered by the police under the direction of Khan Bahadur Mir Abdul Ali, and it was earnestly hoped that Government would be able to see their way to remunerating the Khan Bahadur in a manner adequate to the very responsible duties he is called upon to discharge.

In addressing yet another letter to Government on behalf of Khan Bahadur Mir Abdul Ali, Sir Frank Souter said :—

The Khan Bahadur's general services as Chief Confidential Officer, and head of all Secret Police matter requiring the aid of Native Agency (often of an important political character) have been marked by great usefulness to Government.

It is unnecessary to point out in so important a commercial city as that of Bombay with its immense population gathered together from all parts of the globe, that cases are ever arising which call for the secret and unceasing watchfulness of the Police and which can only be placed in the hands of thoroughly trustworthy, efficient, and experienced officers.

You are aware that I frequently receive from the Political Department confidential references often submitted by the Government of India calling for secret and delicate enquiry and in many cases of such kind I am necessarily obliged to take the Khan Bahadur into my confidence, and I am glad to say after many years' experience that in no single instance have I ever had the smallest suspicion of his having in any way betrayed the trust I have reposed in him.

The Khan Bahadur has had the advantage of a good English education, and in addition to his own language, Hindustani, he is a good Persian scholar, and can speak the Marathi and Guzerati languages. He has also a good knowledge of Criminal Law, and possesses altogether a very rare combination of qualities which mark him as an excellent Police officer.

The rank which the Khan Bahadur now holds is that of 1st Class Inspector of Police, the salary of which is Rs. 175, with house accommodation.

I have long felt that the above remuneration was altogether inadequate for such an officer, but unfortunately it has been out of my power to promote the Khan Bahadur, as the next grade in the Bombay Police is that of Superintendent, and the police officers of this rank are all required to have charge of Divisions with several European Assistants under them, and therefore the rank would not be suitable to the Khan Bahadur, and he could not be spared from his own post which is certainly quite as important and far more difficult to fill.

I would submit that the Khan Bahadur should, as regards emolument, be placed on at least as favourable a footing as a 1st Class Police Inspector in the districts—their pay I understand to be Rs. 250, with Rs. 25 travelling allowance—and therefore considering the additional cost of living in Bombay, I would beg strongly to recommend for the favourable consideration of Government that an additional sum of Rs. 125 per mensem be granted to Khan Bahadur Mir Abdul Ali, which would bring his pay up to Rs. 325 and Rs. 50 above the pay and allowances drawn by a 1st Class Inspector in the mofussil.

Should there seem to H. E. the Governor any obstacle to the granting of the increase above recommended in pay of the Khan Bahadur, then I would venture to suggest whether the amount might not be fairly met as a separate charge in the shape of a personal allowance on the Police Department as remuneration for the numerous police duties (many of a confidential and important nature) which the Khan Bahadur is daily being called upon to perform.

I would mention that I am aware of tempting offers having been made to the Khan Bahadur of employment out of Bombay, and should he at any time be induced to leave the Police of this city, it will be most difficult to supply his place, and I do not hesitate to say it would be a very serious loss to the Bombay Police.

When the late Khan Bahadur Mir Akbar Ali retired, Sir Frank Souter in view of the growing importance of the city and the rapid increase in its population, made certain recommendations for the consideration of Government with the object of establishing a thoroughly Detective Force distinct from the rest of the Police.

A special post of the superintendent of the Detective Police was, thereupon, created for the Sardar on a salary of Rs. 300 (exclusive of horse allowance and horse-rent) rising to Rs. 450 by triennial increase of Rs. 50, and the Detective Force was augmented to a certain extent.

The praiseworthy exertion of this officer and the tact and untiring zeal evinced by him in the discharge of the difficult and delicate duty entrusted to him for making arrangements for granting passports and superintending the despatch of the pilgrims to the Hedjaz in the important pilgrim season of 1881 were promptly brought to the notice of Government by the Commissioner in his report, dated 9th March 1882. The Commissioner then wrote as follows :—

" But even this establishment at times was insufficient to keep down the burden of clerical labour and the other clerks of my office were not unfrequently required to help, and thus inconvenince arose to the disposal of the current police work, and on many occasions so great has been the pressure caused by the sudden influx of pilgrims, as ships were leaving for Jeddah, that but for the untiring efforts and energy of my Detective Inspector Khan Bahadur Mir Abdul Ali, in whose charge I have placed all the arrangements for granting passports and generally superintending the despatch of pilgrims, many would have been left behind in Bombay for considerable periods, and thus lost the auspicious time at which to perform their pilgrimage. I am much indebted to the Khan Bahadur for his praiseworthy exertions and for the tact he has evinced in discharging this delicate and difficult duty."

Government warmly acknowledged their indebtedness in a Resolution, dated 23rd March 1882, which stated "Government are glad to notice the favourable mention made by the Commissioner of Police of the services in connection with the issue of the passports rendered by Khan Bahadur Mir Abdul Ali, Detective Inspector."

In connection with the collection of recruits for the Military Police in Burma, His Excellency the Governor-in-Council in Government Resolution, Military Department, dated 4th April 1887, acknowledged the services of the Bombay Police in the following terms :—"To Sir Frank Souter his special acknowledgments are due. The greater number of recruits were collected through his exertions, and indeed without his hearty co-operation, it would have been difficult for Government to respond so promptly to the Government of India's call." Sir Frank Souter was not slow in bringing to the notice of the Government that "the above acknowledgment of Government was principally due to the most zealous manner in which Khan Bahadur Mir Abdul Ali aided the Police Commissioner in the matter."

In the same year (1887) the Sardar rendered great service to the Junagudh State in the capture of Makrani outlaws, and received Rs. 500 as his share, from the reward given by His Highness the Nawab of Junagadh.

In July 1887 the Khan Bahadur was appointed to act as Protector of Pilgrims in addition to his own duties. The season for the embarkation of pilgrims to the Hedjaz had just then set in. Khan Bahadur Abdul Ali discharged the onerous duties in an eminently satisfactory manner, and for his arduous and zealous services he received a valuable gold watch from Messrs. Thomas Cook and Son.

There are numerous cases of murders successfully traced by Mir Abdul Ali. Some of them were committed under singularly mysterious circumstances. But Mir Abdul Ali has traced them out, often when it was thought they would never be discovered. Though a case might seem hopeless, his unflagging industry did not permit him to relax his ingenious efforts until he had achieved success, and this is the keynote to his phenomenal success in detecting the most marvellous cases. Not a single extraordinary case of murder has occurred in Bombay during the last thirty years in which his knowledge and skill have not been brought to bear upon unearthing it. The successful termination of the cases known as the Parel box murder case (from the fact that the murdered woman was found concealed in a box), the triple murder at Dadar (in which two Parsee ladies and a male-child were brutally done to death), and the Kembekar Street poisoning case (in which five members of a family were killed outright by poison administered in food) were attributable to the skill, dexterity, acumen and perseverance of Sardar Mir Abdul Ali.

Besides, it has frequently fallen to the lot of Sardar Mir Abdul Ali to investigate many mysterious cases. He always does his work with a thoroughness of purpose, which, combined with the instinct of a detective and his knowledge of the criminal law, enable him to present a strong case before the Public Prosecutor. He has his own way of thinking and his own way of acting while engaged in unravelling any mystery. His extraordinary acumen was well illustrated in several other remarkable cases of murder besides those above stated. In the case of the murder of a Mogul and his wife at Oomerkharry, Mookhee Bunde Ali at His Highness the Aga Khan's residence, Nesbit Road, and the Clerk Road murder, his extraordinary police acumen is well illustrated. All these cases were so complicated and mysterious, that it seemed highly improbable that they would be successfully traced. The reputation of the police was at stake, but the Sardar always rose to the importance of the occasion, and succeeded in bringing the culprits to book. Referring to the triple murder at Dadar Mr. Gell, our popular and energetic Deputy Commissioner of Police, in his annual report to the Government of Bombay, while acting as Commissioner in place of Colonel Wilson, remarked: "It is a case worthy of being classed with the now famous Parel murder case, which occurred in November 1887, and is one for the detection of which the Bombay Force and Khan Bahadur Mir Abdul Ali in particular, may well be proud."

Chapter III.

RECOMMENDATION FOR THE RANK OF A FIRST CLASS SARDAR.

SIR FRANK SOUTER, the Police Commissioner, in his report to Government in April 1888 enumerated the past services of Mir Abdul Ali, and recommended him for a title of the First Class Sardar of the Deccan. The Commissioner after narrating the facts of the Parel box murder case, said: "I have deemed it my duty to bring this particular case of murder to the notice of Government as being one committed under circumstances of singular atrocity and planned with extraordinary precaution, such as was calculated to baffle the best detective ability. For some time the bringing to light of this case seemed almost hopeless, but the Khan Bahadur never relaxed his efforts, and it is to his extraordinary perseverance and policeman-like skill that so very satisfactory a result has been brought about. In laying bare the details of a most difficult case of heinous crime of this kind, and bringing the offender to justice, not only are the public inspired with confidence, but a salutary deterrent effect is produced on the minds of the evil-disposed, the value of which is incalculable. The very valuable services which Khan Bahadur Mir Abdul Ali has from time to time rendered are well known to Government." * * * * *

The Commissioner then recounted the remarkable services rendered by this officer in connection with the detection and conviction of eight notorious forgers and utterers of Government currency notes at Aurangabad. The instances in which the Khan Bahadur has received the acknowledgment of Government for approved services, subsequent to the period reported on in the Aurangabad forgery case were then enumerated by the Commissioner who forwarded to Government the highly complimentary certificates which have been granted to Khan Bahadur Mir Abdul Ali by the law officers of Government, Mr. R. V. Hearn, Mr. H. Cleveland, and Mr. F. A. Little. The Commissioner then proceeded to state :—" Khan Bahadur Mir Abdul Ali has descended from a high family of Syads belonging to the town of Manchar of the Poona District, who have been enjoying since the time of the Mogals a permanent net cash allowance of Rs. 395 per annum from the revenues of the village. The present recipient of the allowance is his father, after whose death the son Khan Bahadur Mir Abdul Ali will succeed to the allowance. Khan Bahadur Mir Abdul Ali has the honour of being one of Her Majesty's Justices of the Peace for the City of Bombay, and he fills the most important and responsible office of Superintendent of Police of the Detective branch. He enjoys my entire confidence, and is a thoroughly trustworthy and most valuable officer of the Government, and much respected by all with whom he is brought in contact. I understand that in virtue of his title of Khan Bahadur he ranks as a Second Class Sardar, and I beg now to recommend, which I do most strongly, that in consideration of his meritorious services extending over a period of twenty-two years, that His Excellency the Governor-in-Council will recognise the same by conferring on Khan Bahadur Mir Abdul Ali 'the rank of a First Class Sardar.'"

On the 15th of May 1888 the Governor-in-Council issued a resolution acknowledging with pleasure "the merit of the service rendered by Khan Bahadur Mir Abdul Ali and other police officers in connection with the Parel murder. Police officers, like those of other departments, must look to promotion in their departments as the most appropriate reward for meritorious services. It is only on rare occasion that titles, such as that already conferred on Khan Bahadur Mir Abdul Ali, can be awarded. Government are glad that the officer has, by his abilities and services, continuned to justify the honourable distinction conferred upon him."

The recommendation for the conferring of the title of Sardar on Mir Abdul Ali was supplemented by Colonel Wilson in 1889. In his official report to Government on the detection of the triple murder at Dadar above referred to, Colonel Wilson, after bestowing high praise upon Mr. Gell, the Acting Commissioner, for the zeal and perseverance throughout the inquiry, and giving credit to other officers, said :

"It now remains for me to bring prominently to notice the valuable and important services rendered by Khan Bahadur Mir Abdul Ali. The service being of an exceptional character, richly merits a special recognition by Government. He was the principal officer in charge of the case from the beginning to the end, and displayed remarkable tact and police accumen in tracing out the offender, very skilfully, putting together the evidence and placing it with precision and lucidity before the Government law officers. The successful termination of the case, I consider, was mainly due to his sound judgment and long experience in handling complicated cases of this kind. The accompanying copy of the certificate, given to the Khan Bahadur by Mr. Frere, Public Prosecutor, who conducted the case, will show how valuable his services were to the prosecution. Khan Bahadur Mir Abdul Ali has always been complimented by the Government law officers for the preparation of the most difficult cases and for the clever way in which he pieced evidence together and instructed them. The valuable services of this faithful and meritorious officer are too much numerous to be mentioned here, and most of them have been from time to time brought to the notice of Government. But for ready reference I will give a brief sketch of them before proposing a suitable reward."

After enumerating the Sardar's services extending over quarter of a century, Colonel Wilson proceeded to state: "The Khan Bahadur was highly complimented by the Advocate General and the presiding Judge, the Hon'ble Mr. Bayley, for skilfully detecting the crime and cleverly working up the evidence in the Parel murder case. The Government in their Resolution of the 15th May 1888 left it to the Commissioner to reward the other officers mentioned, by such suitable promotion as he was able to give; but as regards the Khan Bahadur nothing definite was said. Had Sir Frank Souter lived, he would certainly have made a further reference to Government on the subject. In Appendix lettered H will be found the most important services of the Khan Bahadur, acknowledged by Government, during a period of over ten years comprised between the Aurangabad forgery case and that of Syed Gull.

"The reason of my delaying to submit a proposal for a reward to the Khan Bahadur in the Arms case was because I was so impressed with the detection of the triple murder case that I decided to wait for the conclusion of the trial before doing so. Government desired me to acknowledge the services of the Khan Bahadur and other officers engaged in the Arms case. The Khan Bahadur is the eldest son of the famous detective officer Khan Bahadur Mir Akbar Ali, who has retired from the Bombay Police Force on an enhanced pension after a continuously meritorious and distinguished service, extending over a period of fifty-two years. * *

* * * * *

"The Khan Bahadur Mir Abdul Ali's eldest son is a barrister-at-law, and his second son is now studying in London for the Indian Civil Service Examination. His present salary is Rs. 350 per mensem, exclusive of horse allowance and house rent. His pay will be increased to Rs. 400 on the 15th November 1890, and Rs. 450 (being the maximum pay of the appointment) on 1st November 1893. The Khan Bahadur's excellent knowledge of English and Oriental languages and of the Criminal Law, combined with extraordinary detective abilities and the social position he enjoys, especially in the Mahomedan community, renders him a very valuable acquisition to the Police Force of this city. In political matters of importance, particularly in the confidential branch, his services and knowledge are quite invaluable and unique. The family of the Khan Bahadur are hereditary Inamdars and Kazies, and are connected with highly respectable families of hereditary Jagirdars and Inamdars of the Deccan. In point of precedence amongst natives, he ranks as a Second Class Sardar by virtue of the title of 'Khan Bahadur.' I now beg most strongly to urge upon the attention of Government the exceptional and unique nature of the services of the meritorious officer during a period of twenty-four years, and to solicit that they will be pleased to reconsider the recommendation made by my predecessor, the late Sir Frank Souter, and confer upon the Khan Bahadur the title of 'First Class Sardar,' a distinction in my opinion he fully deserves. The Government by acceding to this proposal will not only confer a suitable reward upon one of their most upright, faithful and deserving servants, but it will give an incentive to persons of good families to join the police service."

Chapter IV.

LATER SERVICES OF THE SARDAR.

In the year 1888 Sardar Abdul Ali succeeded in bringing to justice three Afghans, who were in the habit of smuggling arms and ammunitions, which were packed in bales of cotton and sent to trans-frontier outlaws. The Government of India took special interest in the case, and it was after four months' incessant toil, attention and patient inquiries that the Sardar apprehended the gang of Pathans. In bringing the facts of the case to the notice of Government, Colonel Wilson made the following remarks :—'Much time and trouble were expended in this case which required most delicate handling and the greatest patience, and it could never have been brought to so successful an end without the able supervision and great experience of Khan Bahadur Mir Abdul Ali.'

The Government requested Colonel Wilson to acknowledge the services of Khan Bahadur Mir Abdul Ali in this most important and complicated case. The Sardar's services were simply of incalculable value during the visit of His Highness the late Prince Albert Victor of Wales and of the present Czar to this city. The duty was most arduous and severe, and Colonel Wilson was much impressed with the admirable spirit with which he worked at the time, not caring for fatigue, hunger or labour. In the case of the forgeries of postal stamps also the services of the Sardar were represented to Government. The postal stamps were so beautifully executed, and difficult to distinguish from genuine ones without magnifying glasses, that outside opinion inclined to the belief that they were the work of European forgers. The Sardar, however, discovered after lengthened and careful inquiries that they were executed by one Kundoo, who had learnt the art of engraving when serving Government as a surveyor in the Trigonometrical Survey Department. He had also been formely connected with notorious gang of forgers under Dawaria, whose headquarters were at Poona. In his annual report to Government on the Police Administration Colonel Wilson said :—"The way in which the case was handled by Mir Abdul Ali, assisted by his inspectors, is deserving of the highest commendation."

In the beginning of the year 1890, there was a serious strike of the Municipal scavengers, and it must be still fresh in the recollection of the Bombay public what an amount of inconvenience and trouble it produced. The health of the whole city was in danger, and every moment an outburst of some severe epidemic was feared. If the strike had continued longer than it did, the results would have been most serious. The Sardar strained every nerve to put an end to the strike, and his exertions gained for him high praise from Sir Charles Ollivant, one of the most able and popular Commissioners, which the Bombay Municipality has ever had. Sir Charles Ollivant wrote to Colonel Wilson as follows :—" Permit me to repeat my thanks to you and all members of the Police Force for the very valuable and indispensable assistance rendered by the Police throughout the disturbance. Particularly let me bring to your notice the high sense I entertain of the energy, ability and discretion displayed by Khan Bahadur Mir Abdul Ali. I know in what high esteem his services have been held by successive Commissioners of Police and various Government officers, and I trust you will not think I am exceeding my province if after nearly nine years of my present post I add my testimony to the well-deserved record of appreciation which he already enjoys."

In reviewing the annual report on the Police for the year 1890, the Governor in Council "noticed with pleasure the commendation bestowed by the Commissioner of Police on individual Superintendents of the Police Force, and more particularly on Khan Bahadur Mir Abdul Ali, whose services in the detective branch have, since the close of the year, been rewarded by the Government of India with the title of Sardar."

When the title of Sardar was conferred upon Mir Abdul Ali, the news was hailed with joy, not only by the whole Force (European and Native), but by the native community, and more particularly by Mahomedans. Two evening entertainments were held on a grand and magnificent scale, one at Walkeshwar in the bungalow of Mr. Ahmedbhoy Habibbhoy, and another at the bungalow of His Highness Sultan Mahammad Shah Aga Khan, at Nesbit Road. The first entertainment was got up by leading and prominent citizens of Bombay, while the second was held in the Sardar's honour by his countrymen (Hindu and Mahomedan). The Sanad of the title was presented to him by Colonel Wilson at the Police office in the presence of Mr. Gell, the Deputy Commissioner, and all the officers and men of the Force. Colonel Wilson in handing over the Sanad to Mir Abdul Ali remarked that the Sardar had served the Government with loyalty, devotion, zeal and ability, for the long period of twenty-six years, and if all his services were to be enumerated it would take several hours. A report of the ceremony written at the time states :—

In the course of his speech the Commissioner pointed out that it was well known how the Sardar would never rest until he had satisfactorily unravelled the crimes he had been deputed to track out, and his abilities were such that he knew not how they could well do without him. Those services had been prominently brought to the notice of the Government of Bombay, and subsequently to that of the Government of India, who had recognised them by conferring on him the title of 'Sardar.' To illustrate the nature of the services performed by the Sardar, he alluded to the visit of the present Czar to this city. What those services were, and how arduous were the duties in relation to them, was best known to himself (the speaker). He would add, however, that those were carried out entirely to his satisfaction.

As he handed over the Sanad to the Sardar, the Commissioner wished him a long life to enjoy the honour, and said that the document would become a precious heirloom in the Sardar's family for many generations to come.

The document runs :—'To MIR ABDUL ALI, Khan Bahadur, Superintendent of the Bombay City Police. I hereby confer upon you the title of Sardar as a personal distinction.—(Sd.) LANSDOWNE, Viceroy and Governor-General of India. Simla, the 30th May, 1891.' The document is on vellum, surmounted at the top by the Royal Coat of Arms, the seal of the Governor-General of India being affixed at the end.

The Sardar, in tendering his thanks, said he felt indebted to the Commissioner for the title, which he owed to Colonel Wilson having powerfully supplemented the previous recommendation of his worthy predecessor in office, Sir Frank Souter. He felt greatly honoured by the title so graciously conferred on him by the Viceroy, and it would stimulate him to renewed vigour and energy, and he would never spare to do anything in his power to maintain the good name of the force.

Addressing the men on parade in Urdu, the Sardar added that whenever Government services were performed with devotion and loyalty, they were never left unrewarded. Consequently he exhorted them to exert their best energies and execute their duties in a trustworthy manner.

The "splendid services," which Sardar Mir Abdul Ali, Khan Bahadur, rendered during the Mahomedan and Hindu riots in Bombay were acknowledged by Mr. Vincent, who himself was always to be found in the thick of the fray. Efforts of Mr. Vincent and his men were beyond all praise, and the public were afterwards gratified to learn that the services of Mr. Vincent had been acknowledged by the Government of India conferring upon him the distinguished title of C. I. E. Sardar Abdul Ali's work was anything but light. He was seen everywhere during those eventful days. It was due to his exertions (supported by two of the leaders of Mahomedans, Khan Bahadur Kassam Mitha and Mr. Oomar Jamal) that the Sidis who did most of the fighting in the anti-Parsi riots of 1874, took no part in the disturbances of 1893. The reports in the daily papers at the time bear sufficient testimony to the excellent work done by the Sardar during the riots. He assisted in checking the disturbances, arresting the rioters, sheltering and protecting the helpless and poor persons, and above all in restoring peace and bringing about a reconciliation between the two communities. In conjunction with Mr. Brewin, he was specially appointed to prosecute the rioters before the magistrates and at the Criminal Sessions ; and he discharged the duty in a most efficient and satisfactory manner. His services were duly acknowledged by Government and its law officers.

When the Police Force was recently augmented, special arrangements were made by the Government on the recommendation of Colonel Wilson with the sanction of the Secretary of State for an increase in the salary of Sardar, whose maximum pay was fixed at Rs. 600 exclusive of the house rent and horse allowance. The Sardar in ordinary course would have obtained the maximum salary of his post in 1899, but on the strong recommendation of Mr. R. H. Vincent, and supported by the Government of Bombay, the Secretary of State only in August last sanctioned the payment of maximum salary to the Sardar at once in consideration of his most faithful and valuable services.

In the case in which Fonseca, a bailiff of the Small Cause Court, was sentenced to be executed, for causing the death of one Duarte, the Sardar rendered very valuable assistance to Mr. Brewin, an able officer in whose hands the case was placed by Mr. Vincent. As was remarked in the annual report of the Police for the year 1894, the Sardar exerts himself to the utmost in all matters small or great, and sets a splendid example to his subordinates. In the last annual report of the Police for 1895, Mr. Vincent said :—" Of the Superintendents, I would specially mention as deserving of commendation, is Sardar Khan Bahadur Mir Abdul Ali, who, in the numerous, intricate and delicate matters he had to undertake, proved himself again to be a most loyal, energetic and intelligent servant of Her Majesty." In the Police report for 1888, Colonel Wilson said : " Khan Bahadur Mir Akbar Ali, the Superintendent of the Detectives, has performed his duties in his accustomed, zealous and efficient manner. I have never in the whole course of my service met with an officer of his calibre, keen as a blood-hound when crime has to be detected, and unflagging in his zeal and devotion to duty."

Such are the official testimonies in regard to the career of this remarkable man, who is a bright example of all that a good policeman should be: upright in conduct, devoted to duty, and full of energy and zeal. But at the samo time his zeal does not carry him away to do wrong to an accused person. The foregoing brief summary of his services and the following pages, which contain a fuller account of many of his cases, will show that there is not the least exaggeration in the remark of Colonel Wilson that he did not know how they could do without the Sardar.

When Lord Lansdowne visited this city in March 1891, the Sardar accompanied the gabernatorial party on the occasion of the Viceroy's visit to several places of interest. At the Matunga Leper Asylum, Lord Harris, the then Governor of Bombay, called Sardar Abdul Ali and presented him to His Excellency. Lord Lansdowne shook hands with the Sardar and said: "I am very much thankful to you. I did not know that I was looked after by you." The Sardar bowed his acknowledgments to the Viceroy, and made a graceful reply to the effect that he was simply doing his duty.

During the recent visit to Bombay of Shahzada Nasrulla Khan, second son of his Highness the Amir of Kabul, the Sardar specially looked after the Prince, who was so much pleased with the attention paid to him by the Sardar, that he sent two valuable shawls to the Police Commissioner for presentation to the able and amiable Chief of our Detective force. The shawls were presented to the Sardar with the special permission of H. E. the Viceroy.

The Sardar's private life is not without many bright features. For the promotion of the welfare of his Mahomedan brethren he has been striving hard. He is the pioneer of liberal reforms among his community. In conjunction with Mr. Vincent, he has been trying hard to put on a permanent and sound footing the Mahomedan Orphanage for the foundation of which Mr. Haji Jakeria Haji Ahmed Patel has given two lakhs of rupees. The Sardar holds enlightened and broad views on social matters. He is a high Mason, and is a Past Worshipful Master of the Lodge Islam, of which he is one of the founders. He is always a friend of the poor, and no one really deserving support would ever go away without being helped by him. His advice is often solicited even by men of light and leading. He is acknowledged to have great natural abilities for his own profession, but his abilities are such that he would have been an ornament to any liberal profession. His motto is that 'contentment is the true philosopher's stone.' He does his work in a most modest and unostentatious manner, and even a child is not afraid of going to him.

The Sardar had a natural bent for the detective's work, and even in his school-days his detective abilities had gained him great distinction. A silver cup, which was to be run for, was stolen from the Byculla Club three days before the race. The young Mir Abdul Ali, who frequently used to go in his father's company to detect crimes, succeeded in recovering the cup, which was buried under the ground by the thief, actually twelve hours before it had been run for, and obtained a reward of Rs. 100 from Mr. Forjett. After passing his Matriculation Examination he studied Medicine for two years; but so struck was Colonel Henderson with his detective skill that he offered Mr. Mir Abdul Ali an appointment in the Police Force which was accepted, and as the events have proved he has been eminently successful in his Police career.

The Sardar had recently the great misfortune to lose his eldest son, Mr. Mir Sarfraz Ali, who died at Karachi on Sunday the 11th of October 1896. The late Mr. Mir Sarfraz Ali had received very liberal education in England, and was called to the Bar in 1890. He was a most promising Mahomedan counsel, and it is to be deeply regretted that he has been cut off so prematurely. Mir Sarfraz Ali was in the prime of young manhood, being only twenty-nine years of age at the time of his death. He was very popular among his wide circle of both European and Native friends, and his death is deeply regretted by all who knew him. By his genial disposition and suavity of manners, he had gained the love and affection of all with whom he came in contact. His services were often engaged in important cases in the Mofussil. In the dispute of the Khojas of Mahuva, in Bhavnagar, about some property, he was engaged by H. H. the Aga Khan. He conducted the case with marked ability. In the great Hyderabad jewel robbery case, in which some Nawabs of Hyderabad were charged with theft of jewellery, worth about seven lakhs of rupees, he was engaged to defend one of the accused. Only last year he ably defended a case at Bhavnagar, in which some Borahs were charged with murder. All the accused in that case were acquitted, and Mr. Mir Sarfraz Ali was complimented by the Judge on the able manner in which he conducted the case. He was a shrewd man of the world, and had inherited many of his father's intellectual attainments. He always took a very great interest in the promotion and welfare of the Mahomedan community. It was the late Mr. Mir Sarfraz Ali who convened a meeting of Mahomedans, a couple of years back, to protest against the dissection of dead bodies of Mahomedans in the hospitals. A petition was forwarded to Government, who passed a resolution, the effect of which was that the bodies should be handed over to the proper parties for burial. When the Dr. Mackichan Memorial Fund was started, he took a prominent part in the movement. By reason of his amiable qualities and obliging nature, he had won the esteem of all with whom he came in contact. He was suffering from lung diseases for some time past.

In 1894 he went on a long sea voyage, and journeyed to England and other countries of Europe. He returned from Europe in January 1895, the change having done him a world of good. About nine months' back the symptoms of malady again showed themselves, and he was ordered to try a change at Karachi. He remained at Quetta, Hyderabad, and Karachi, and proposed to go to Australia in December next. All that best medical skill can do was done to spare his life, but he succumbed to the disease. The deceased was married in a nobleman's family at Gwalior, but the death of his wife, three years ago, cast a gloom over his own life. He took greatly to heart the death of his wife, and now he himself has gathered among his forefathers. He leaves behind an only son, who is now at Gwalior. The greatest sympathy was felt for the Sardar in his sad bereavement, and he was the recipient of numerous telegrams and letters of condolence and sympathy, the senders including His Highness the Maharaja of Gwalior, His Highness Sultan Mahomed Shah Aga Khan, His Highness Aga Akbar Shah, and Mr. Dosabhoy Framji Karaka, C.S.I. Expressions of sorrow and grief were manifested on all hands, which gave an idea of the high esteem in which the deceased was held. His remains were brought to Bombay and carried to Manchar for burial by the side of his great-great-grandfather whose shrine is worshipped even now as that of a saint, not only by Mahomedans, but also by the Hindus of Manchar and other surrounding villages. The funeral procession was a very grand one, and was on a scale never witnessed before in Bombay, the death of Mr. Mir Sarfraz Ali having filled the hearts of the Mahomedan community with the deepest sorrow and regret, which was shared by a host of European, Parsee, and Hindu friends of the deceased. A mass meeting of the Mahomedans was held at the bungalow of Syad Mahomed Makba, and it was resolved, on the motion of Nabob Mohshun-ul-Mulk Mehdi Ali, to forward a letter of condolence to the Sardar in his sad bereavement. The letter was personally handed over to him by Nabob Mehdi Ali, Mr. Nazmudin Tyabji and Molvi Hidaetulla at the bungalow of Mr. Mir Aun Ali. The Mahomedans have started a fund to perpetuate the memory of the deceased by opening a hospital, bearing the name of Mir Surfraz Ali, in connection with the Mahomedan orphanage at a cost of nearly Rs. 25,000. The European, Parsee and Hindu friends have also subscribed money to found a University scholarship in the name of the deceased, while a similar movement is set on foot by Hindu and Mahomedan residents of Manchar and other villages in the Deccan.

The second and the eldest surviving son Mir Aun Ali is a very promising young man. He has a literary turn of mind, and is conversant with several European and Oriental languages. As he showed signs of great talent at a very early age, the Sardar sent him to England to compete for the Civil Service Examination but he failed. He was, however, called to the Bar in 1894. He stayed in England, France and other countries of Europe for about eight years, and he thereby acquired a good knowledge not only of different languages, but of the customs and manners of different countries. His contributions of miscellaneous articles to the columns of the *Bombay Gazette* have been well received by the public. His views in regard to certain University reforms were well expressed in some of these articles. He is a pioneer of sound liberal reforms and not a blind advocate of mere sham advancement. His professional services have been already several times engaged in important Native States in political matters, and he has acquitted himself in an admirable manner. He is also a Justice of the Peace. He has a very wide circle of European and Native friends, and he is a *personna grata* in society. He is the Honorary Secretary of the Mahomedan Orphanage, and as such he is doing his best to place the institution on a most firm and permanent footing. The third son, Mir Hasan Ali, is now a student in the school, and gives hopes of a brilliant future career.

A man of remarkable ingenuity and great resourcefulness, the Sardar has never been slow to do good to his countrymen, whether Parsees, Hindus, Christians or Mahomedans. He is respected by his superiors and loved by his subordinates for his numerous qualities both of head and heart, and for his sterling character. He has an exemplary love for his superiors, and always talks of them with veneration. Such a man combining the many-sided qualifications and virtues to which we have referred, cannot fail to secure appreciation at the hands of his superiors and the approbation of the general public. Though the task of a detective is often thankless, the Sardar has many admirers and friends and few foes; which is indeed high praise for a police officer. It is a source of delight to the native community that one of their own countrymen should have succeeded so well in this most arduous and responsible position. "Every man is the architect of his own fortune, for character is fate," says a well-known proverb, and this is strikingly exemplified in the case of Sardar Mir Abdul Ali, as are also the aphorisms that "honesty is the staff upon which the pilgrim of life may lean with confidence," while "perseverance is the helm in the hand of a skilful pilot, enabling him to steer safely over the stormy sea of opposition, and to land safely at his wished-for destination." Sardar Mir Abdul Ali's laborious life has been spent in exerting his powers of body and mind in the service of the Government and the public, and he has won the golden opinions of all with whom he has come in contact. The Sardar belongs to the class of men who are always ready to sacrifice popularity on the altar of duty. This is a crowning beauty of his noble career, and we may regard his public labours for the prevention and punishment of crime as forming an enduring monument—far more enduring than marble busts or statues—of a life spent in the service of the Government and the people.

THE WILFUL DESTRUCTION OF THE S.S. "AURORA."

At no time in the annals of the criminal history of Bombay—nay even of India—was such general interest was aroused as when what was subsequently known as the great "Aurora Frauds" were perpetrated. In June 1870, commercial circles, not only in Bombay, but also in Liverpool and elsewhere, had their attention almost absorbed by, first, the suspicious circumstances attending the loss of the ship "Aurora," and then by extraordinary confessions made by those who planned and carried out the destruction of that vessel. The suspicious circumstances were the loss of the vessel by fire the very first morning after she sailed from Bombay; the mysterious origin of the fire; the total absence of any effort to extinguish it; the fact that bills of lading representing large consignments of valuable cotton had been signed by the captain and turned to account at the Underwriters' offices and the banks while no such consignments had gone on board, and substitution of rubbish purchased at Rs. 16 or Rs. 20 a bale for good cotton and wool as cargo. So serious were the rumours afloat before the "Aurora" sailed, that efforts were made by the Underwriters to have her departure delayed by the police, but that could not be managed in time, and she left the port to be burned a few miles out. Grievous as these suspicions were, the extensive nature of the fraud was not known until first one and then another of those implicated related the whole of their connection with the transaction. Fearing detection, and probably knowing that the police were collecting evidence against him, one Soonderji Shamji, a native merchant or broker, who had chartered the ship, related to the police all that he knew of the affair. He had been privy to the plot, which seems to have been originated and matured by a man, named Elmstone, and he procured and shipped the greater quantity of the rubbish. His statements led to the arrest of Messrs. Elmstone and Whitewell, the brokers for the ship, and of Captain Harriott, who had been her commander. The captain followed suit with a voluntary confession on his part to the effect that he had been led to sign the bills of lading under a guarantee from Messrs. Elmstone and Whitewell, that the goods would follow; that he knew these bills of lading had been used to procure advances from the banks; that every effort he put forth to obtain the goods they represented was vain, and that in despair he listened to Mr. Elmstone's suggestion to destroy the ship, resisted long, but at last consented under the assurance that it would mean the making of his fortune. Messrs. Elmstone and Whitowell told the same story in different words, and the carpenter, who by this time was in custody, related how he had been engaged to do the job for £600. He was to scuttle the "Aurora," but finding an opportunity to spill the turpentine in the lazarette he threw in a piece of lighted oakum and burned her. The origin of it all was the dishonest and ruinous practice some captains had got into of signing bills of lading before the goods had been received, a practice which, though punishable by law, had become somewhat prevalent in Bombay. Banks had long refused to advance money to shippers with "documents to follow;" but the fraudulent or impecunious shippers got behind the north wind and flaunted the documents in the bankers' faces with even "goods to follow," and as in this case, it happened in several cases that no goods followed. Mr. Edgington, assisted by Mr. Mir Abdul Ali, took a prominent part in throwing light on this most extraordinary case of the most astounding audacity. Although the task of the police was, to some extent, lightened by the confessions of the prisoners, it was not until the police obtained sufficient proofs to secure a conviction that the confessions were first made before the Commissioner of Police and then before the Presidency Magistrate. The revelations in the case actually caused a panic in commercial circles, and it was the subject of conversation in every quarter for some days. On each occasion of the hearing of the case, first at the Police Court, and subsequently at the Criminal Sessions, the Court was densely crowded by merchants and others who took the greatest interest in the case. Both the English dailies issued supplements, containing the full report of the case, every evening, and the native papers teemed with accounts of the trial.

But the excitement was at its height when further disclosures of gross commercial immorality in certain sections of the community continued to be made day after day in Bombay, and the greatest uneasiness prevailed in the mercantile world. The burning of the "Aurora" formed the centre-piece, around which the other figures grouped themselves, and other vessels than the "Aurora" and captains of sterner stuff than Harriott appeared in the ugly tableau. Several arrests were made, and the police were known to have a bundle of warrants in hand and to be on the look-out for the men who had disappeared. One well-known man, Karsondas Madhowdas, was arrested. He was one of the prominent figures of the breezy days of 1865, one of Mr. Premchand Raichand's lieutenants, one of those who had passed splendidly under Act XXVIII. (Insolvency Act), and who had afterwards been doing a good deal in the cotton trade. He knew something about the "Aurora" fraud, and would probably have given information to the police, only his offer to do so came too late. Karsondas and Captain Brown of the ship "Theresa" were arrested for conspiracy to defraud Messrs. Finlay, Scott and Company by signing bills of lading for one thousand bales of cotton, before they had shipped a single bale. On this fictitious shipment Messrs. Finlay, Scott and Company advanced £8,500. The captain confessed to having signed the bills of lading, and Karsondas Madhowdas to having deceived Messrs. Finlay, Scott and Company, as to the real state of the circumstances.

Further connected with the "Aurora" frauds and other shameful dealings of a like nature was the suicide of a well-known Parsee cotton broker and opium agent of Bombay. This man also had a history. In 1862, when he was only twenty-four years of age, he began mercantile life as a member of a firm which failed in 1866. The liabilities of the firm amounted to upwards of fifty lakhs, the reliable assets being under half-a-lakh. In November of the following year the Parsee broker was sentenced to a term of imprisonment, at the expiry of which he again began life—this time in some business relations with Mr. Karsondas Madhowdas and as a broker to one of the first European firms. This man was mentioned in the "Aurora" case, as having given guarantee for some of the cotton on board that ship, but this he denied to his brother before his death. He confessed, however, that he had stood guarantee for certain cotton on board the ship "Greyhound." He said that as the shipper, Karsondas Madhowdas, mentioned above, was unable to place the bales of cotton on board the ship, all the liabilities would fall on himself, and as he was unable to save his reputation he had determined to destroy his life. This he effected by swallowing a poisonous dose of opium.

In addition to this, similar frauds were committed in respect of cargo on the ship "Theresa." The cargo stank so horribly, that the surveyors who went on board to examine it for the Underwriters, found it barely possible to remain below. Such was the putrefaction going on in the rubbish of which some of the bales consisted. The "Greyhound" was also under suspicion. The confession of the Parsee implicated that vessel to which the finger of popular rumour had already directed attention, and the sudden and unexplained disappearance of her captain, who was also a part owner, lent colour to this suspicion. In addition to all the foregoing, three Bhattias were arrested on a charge of cheating Messrs. Volkart Brothers to the extent of £1,380 by shipping rubbish in place of cotton, and the total sum involved in these fraudulent consignments of sweepings instead of cotton was estimated at £100,000.

Captain Harriott's confession showed that he was instigated by Elmstone and Whitewell to destroy the ship. Elmstone told Whitewell respecting him, "I have put a fortune in this young fellow's way, doing good for his owners and himself." Whitewell with a view to induce the captain said that such chances as that rarely occurred, and he saw a clear way to make a fortune for themselves. The captain yielded, and received £1,000 as his share for consenting to the destruction of the ship. In his confession the carpenter, who was asked to scuttle the ship, admitted having received for the purpose £600, the major portion of which he remitted to his wife in England. He said that he did not scuttle her, although he told the captain that he had done so. After giving the details of conversation with the captain he said, "The idea suddenly occurred to me that I could easily set fire to the ship. On the impulse of the moment I struck a match, lighted a bit of oakum, opened the door of lazarette, and threw the burning oakum towards the spot where the turpentine had been spilt. I closed the door of the lazarette instantly, and immediately heard an explosion inside and found the ship was on fire, and I heard the cry of fire from the deck. I am very sorry that I yielded to the impulse of the moment and fired the ship. I had previously determined not to do anything towards destroying her, and had even written to my wife telling her to write to the owner of this and inform him that things were going on very strangely, and I did not half like it. I have not the least doubt that my wife did so write. I previously forgot to state that soon after the proposition to destroy the ship had been made, the captain took me with him to Colaba, and left me standing on the road while he went into a bungalow and brought Mr. Whitewell out, and the captain then introduced me to him. Mr. Whitewell said: "Well, carpenter, do you think you can manage this little affair?" I said, "Yes." He went on to say, "This is a chance that happens but once in a man's life." Then speaking to the captain he said: "It is a pity we did not think of this before—a large fortune might have been made for each of us. However, we shall do very well as it is."

At the Sessions Court, which was presided over by the Hon'ble Mr. Justice Bayley, tho following points were raised by the counsel for the prisoners :— "Whether the prisoners C. T. Elmstone, Alfred Whitewell and George Harriott are or any of them could, in point of law, be convicted upon all or any of the additional heads of charges of which they have been respectively found guilty, it appearing that the British ship called the "Aurora" was destroyed by Richard William Marks, a British subject, by fire on the high seas, and at a distance of fifty miles or thereabouts from the Harbour of Bombay." Briefly the question was whether the High Court of Bombay had jurisdiction to try the case. Mr. Justice Bayley having reserved the point, it was argued before a Full Court consisting of Sir M. R. Westropp, Chief Justice, Mr. Justice Bayley, and Mr. Justice Green. The Full Court held that the prisoners were all subject to the Admiralty Jurisdiction of the High Court of Bombay, and that they were liable to punishment under the Statute Law of England. They were accordingly tried and found guilty.

Mr. Justice Bayley, in passing sentence, said : "Prisoners at the Bar,—It is indeed a most painful and melancholy spectacle, not only to those present in this crowded Court, but to all Englishmen in India, that four of our own countrymen—persons of intelligence and the majority of you, doubtless, men of some education—should stand in that dock convicted of a crime of such astounding audacity. In this land, so far away from our own homes, where we are but little else than a handful of men as compared with the uncounted millions of India—where the acts and deeds of most of us are watched and criticised by the keen eyes of those among whom we dwell, and where force of character and force of example have such a mighty influence for good or for evil—one cannot but reflect upon the shock which your acts of conspiracy and crime must have occasioned to the mercantile classes of this city, which have long been accustomed to respect the honourable dealings of Englishmen engaged in the lucrative pursuits of commerce and trade. It is, I believe, upwards of a quarter of a century, since a similar crime was planned in Bombay, and it was at the October Sessions in the year 1844 that Sir Erskine Perry, then a Puisne Judge of the late Supreme Court, awarded from this bench the punishment of transportation for life to the wealthy native merchant Aloo Paroo, and passed sentences of less severity on the two other natives, who were concerned in conspiring to burn the ship 'Belvedere' on the high seas on her voyage from Bombay to China. As to you, Elmstone and Whitewell, I can see no extenuating circumstances whatever in your conduct. You contrived between you this most infamous plot ; you corrupted Harriott, and, through him, Marks, and you seduced them both from their duty to their employers. Then you obtained large sums of money on three bills of exchange, two of them for £3,000 sterling and the third for £1,200 sterling, and the evidence of your clerk, Anandrao Krustnarao, proves that the copy of these three bills was in Elmstone's handwriting, while the endorsement of your firm's name at the back was in the handwriting of Whitewell. Upon these bills and upon other documents equally valueless, you obtained from the Agra Bank advances at the rate of £10 sterling per bale against what was supposed to have been 600 bales of cotton, whereas with respect to 500 bales not a particle had been shipped, or was ever intended to be, and with respect to the 100 actually shipped, the cotton in them was the refuse of the bazaar—what was described in the evidence as 'droppings'—of which you purchased a portion at the rate of Rs. 40, and the rest Rs. 48 per bale. Conduct, more disgraceful and more criminal it is impossible to conceive. You, Harriott, and you, Marks, allowed yourselves to be drawn into the scheme, and after due reflection, you consented for, what to you were large sums of money, to aid in the destruction of the 'Aurora.' Your respective shares in the transaction, though highly criminal, appear to me to require a much lighter punishment than that which will be awarded to Elmstone and Whitewell, but still your sentences will be severe. I have listened attentively to what has been urged by the learned counsel acting on behalf of all of you, but contrition and confession of guilt after the commission of a crime so carefully planned and of such gravity, cannot, in my opinion, be accepted as a plea in mitigation of punishment."

Elmstone and Whitewell, the brokers, were sentenced to penal servitude for life; Harriott, the captain, to penal servitude for fifteen years, and Marks, the carpenter, to penal servitude for ten years. Thus ended the most remarkable case of the felonious destruction of the 'Aurora.'

In one of his despatches to Government, Sir Frank Souter in enumerating "some of the big cases in which his (Mr. Abdul Ali's) services were most conspicuous," said as follows: "There was great 'Aurora' case in which the ship was deliberately and fraudulently burnt, and on which the services of the police were acknowledged and brought to the notice of Government by the Underwriters. Mir Abdul Ali took a prominent part in the work of throwing light on this heavy case, which was of such a vital importance to the mercantile community of Bombay."

CLEVER CAPTURE OF A NOTED MUTINEER.

THE Sardar Bahadur rendered excellent services to the State in the case of Moulvi Liakat Ali, who as the pretended Viceroy of the King of Delhi, deluged the streets and courts of Allahabad with English blood on the 6th of June 1857, and perpetrated barbarous atrocities, which filled with dismay the hearts of even native beholders. The capture of the mutineer, fourteen years after the Mutiny of 1857, was most remarkable. The most sanguine could not even have dreamt that the miscreant could be run down to earth in Bombay after a long lapse of time during which nothing was known of his whereabouts. Curiously enough he was arrested at a time when his continuing at large would have been a direct menace to the public peace, for he was secretly engaged in seditious preachings which might easily have led a band of disaffected persons to flock round his standard. There is, therefore, no wonder that Sardar Abdul Ali's strenuous efforts to secure unimpeachable documentary evidence of sedition against the Moulvi were duly appreciated and promptly recognised by Government. The following facts will give the readers an idea of the enormous magnitude and atrocity of the dark crimes of the Moulvi. The momorable 6th of June 1857 has not yet been forgotton by the oldest residents of Allahabad. At 9 o'clock that evening a rocket was fired from the direction of Popamaw, and was quickly answered by another shot from the cantonments. The flash hardly left the sky when the roll of musketry told the panic-stricken Englishmen that the smouldering embers of disaffection and disloyalty had been fanned into open mutiny. The 6th Regiment of Native Infantry had proved faithless and mutinied, slaughtering their officers who were, all told, fifteen in number at their mess-house.

By a strange coincidence a letter of thanks for their loyalty from H. E. Lord Canning, the then Viceroy of India, had been read over to this very regiment while on parade, a few hours before the outbreak, when amid lusty cheering they cried out to be led against the rebels of Benares. Next day the green flag of the Prophet of Islam was seen flying over the city Kotwali, and the Europeans in the station were butchered to death in a most terrible and shocking manner. Those who had taken the telegraphic warning of General Wheeler from Cawnpore, and had promptly acted on it by leaving their abodes and taking refuge in the Fort were the only persons saved from the onslaught. Allahabad was taken possession of by Moulvi Liakat Ali, a native of Mogaon, which was the most disaffected and turbulent village of Chail. The Moulvi, who was a handsome fellow, belonged to the caste of weavers, and in 1857 was a school master by profession. The hyper-sanctity of this bigot had gained for him the respect of the whole people of the village, who were too ready to follow any leader. The Mahomedan zamindars of

Chail and others accepted the Moulvi as their leader, and marched to Allahabad, and there they proclaimed him the governor of the district in the name of the King of Delhi. Khooshro Bag was chosen for his head-quarters, and there the rebel courts were held, and to secure the place two nine-pounder guns, which had been sent by Colonel Simpson the day previous with a party of the 6th Native Infantry to Daragange, were secured by the rebels and placed inside the garden gates. With full powers the Moulvi reigned in the place for a week, during which even the natives were struck with horror at the fires, the murders and rapine which were the order of the day. But there was no system in the outbreak, no concert between the mutineers. The Moulvi headed the Mahomedans, the Pragwal Brahmins carried with them the hinder population, while the troops fought on their own account. On the 11th of June Colonel Neill arrived in Allahabad, and assumed command of the Fort garrison, and on the 15th a grand attack was made by the Fusiliers, the Sikhs, and the Irregulars on Kydgange and Moteegange, supported by a steamer moving up the Jamna, with a howitzer and some riflemen on board. The rebels were beaten at every point, and our troops followed them up closely. The terror of approaching disaster soon broke up the Moulvi's camp in the Khooshro Bag, and on the night of the 16th Moulvi Liakat Ali and all his followers fled, leaving behind them the two guns and a number of prisoners, among them the brave young Cheek, who died the same evening, his body covered with wounds and sores, and his mind wandering. Conductor Coleman was also among the Moulvi's prisoners, and died soon after his release from the wounds he had received.

Meanwhile the Moulvie had escaped. For no less than fourteen years he wandered about the country, trying to stir up the people to bring them to the days of his former glory at Khooshro Bag. For the capture of the notorious Moulvi, who had cleverly disguised himself, handsome rewards were offered, as his freedom was a source of great anxiety to the British Government in the country, but he was nowhere to be found. After his flight from Alahabad, the Moulvi seemed to have lived in disguise as a respectable Mahomedan gentleman, and those amongst whom his lot was cast had not the faintest idea that he was the person "wanted." In this position he lost no opportunity of inculcating sedition, and preaching a new Zehad to those around him. Two years before his arrest the Moulvi was preaching sedition in the neighbourhood of the residence of the Nawab of Sachin, a few miles from Surat. The Nawab at once conveyed this intelligence to Mr. Hope (afterwards Sir Arthur Theodore Hope), the then Collector of Surat, and an inquiry was instituted, which resulted in the discovery of the fact that the Moulvi had been living in the State for more than five years.

The Sachin Nawab had his suspicions roused from the Moulvi's surreptitious ways of coming to and going out of his State, and from what he had heard of the holding of secret meetings, and when attempts were made to arrest him, it was found that he had made himself scarce. From the parties sent out to gather information, Mr. Hope obtained sufficient information to believe that the man was exciting disaffection among the people, and that he was an agent of some party sent out for the purpose. A warrant was issued for the Moulvi's arrest, and although it was suspected, it was not definitely known at the time that he had been a primemover in the Mutiny. Diligent search was made, but to no purpose. Finding the place too hot for him the Moulvi left the Sachin State and for some time remained in hiding at Baroda, which place he appeared to have left some two months prior to his arrest in Bombay. In Bombay he passed himself off as a pious devotee, and was known to be engaged in praying for the birth of a son to the Ranee of Baroda. The Bombay Police, however, had some doubts as to his anticedents. At that time a man acquainted with the fact of the issue of the warrant by the Collector of Surat, happened to be in Bombay. The Moulvi had, meantime, assumed the name of Abdul Kareem, and though his real name and identity were unknown, this man entertained suspicions that Abdul Kareem was the person "wanted" by the police. He accordingly communicated with Government of Bombay on the subject. The Governor-in-Council referred the matter to Mr.

Edginton, the then Acting Commissioner of Police, Sir Frank Souter being on leave at the time.

Inquiries were instituted, but the circumstances alleged against the man were found insufficient to justify his arrest, and the result was that the Collector of Surat was communicated with on the subject, and a request was made to send a man from Surat armed with a warrant to identify the man. The warrant was accordingly sent by Mr. Hope with a letter stating that *he was not in a position to prove any offence* against the man. On the receipt of the warrant, Mr. Edginton personally made careful enquiries into the matter, and ultimately came to the conclusion that the man must have in his possession some documents which would lead to the detection of the offence alleged against him. Mr. Edginton, as was subsequently ascertained, was not wrong in his opinion. He reported the matter to Government, at the same time requesting to be allowed to use the warrant issued by the Collector of Surat for the arrest and search of the man against whom the police had the strongest suspicion. At this juncture Mr. Souter returned to duty, and on receiving orders from Government, the Moulvi was arrested at the Byculla railway station by Mr. Edginton and the late Rao Bahadur Daji Gungaji Rane as he was about to leave Bombay for Central India. Nobody could have dared to assert that the man who was arrested was Moulvi Liakat Ali, an accomplice of the notorious

Nana Saheb of Bithoor, for up to the time of his arrest there was no proof of his identity. Baker Ali, a respectable Mahomedan gentleman, with whom the accused lived in Bombay, did not suspect for a moment that he was harbouring tho noted mutineer.

The case was at once placed in the hands of Mir Abdul Ali, who found in the possession of the accused a number of seditious papers. It was due to the very great skill and indefatigable exertions of Mir Abdul Ali that it was proved beyond doubt that the man who was caught was no other than Liakat Ali. In conjunction with the Oriental Translator Mir Abdul Ali was engaged for over a fortnight in translating the papers found upon the person of the Moulvi, on whose head a very heavy price had been set by the Government of India. There was also a secret code found upon him, and it was cleverly deciphered by the Sardar. The Moulvi was so popular that the task of his arrest was considered next to impossible, and that of identification much greater. It was anticipated that some little difficulty would be experienced in procuring the conviction of the accused, but thanks to tho labour of Mir Abdul Ali unimpeachable documentary evidence was available to establish the clear identity of the mutineer and his future plans to attempt an overthrow of the British Raj in India. The feeling in favour of the Moulvi was very strong among the Mahomedans. On the occasion of the marriage of a son of the Moulvi, the family, owing to the confiscation of their property were unable to celebrate the event with befitting *eclat*, but the Mahomedans of the district subscribed among themselves all his marriage expenses. Two natives, who knew the Moulvi when he held temporary sway at Khooshro Bag in 1857, were sent down from Allahabad, and they at once recognised him as the veritable mutineer for whom all search had hitherto been made in vain. Hence the Moulvi was sent to Allahabad for trial. News of his journey seemed to have gone on in advance of the train by which he travelled, for all along the route the stations were crowded with persons anxious to see the man under whose direction so much innocent blood had been shed during the Mutiny. At Jabalpur, a European, who in 1857, at Allahabad, had a most marvellous escape from death at the hands of this man, identified the Moulvi at a glance. The scene at the Allahabad railway station was one the like of which had not occurred there for many years. Thousands of natives had assembled, and when the arch-rebel made his appearance they gave vent to their indignation by prolonged hootings, hissings, and groanings. At Allahabad he sat with evident pleasure and ease to be photographed, and some capital likenesses of him were taken.

In appearance the Moulvi was a handsome fellow, apparently about fifty-five years of age, with regular features, a tall and commanding aspect, and short-cut grey beard, whiskers and moustaches. Shortly after his arrival an inventory of his property was taken. A bag was found containing over Rs. 100, and there was also a peculiar bamboo stick with a brass ferrule at one end and a glass or crystal knob at the other. It was at first suspected to be a weapon, but on a close examination it was found that the crystal only served as a screw, and the entire hollow of the stick contained gold ingots of the aggregate value of Rs. 2,000. The prisoner did not now attempt to deny his identity, though he gave a false name when first examined. An advertisement in the *Pioneer* asked for information as to the whereabouts of the family of Conductor Coleman, who was murdered in 1857, and whose family, if surviving, would be able to give valuable assistance to the present case. The Moulvi was first tried before Mr. C. J. Robertson, Magistrate of Allahabad, who committed him to the Sessions on a charge of complicity in the rebellion of 1857, having in June of that year held a court at Khooshro Bag, Allahabad, headed the mutineers and waged war in the field against the troops of Her Majesty.

Tho captured seditionmonger pleaded guilty to the charges, but stated that his only crime was that of rebellion. He submitted that he had saved the lives of several gentlemen and ladies at Allahabad. In one particular case a lady was protected by him from Nana's forces at Cawnpore, and to effect her concealment better he dressed her in native clothes and passed her as his sister, but he failed to identify the fugitive. In a statement made before the Magistrate on being first arrested and brought to Allahabad, the Moulvi gave his own version of the part he took in the Mutiny, and narrated his subsequent career. He stated that in all he did, though seemingly hostile to the British Government, he was actuated by fear of Nana. In reality he did his utmost to support the British Power, and to protect the lives and property of Europeans. In one case he actually misled Nana about the arrival of British troops and trusting the statement Nana had remained careless, with the result that he was taken by surprise by the British troops and was completely routed. He further related how he escaped from Allahabad after the British troops entered the city and joined Nana at Cawnpore, but he affirmed that though at the risk of his life he always endeavoured to thwart the movements and intentions of the arch-rebel. He was released, and after the capture of Delhi he fled to Muttra, and went afterwards to Faraccabad and Lucknow. When the game was up, he disguised himself as a *fakeer*, crossed Rewa and Manikpore with three or four men, and took refuge with the Nawab of Sachin, in Bombay Presidency, who, he said, was kind to him.

After staying at Sachin for some time the Moulvi went to Guadar, thence to Muscat, when, on the outbreak of disturbances there, he returned to Sachin, and lived with the Nawab until his arrest. He averred that he never afterwards returned to Allahabad and went only once to Bagdad, and never to Mecca. Mr. A. R. Pollock, the Sessions Judge, in passing the sentence of transportation for life on the Moulvi, remarked that whilst the rebellion lasted at Allahabad and Cawnpore, Liakat Ali devoted himself to the rebel cause, and had been brought to trial not by any act of submission of his own, but through *his being captured by the Bombay Police whilst living under another name.* In a case of such a magnitude as that, and where the accused had shown such determined hostility which, but for total absence of courage, might have been carried further, the Court had but one course left to it, and that was to pass a heavy sentence. The Moulvi, who was sent to Port Blair, declared that he had left property at Allahabad to the extent of three and a-half lakhs of rupees which had been confiscated by the Crown, and that he had saved the lives of Europeans, men, women and children, during the Mutiny.

The reader must have perceived how great were the services in this case of Mir Abdul Ali, who was highly spoken of by Major Parsons, who prosecuted the Moulvi. Sir Frank Souter recommended that the valuable and faithful services of Mir Abdul Ali be marked by Government conferring upon him the title of Khan Bahadur.

In accordance with this recommendation Government conferred the title of Khan Bahadur on Mir Abdul Ali.

THE DeGA CONSPIRACY CASE.

On Tuesday, the 12th of November 1872, the whole native community was thrilled with awe by the report of a most diabolical tragedy enacted almost simultaneosly at the house of a Mr. DeGa, an accountant in the Bank of Bombay, opposite the Royal Theatre, Grant Road, and at two small bungalows at Bandora. It resulted in the death of four persons and the illness of several others. The dire deed seemed to be the result of a deep-laid and diabolical plot conceived and carried out secretly and carefully. The crime was rendered the more revolting and detestable when it was discovered that the perpetrators had not only struck at the intended victim or victims, but the blow had felled two innocentpersons not included in this evil design. The time selected for the accomplishment of the devilish purpose was, unhappily, but too well suited to the success of the plot, and there was a method in which the whole affair indicated a carefully laid plan and pointed to shrewd and wary designers. The plot appeared to have been laboriously matured, and offered a tangled web for the detectives to unravel.

A person dressed or disguised as a peon, but who was not seen by any member of the family, brought to the "Prospect Lodge," the town residence of the DeGa family, a couple of confectionery cakes, and devliered them with the compliments of a near relative. The message itself was plainly calculated to evade the suspicion of the DeGa people, and to induce them to accept and partake of the articles sent by a trusted and near relation. The scheme succeeded too well. Not a single question was asked. The cakes were accepted, and placed on the table after dinner, and Mr. J. M. DeGa and his sister Miss Amelia DeGa partook thereof. Shortly afterwards both of them were seized with very violent vomiting fits and excruciating pain. Three of the servants, who also consumed a portion of the confectionery, were likewise attacked. Unfortunately, the sad affair did not end here. A portion of the present was sent to a relation of Mr. DeGa. The relation Mr. A. DeGa sub-divided the sweets and sent some to a Mr. J. D. Pereira, a managing clerk of Messrs. Dallas and Lynch, Solicitors. Mr. and Mrs. DeGa and Mr. Pereira and his mother partook of the sweets. They were all seized with vomiting fits and violent pain. Medical assistance was at once called for, and all medical men could do was done, yet Mrs. Pereira and her son soon expired. Two members of DeGa family also died, but the surviving members had no suspicion of evil designs against any particular person. As far as was known they had no enemies. The motive of the deed seemed inexplicable. Whether it was prompted by a petty but virulent malice or deep revenge, or whether it was done for the sake of filthy lucre no one could say. In respect of the latter suspicion it was suggested that investigation should be made as to who would have been pecuniarily benefited, and in what manner by the removal of any one of the family who might have been in actual possession of ancestral property with reversionary rights to others. This was a painful and delicate task, but the cause of justice and protection of society demanded such an enquiry. A reward was offered for revealing the mystery, with a view to whet the keenness of the detective force, or tempt some wretched accomplice to make a clean breast of the horrible crime.

At this very time Bombay was honoured by Viceregal visit. The unusual and to some extent irresistible declaration of Lord Northbrook's official visit to this city contributed to withdraw the attention of the public, if it did not paralyse the endeavours of the police in some degrees from investigating the particulars of the diresome quadruplicate murder. So great had been the influence of the engagements into which the public of Bombay had been plunged a couple of days after this sad bereavement in the DeGa family, that many who came in contact daily with the men who were so diabolically done to death, scarcely visited his house. The story of their sudden and awful end fell on ears perturbed with the sounds of a Royal Salute and expressions of condolence or enquiries were for the nonce sacrificed to the main run of conversation regarding the great display and splendour consequent upon the Viceregal visit. Nevertheless the woeful fact remained that when in our midst all was joy and revelry, a crime was consummated which called for the deepest sympathy of the public, and which for the extent of desolation that it had wrought among well-to-do and much-esteemed people was almost without parallel in the annals of the city. The public demanded that the best penetration of the police should be turned to the task of unearthing the perpetrators of the deed. There never was a better example of unloosing the belt of Orion than this. The circumstantial evidence pointed to the fact that a net was laid for only one of the DeGas, but unfortunately more persons were drawn into it unwittingly. A man who enters upon the execution of a crime can never at any time limit its ultimate effects, and in this case the results were far more terrible than the culprit himself could have thought of. A suspicion rested on Michael DeGa, a younger brother of the deceased, who was living separately in the neighbourhood of Mazagon. He was taken into custody, but no evidence could be gathered against him. Pestonji Dinshaw, a Parsee Solicitor, was also suspected of complicity in the affair, but the police enquiries were baffled in consequence of the absence of the cooli, who took the cakes to the DeGa family, and who was supposed to have been murdered and buried in a field so that he might not give evidence against the culprits.

The inquest on the body of Mr. A. G. DeGa and the three other unfortunate persons who died from eating poisoned confectionery, resulted in the jury returning an open verdict and the discharge from custody of Michael DeGa, who had been all along supposed rightly or wrongly to know more about the affair than he chose to divulge. On the evidence before them the jury could have arrived at no other decision but the verdict was eminently unsatisfactory, and people began to ask if there was to be a failure of justice—if the author of this horrible tragedy whoever he might be was for ever to remain unknown. A very uncomfortable feeling pervaded the minds of many persons. The *Times of India,* commenting upon the verdict of the jury, remarked, "Where, let us ask, is that distinguished head of the Detective Police, Khan Bahadur Akbar Ali, and his clever son Mir Abdul Ali, who speaks English with such wonderful fluency, and gives his evidence in a policeman-like manner. * * * * Public interest is so absorbed in the event that no efforts will be spared to secure the arrest and punishment of the miscreant."

The task of the police was peculiarly difficult, and although no efforts were spared, the mystery was not fully cleared up. However, it was explained to some extent by what subsequently followed. When the case was under investigation the public mind was exercised and agitated over the report of a diabolical attempt to murder the surviving DeGa brother. One morning in December the public were startled by the following announcement in a leading journal : " The excitement in Bombay consequent upon the disclosures regarding the DeGa poisoning case was intensified on Saturday morning when it became known that Mr. Pestonji Dinshaw, the well known Parsi Solicitor, had been apprehended by the police on the charge of instigating to poison Mr. Nicholas DeGa and his wife Rose Mary DeGa." The extraordinary story of the narrow escape of another branch of the DeGa family, and the arrest of a Parsee Solicitor, created a most profound sensation in Bombay.

On the 9th December, Ali Mahomed Borah, who was a confidential friend of Pestonji Dinshaw, went to the head detective Khan Bahadur Mir Akbar Ali, and informed him that Pestonji Dinshaw and Saccaram Raghoba had been consulting him as to the manner in which by secret means they could bring about the death of Nicholas DeGa and his wife Rose Mary DeGa. The Borah further told the head of the Bombay detectives that there were reasons to suspect that Pestonji Dinshaw and Saccaram had also been concerned in the DeGa family poisoning case. The matter was immediately reported to Sir Frank Souter and Mr. Vincent, the latter being the then Acting Deputy Police Commissioner. A plan was at once devised with the object of ascertaining the truthfulness of the informant, and the facts of the case and the extent of Pestonji and Saccaram's criminality. It was, therefore, determined that Mr. Vincent, Mir Akbar Ali, and Mir Abdul Ali, with Superintendent Mills and other officers, should conceal themselves in the house of Fakir Khakisha to whom the Borah was to introduce Pestonji and Saccaram. They proceeded to the house in 3rd Kamatipura Lane. Mr. Vincent, in relating as to what took place there, said : " After we had waited there for some half hour or three-quarters of an hour in such concealment, three persons came upstairs, and sat down in a room adjoining the one wherein we were so concealed, one of these persons being Pestonji Dinshaw, a Solicitor of the High Court, and another being a Gujarati Brahmin, whose name I have since ascertained to be Saccaram Raghoba, the third person being a Borah, named Ali Mahomed. After the usual salutations, Khakisha asked the three persons the object of their visit, whereupon Saccaram Raghoba introduced the subject by saying that there were certain persons, a man and his wife, who were very obnoxious to the Sheth (meaning thereby Pestonji Dinshaw), and whom they wished to make away with. That it was not on account of money they wished to kill them, but simply on account of their being source of great trouble and annoyance to the Sheth. In answer to Khakisha's enquiry as to the caste of the persons referred to, Saccaram said that they were Christians (the word used being 'Kristees'). Some conversation then followed about the remuneration to be given to Khakisha for the part he was to take in this matter. Pestonji Dinshaw there and then agreed to give the sum of Rs. 500 on the day that Mr. Nicholas DeGa should fall ill, and a further sum of Rs. 2,000 if he, Nicholas DeGa, died on the third day from the time of his being so made ill; and the same terms were agreed to by Pestonji Dinshaw with reference to Rose Mary DeGa, wife of Nicholas DeGa. It was stipulated that the thing should be done as soon as possible, and, if practicable, within twenty-four hours from the time of this agreement. Khakisha then said it was necessary for him to see these persons himself, and it was agreed that he should be taken the next day at 11 o'clock a.m. in a shigram to some place where Nicholas DeGa would be shown to him. I heard the mode by which Nicholas DeGa and his wife should be got rid of discussed by Pestonji Dinshaw, Saccaram Raghoba, and Khakisha. The latter particularly asked the names of the persons who were to be got rid of, and they were given to him both by Pestonji Dinshaw and Saccaram Raghoba as Nicholas DeGa and Rose Mary DeGa, his wife."

The cause for this dire design against the lives of two persons was explained by Nicholas DeGa. Nicholas DeGa, whose life was supposed to have been threatened, was married in February 1872 to a young lady, named Rose Mary Stephens, whose father had died, leaving Anne Pennell and Pestonji Dinshaw as executrix and executor. A plaint was filed in October 1872, and rule granted on 4th November 1872, calling on Pestonji Dinshaw and Anne Pennell to show cause why they should not be debarred from meddling with the affairs of the estate, and that a proper account of the receipts and expenditure should be rendered. Negotiations were entered into by both parties for settling the affairs out of Court. The first offer made by the exceutor and executrix was that they were to hand over to Mrs. DeGa the sum of Rs. 10,000 and a house of the estimated value of about Rs. 8,000, in full settlement of all claims against the estate. This offer was declined. On or about the 5th of December another offer was made which was accepted, *viz*., that a sum of Rs. 12,500 should be paid to Mrs. DeGa in one month's time from the date of the agreement, as well as the house. This brought the date of settlement to the 5th January. About this date, Saccaram Raghoba, who was connected with Pestonji, applied to a Borah, one Ali Mahomed, a man of indifferent character, to relieve Pestonji of one or two troublesome people. The plot happily remained unexecuted through the timely intervention of the police. Pestonji Dinshaw and Saccaram Raghoba were committed to take their trial at the Sessions. The interest centred in the case was unprecedently great. It was tried by the Hon. Mr. Justice Bayley and an enlightened jury.

Mr. Scoble (now Sir Andrew Scoble), the then Advocate General, with Mr. Ferguson, represented the Crown. The late Mr. Anstey, the eminent counsel, and Mr. Inverarity were engaged to defend Pestonji Dinshaw, while Mr. Marriot and Mr. B. Tyabjee defended Saccaram Raghoba. During the trial the Court was densely crowded, principally by Parsees, who seemed to take a most lively interest in the proceedings.

The Advocate General in opening the case remarked: "My Lord and Gentlemen of the Jury,—The case which will be brought before you to-day for investigation is one of the greatest importance, and possesses features of the highest interest, and will, I will assure, receive your most careful attention. The first prisoner, Mr. Pestonji Dinshaw, was, until this grave charge was brought against him, an officer of this Court, a man of good education and position. I have known him personally since my arrival in this country, and he has always held a high position in society. But in the present instance all this must be forgotten, and not taken into consideration. The case which is now before you relates to the family of the DeGas, and must be decided on its own merits. It must not be mixed up, or in any way connected in your minds, with the Grant Road poisoning case." The learned counsel at the conclusion of his opening remarks said: "The proposal of the accused was that DeGa and his wife were to be made to sicken, one at the time, and in two or three days to die, not from the effects of poison, but by 'ellum' or sorcery on the part of the witness Khakisha. The bargain made was that as soon as either of them became ill Rs. 500 were to be paid, and on the death of either Rs. 2,000 in addition, making a total of Rs. 5,000, for the deaths of both these persons. The motive, therefore, for the commission of this crime would be the gain of a sum of about Rs. 15,000, being difference between the Rs. 12,500, and the value of the house (Rs. 8,000) and the amount of Rs. 5,000 to be paid to Khakisha, provided he succeeded in putting Mr. and Mrs. DeGa out of the way. It must be borne in mind that Pestonji persistently objected to the use of poison. He said it must be done in some or any other way, but he would not hear of poison as a means of getting rid of them. He told the sorcerer that if poison were used, analytical skill would soon discover its presence. He said, '*Hei kooch ellum que vaste tujbeej kurna chai hai.*' It may be suggested by the learned counsel for the defence, that an intelligent man, such as Pestonji Dinshaw, could hardly believe in the effects of 'ellum,' but it is not many years since that sorcery was believed in and practised in England, although it was made punishable with death, and even Sir Mathew Hale, a man of intellect and intelligence, admitted that sorcery could be used to compass death. If it could have been believed in at that time, it is not incredible to hear that Pestonji might believe in it as a means of death. All over India it is still believed in, and it is not astonishing that Pestonji should still retain some of its old traditions. At the present time, in England, men holding high positions, and of undoubted intelligence, believe in table-turning, spirit-rapping, and other vagaries."

The evidence for the prosecution was complete, and not in the least shaken in the cross-examination by Mr. Anstey, Mr. Inverarity and Mr. Marriott.

Mr. Anstey in addressing the jury said "that in the Mofussil they have not the same disciplined body of police we have in Bombay, but I cannot blame them for resorting to traps which have been baited by the very parties who fall into them. The learned counsel after reviewing the case, as stated by the Advocate General, proceeded, saying, the facts I have just enumerated, form, as my learned friend opines, the ground-work of the plot, referring to the suit and attempted compromise. It may be suggested that a learned man like Pestonji Dinshaw could not possibly believe in 'ellum.' But as I am aware that you are nearly all as well acquainted with English history as myself, I have only to call your attention to the severe laws which were in force, not many years ago in England, against practising witchcraft, which was a crime punishable with death. My learned friend spoke of it in his opening speech, and mentioned Sir Mathew Hale as a man who believed that death might be caused by sorcery. This presidency is now asked to vindicate its own character as to whether it is the most benighted presidency in India or not, and to say whether or no all persons practising witchcraft shall be brought before any petty magistrate in the presidency." The learned counsel quoted several cases tried in Calcutta and elsewhere, in which persons similarly charged were set free, owing to the fact of no harm having happened, and proceeded to remark: "It was a favourite amusement among the privates in the British Army to shoot their officers. On one occasion, a private in the 45th Regiment attempted to shoot his superior officer, and on this being conducted to the guardroom, expressed his regret that he had omitted to cap his gun. On his being examined, it was found loaded with powder and ball. Hence he was not convicted. Now if Nicholas DeGa had been accidentally killed, or Mrs. DeGa had died in labour, would it be possible to connect the death of either or the other to the prisoners at the bar. You would not do so, without you thoroughly believed in witchcraft, which would be a very poor compliment to pay you. I am bound to go through the whole of the evidence, and hope you will weigh well the whole of the evidence, as it is heard from my lips. The tedious evidence relating to the wills will be passed by me, although my learned friend appeared to attach great importance to them. Even in the event of Pestonji having succeeded in his proposed nefarious intentions with regard to Mr. and Mrs. DeGa, how could he be the gainer. Mrs. DeGa has two half-sisters, besides the child just born, who would have come forward with a claim on her estate. I do not deny Pestonji's going to Khakisha's, neither do I disbelieve the main evidence of the police; but it is very unlikely that

Pestonji should really believe that it is in the power of any man to have the supernatural gift of healing or killing people within any given time. I have heard of a great many beliefs, such as Darwin's system, spiritualism, &c., the former of which I consider the most sensible of all. The great and philosophic Seldon is quoted by me, as I am a great admirer of his writings, but do not necessarily believe all I read. The laws relating to the punishment of sorcerers in England was not repealed till the reign of George II. Then I ask, why should Pestonji Dinshaw be considered superior to prejudices which exist among the very highest and lowest in Europe and America. When any person, either adult or not, is supposed by others to possess some supernatural gift, the person immediately labours under the impression that he or she is actually endowed with that gift, in fact it turns the brain, upsets the seat of reason, and ends in their becoming mad. There is a sort of fascination in being considered something beyond the natural. In England people allow themselves to be duped by such men as Hume and other adventurers: then why should Pestonji Dinshaw prove an exception. He is only a Parsee, and when such men as Bacon, Hale, and Coke believed in the existence of witches, and framed laws for the extinction of the race, can it be wondered at that my client should have had the veniel curiosity to test the powers of this Khakisha. I should regret extremely that it should go forth to the world, that a man like my client should be convicted for trying a simple experiment. According to the evidence of the prosecution, he wanted to get rid of somebody ; the Borah agreed to find the instrument, but informed the police first. This word 'ellum,' the meaning of which has been so frequently disputed, appears to mean sorcery, magic, black art. There were two alternatives offered in this case, *viz.*, poison or 'ellum.' All the witnesses agree that Pestonji Dinshaw objected strongly to the use of poison, but gave Khakisha permission to use his skill in 'ellum' upon the persons of Mr. and Mrs. DeGa. They were not to be killed together or suddenly. The husband was to sicken first, and after three days to die. The wife was to be served in the same way. A stupor was to be produced, so that they should not recognise any one who came near them, and no clue could be discovered. Khakisha stated that he must have the names in his book of divination. These books are still in vogue in Persia, and are believed in by a great part of population. He said it would be no use without the names and also the name of the principal party interested. When these requests were complied with, Khakisha went into his inner room, and after remaining inside a few minutes, came out with a book, and told the prisoners that the affair would be completed satisfactorily." Mr. Anstey next detailed what took place when Nicholas DeGa was informed of the supposed plot, as to his going to the Magistrate to swear an information which the latter would not receive without Mr. Vincent's affidavit, which was afterwards given in. He then appealed to the good sense of the intelligent men who formed the jury, and continued as follows : "It is not by such means as those at present adopted, that these malpractices can be put down. Mr. Vincent states that the executive must have proof that charges have been made, and fees received before a conviction can be secured. Who or what could have induced the two prisoners to mix themselves up with bazar gup, Police Courts, and then to find themselves here in this Court. In my opinion the Borah and Mr. DeGa were the investigators, the former a tool in the hands of the latter to enable him to throw suspicion from himself, and put it on the shoulders of others. It must be remembered that the investigation in the Grant Road poisoning case was going on about this time before Dr. Hewlett, the Coroner, and that the police were engaged in both affairs. Saccaram was arrested before DeGa was liberated. After his liberation, he was running all over the city, in the company of Mir Akbar Ali, in search of apochryphal cooli, whom he suspected of having brought the plate of poisoned sweetmeats to the houses of his murdered brothers, and when he could no longer bolster up the authorities with this excuse, he commenced to endeavour to fasten suspicion upon innocent people. Some of the witnesses have told you that when they went to Khakisha's house on the 11th December, it was with the expectation of hearing something in connection with the poisoning case. It is credible that Pestonji and Saccaram should have almost daily importuned the Borah to procure them an illumwalla for about two months incessantly, and this while the poisoning case was being investigated. The Borah finds a man put forward by the police for the purpose, and the prisoners fall into the trap. I do not blame the police for watching a trap into which those who have baited it fall, but I cannot possibly admit the veracity of all the evidence brought forward by the prosecution. The prisoners went to Khakisha's house with a view to find out whether or not it was possible for this man to hold in his power the issues of life or death. As no crime has resulted from this visit to the Fakeer, no punishment can be given. You can only put them on an equality which the English celebrities above quoted."

After Mr. Anstey had finished his address, the Court adjourned for a few minutes. When it reassembled, Mr. Inverarity said that his learned friend Mr. Anstey had desired him to apply to his Lordship for the point of sorcery to be reserved for being argued. His Lordship declined.

Mr. Marriott, in addressing the jury, confined himself to the arguments used by Mr. Anstey. It seemed to him that there were three most material questions for the jury to consider in coming to their decision. The first was whether the prisoners went to Khakisha's hut with any serious intention of causing injury to DeGas, because he apprehended that if—as he intended to urge upon them—the prisoners went simply as a joke, and not for the purpose of really causing injury, they were entitled to an acquittal. The second question was whether, if any injury was intended, that injury was intended to be caused by "ellum," or, as he preferred to call it, by supernatural means. And the third question was whether, if injury was intended, that injury was to be caused by material means. The counsel urged that Pestonji and Saccaram went to the hut simply as a joke for the purpose of ascertaining from the sorcerer the extent of his alleged powers. In looking at the conversation that passed at the sorcerer's, the jury must bear in mind that Pestonji and Saccaram when they went there, they did so with the intention of giving a serious air to the matter of leading the *Fakeer* to believe that they really did believe that he had power to cause death by *ellum*. The fact, then, that the conversation between Pestonji and Saccaram gave an air of reality to the transaction would excite no surprise. Looking at the whole facts of the case, and of the conversation in particular, he thought that the jury would conclude that an air of probability and earnestness was wanting about it, which certainly would have been there, had there been any intention on the prisoners' part to have caused injury to DeGas. They should not merely consider the question of intention, but also whether it was intended that the act should be committed by means capable of causing death. The mere intention of causing death, he submitted, without reference to means, did not amount to murder or attempting to murder.

His Lordship, in summing up after explaining the charges, said that the learned counsel on both sides had stated with great truth the gravity of the crime, the first prisoner, an attorney of the High Court, was charged with an offence if he was found guilty of which would stamp him with infamy for life. As to the other man, it would for ever prevent his earning any honest livelihood. His Lordship thought the learned counsel were somewhat hard upon Nicholas DeGa in the matter of the suit, and said all the facts had not been made known to the jury, which would place matters in a different light. He then described how under the three wills (1) of Anne Stevens, dated June 1863; (2) Henry Stevens, dated February 1868; and (3) of Eliza Phillips, the girl Rose Mary took a considerable interest on coming of age or on marrying, and said that it was quite justifiable on DeGa's part to experience a hostile feeling against the representatives of the legatees (*i.e.*, the executor and executrix), and to file a suit against them. His Lordship then reviewed the evidence carefully to the jury, asking them to decide conscientiously upon what they heard, and further stated that section 115 of the Indian Penal Code provides that persons abetting the commission of an offence are punishable with death, but in this case Pestonji wanted to kill Nicholas and Rose Mary DeGa, not by poison, as witnesses had proved, but by " ellum."

The case was summed up by his Lordship at 7-55 p.m., when the jury retired, and after a consultation of five minutes, returned into Court with a unanimous verdict of guilty against both prisoners. The Clerk of the Crown on having asked Pestonji Dinshaw why sentence should not be passed upon him, the prisoner did not answer, whereupon Mr. Marriott stated to the Court that by section 115 of the Indian Penal Code this Court had no power to pass any sentence upon his client Saccaram Raghoba. His Lordship stated that it was for him to pass a lenient sentence upon him.

Mr. Marriott requested his Lordship to take notice of the objection stated by him. Mr. Inverarity raised a similar objection on the part of his client. The Clerk of the Crown then asked Saccaram Raghoba why sentence should not be passed upon him. Saccaram replied, I am innocent. I am a Brahmin, and pray your Lordship will pass a lenient sentence upon me, and at the same time make some arrangements about taking my meals separately. I am 60 years old. His Lordship passed sentence of seven years' rigorous imprisonment on each of the two prisoners in the House of Correction.

The case did not end here. Application was made to the Advocate General, under clause 26 of the amended Letters Patent of the Court, which provided " that on its being certified by the Advocate General that in his judgment there is an error in the revision of a point or points of law decided by the courts of criminal jurisdiction, the said High Court shall have full power and authority to review the case or such part thereof as may be necessary, and finally determine such point or points of law, and thereafter alter the sentence and pass such other sentence as to the High Court shall seem right." The matter was brought before the Advocate General by the Solicitors for the prisoners upon the certificate of the two learned counsel who appeared for the prisoners at the trial, that Mr. Justice Bayley had, in summing up the case to the jury, directed them that evidence of simple intention to kill without reference to means to be employed to cause death was sufficient to warrant a conviction. On this representation, the Advocate General granted a certificate under the 26th clause of the Letters Patent of 1865. In granting the certificate the Advocate General reserved to himself the liberty to contend before the Full Bench that Mr. Justice Bayley did not so direct the jury. The review of the trial came on before the Full Court consisting of the Hon'ble Sir M. R. Westropp (Chief Justice), the Hon'ble Sir Charles Sargent, the Hon'ble Mr. Justice Gibbs, the Hon'ble Mr. Justice Bayley, and the Hon'ble Mr. Justice Melvill. The High Court was densely crowded, principally by the Parsees, who seemed to take a most lively interest in the proceedings and considerable amount of money was staked on the result of the case. Their Lordships confirmed the conviction and sentence upon the prisoners, having held that nothing had been said by their brothor Bayley that did or was calculated in any manner to mislead the jury, but that on the contrary he had correctly addressed them.

The police then ascertained that the cooli who took cakes in the first case was also murdered so that he might not tell any tales. Succaram Raghoba then offered to make a confession, but before the police could go to him he died in the jail at Thanna, and the curtain dropped on the tragic drama.

THE GREAT AHMEDABAD CONSPIRACY CASE.

In some of the most interesting and important cases Sardar Abdul Ali, along with his father Khan Bahadur Mir Akbar Ali, the eminent detective, worked shoulder to shoulder with Mr. Vincent, the present popular Commissioner of Police, who at that time filled the responsible post of Deputy Commissioner. The case known as "The Great Ahmedabad Conspiracy" taxed all their energies, for the parties concerned were very wealthy and influential men, and did their best, not only to tamper with the witnesses and the police, but also to bribe members of the jury. No less than fourteen counsel were engaged for the defence, and although every effort was made to thwart the police, the prosecution was successful. On Saturday the 6th of July 1872, at the Criminal Sessions of the High Court, the case of conspiracy presenting some singularly novel phases of native chicanery and low cunning, was called on for trial before the Honourable Mr. Justice Bayley and a Common Jury. It was a case of great importance, and it would be difficult to conceive of a more infamous and iniquitous conspiracy than that established against the prisoners. Five months prior to the discovery of the plot there were three men in Bombay upon whom their neighbours or relations sought to be avenged; and the latter, to carry their designs into effect, procured the assistance of some of the members of a gang who had made it their profession to trump up charges against innocent persons for a consideration, and to get them punished in proportion to the amount of the fee. Accordingly, for Rs. 2,000 in one instance and Rs. 1,000 in another, it was agreed that the three obnoxious persons should be accused of a serious offence and punished. At a meeting of members of the gang held in Bombay, it was resolved that the operations should commence forthwith, as the consideration money was paid in advance. One of the conspirators agreed to be wounded by two others of their number. In order not to excite suspicion by acting too near home, where instantaneous detection would be inevitable, it was arranged to commence operations at a safe distance from Bombay ; and one fine morning in the month of February, the conspirators travelled by rail to Ahmedabad, where one of them was wounded with a knife by his comrades. A charge was laid before the Magistrate of that city against the three obnoxious persons in question as being the authors of the crime. Warrants of apprehension came down to Bombay, and the three innocent men were sent as prisoners for trial at Ahmedabad. Fortunately before their conviction, the ramifications of the plot were disclosed to the Bombay police, and the conspirators were pounced upon in a manner highly creditable to the vigilance of Mr. Vincent, Sardar Mir Abdul Ali and his father at the Criminal Sessions was the result. There were eight prisoners in all, but three of them were minor actors in the drama and were policemen of Ahmedabad who came upon the scene at a late stage of the proceedings.

The prisoners Bhama Narsee Buggywalla, Premji Lalji Joshi, Ismail Russool Godur, Abdool Rahimon, Haji Cader, Poonja Sowa Lohar, Noor Acha and Oomajee Ballajee were charged on fifteen different counts. The principal charges were as follows :—That Doolab Shamjee and Pitamber (not before the Court) fabricated false evidence at Ahmedabad, intending to cause Walljee Khemjee, Carrimkhan Sodurkhan, and Haroon Latiff, to be convicted of voluntarily causing grievous hurt to Cooverjee Jetha ; and that all the prisoners abetted such offence in Bombay by conspiracy. That Doolab Shamjee and Petamber fabricated false evidence at Ahmedabad, intending to cause Walljee, Carrimkhan, and Haroon to be convicted of robbing Cooverjee Jetha ; and that all prisoners abetted such offence at Bombay by conspiracy. That Cooverjee Jetha at Ahmedabad, with intent to injure Walljee, Carrimkhan and Haroon, falsely charged them with voluntarily causing him grievous hurt ; and that all prisoners abetted such offence in Bombay by conspiracy. That Cooverjee Jetha at Ahmedabad, with intent to injure the abovenamed persons, falsely charged them with robbery, and that all the prisoners abetted such offence. And that all the prisoners in Bombay abetted the offence of making the false charge at Ahmedabad against the abovenamed persons.

Mr. Anstey, with Mr. Farran, instructed by Messrs. Jefferson and Payne, appeared for the prosecution. Mr. Inverarity appeared for the first, second and fifth prisoners. Mr. Marriott and Mr. Leith, instructed by Mr. C. Tyabjee, appeared for the third prisoner. Mr. Branson and Mr. Lang, instructed by Messrs. Hearn, Cleveland and Peile, appeared for the fourth prisoner. Mr. B. M. Wagle, instructed by Mr. Vinaek Harrichand, watched the proceedings on behalf of Carrimkhan. The sixth and seventh prisoners were undefended.

The principal witnesses were Cooverjee Jetha, Doongersi Narayen, Mr. Vincent, Khan Bahadur Akbar Ali and Khan Bahadur Abdul Ali. Doongersi Narayen was the informant in the case. He said that about the 10th of February he went to Ahmedabad to assist in the conduct of a criminal charge against somebody for cheating. On the platform of the Ahmedabad station he noticed the arrival of one of the prisoners. Knowing this man to be a Bombay buggywala, and knowing something of his antecedents, he suspected that all was not right, and on his arrival in Bombay he communicated his suspicion to Khan Bahadur Akbar Ali, who took him to Mr. Vincent. In consequence of his statement Mr. Vincent, Mir Abdul Ali, and another police officer went to Doongersi's house, and by concealing themselves in an adjoining room, overheard the conversation between some of the prisoners. The prisoner, unaware of the presence of the police officers, related to Doongersi what had taken place at Ahmedabad. He said that Cooverjee Jetha had allowed himself to be stabbed, on receiving a sum of Rs. 500, and that the man who stabbed him was Doolab Shamjee, who twice before did similar tricks at Surat and Poona. Doongersi was requested to assist in the matter by giving his evidence against an innocent man, for whose apprehension a warrant had been issued by the Magistrate at Ahmedabad. That innocent victim of the plot was no other than the uncle of the fifth prisoner, and his only fault was that he belonged to an opposite section in the caste and was instrumental in getting his nephew excommunicated for four years.

In summing up the case his Lordship pointed out that the evidence of Mr. Vincent and the detectives was unimpeachable, and it supported the evidence of the approver. The Jury unanimously found all the prisoners guilty. His Lordship, in passing sentence, said: "Prisoners at the bar, you have been found guilty upon the clearest and most satisfactory evidence of a most infamous conspiracy; and from the intimate acquaintance which three of you—as was shown in the evidence—have with another false charge, it is quite evident that you belong to a gang of persons who are banded together to deprive persons of their money and their liberty; and there is the clearest evidence in this case that one of you lent your own servant for being stabbed in the Surat case, by which three Brahmins were sentenced to three years' imprisonment. No man's liberty is safe while persons of your description are at large. I am much afraid that the attempt which was made in the interval between the rising of the Court on Saturday and the sitting of the Court on Monday, to bribe a gentleman of the jury, was instigated by some one of your friends out of jail. The sentence upon you 1, Bhawa Nensee Buggywalla; 2, Premjee Lalljee Joshi; 3, Ismail Russool Cadar; 4, Abdool Rahimon Hajee Cadar; and 5, Pooja Sowa Lohar, is that you and each of you be kept to rigorous imprisonment for seven years. And you 6, Noor Acha, and 7, Oomajee Ballajee, your case stands in a different aspect; and I feel I have not the power of inflicting a heavier sentence upon you than what I am about to pronounce. You did not come upon the stage until a comparatively recent period. The sentence upon you is that you be respectively kept to rigorous imprisonment for twenty-one months."

In his report to the Government, dated 27th July, Sir Frank Souter brought to the notice of the Government the conspicuous services rendered by Mr. Vincent, Khan Bahadur Mir Akbar Ali, Mir Abdul Ali and other officers, and expressed a hope that Government would acknowledge the samo in such manner as they might think fit. A Government Resolution was passed on receipt of the Hon'ble Mr. Bayley's letter, in which the acknowledgments of Government were expressed, for the very important services rendered by Mr. Vincent and other officers.

The Sardar then successfully prosecuted some members of the gang in the Surat conspiracy case, and they were all sentenced to a long term of imprisonment.

In recounting the services of Mir Abdul Ali, Sir Frank Souter in his letter to Government, dated 18th October 1872, referred to this case in the following terms: "In the recent Ahmedabad conspiracy case, which caused so much sensation, and in which I know that extraordinary effort was made to tamper with the Bombay police, the services of Inspector Mir Abdul Ali have received the well-deserved acknowledgment of Government as per their Resolution, dated 9th August 1872, Judicial Department."

KIDNAPPING A CIRCASSIAN GIRL.

One of the most sensational and romantic cases of kidnapping a Turkish girl—a damsel of great beauty—was unravelled by Mir Abdul Ali in 1873. The facts of the case prove the old adage that "Truth is stranger than fiction." The heroine of the kidnapping case was one Fullucksoor, whose beauty was indeed to her the "fatal gift." She was originally a resident of Constantinople. Her father took her to Egypt, where she remained with a relation. In the beginning of the year 1873 her father died, and subsequently she made the acquaintance of one Syed Mahomed Burgunzi, who promised to marry her at Mecca. Under this promise he induced her to leave Egypt. When she arrived in Bombay, Syed Mahomed told her that it was Jeddah. He was accompanied by two other women, whom he called his wives, and three men. He was provided with a pass from the Egyptian Government, under the signature of a Pascha, which certified that he was accompanied by his *zanana,* and had permission to travel for the purposes of trade. Having arrived in Bombay he took a house in Memon Mollah, and resided there until the 1st of August 1873. On that day he placed his wife Aysa and his maid-servant Syda in charge of the house, and he in company with Fullucksoor, whom he called his second wife, and Koochook Fullucksoor, whom he called his daughter, and two servants, Suroor and Furroz, left Bombay by rail for Hyderabad. While leaving Bombay for Hyderabad, he told Fullucksoor that they were on the road to Mecca. They were accompanied by a lad named Mahomed Saleh. They reached Gulburga safely, and from there they proceeded on their journey to a place called Humnabad, about 20 miles from Gulburga. After they had proceeded on their journey about two miles from Humnabad, they were all suddenly arrested by the police on the strength of telegraphic advices from Bombay—it being known that the object of Syed Mahomed was to sell Fullucksoor and the lad to a wealthy gentleman of Hyderabad. They were taken under arrest to Gulburga, where they were kept in close custody, each apart from the other, and were subsequently brought down to Bombay.

The Syed was placed before Mr. John Connon, the then Senior Magistrate, and charged under the Penal Code with kidnapping. On the application of his Solicitors, Messrs. Jefferson and Payne, he was released on depositing Rs. 5,000 in cash and procuring securities for Rs. 5,000, and entering into his recognizances for Rs. 10,000. Syed Mahomed then at the instigation of some Memons took out a writ of *habeas corpus* against the Police Commissioner to show cause why his wives and daughter had been detained by the police against their wishes. On the 18th August the Advocate-General appeared before Mr. Justice Green to show cause against the writ. Aysa and Ameena, the wives of Syed Mahomed,

Fullucksoor, his alleged daughter, Syda, the servant of Aysa, and Suroor, the servant of Syed Mahomed, were all in Court, the first four being closely veiled. Syed Mahomed in reply to questions put to him by the Advocate-General, through an Arabic interpreter, said that Fullucksoor was his daughter by Ameena, who was between 30 and 35 years of age. Ameena on being questioned, stated her age to be 20 years, and that of her daughter 12. Fullucksoor denied being the daughter of either Syed Mahomed or Ameena. The Advocate-General then said that he was instructed to state that these women were under no restraint whatever, but had merely been provided with accommodation in Bombay until a charge against Syed Mahomed for importing the said women to Bombay for the purpose of kidnapping or abducting them, which was at present before the Senior Magistrate of Police, was heard. On being questioned by the Advocate-General, Fullucksoor said, "I am in no way related to Syed Mahomed. I came with him to Bombay. I went with my father from Constantinople to Egypt, and there he died. I met Syed Mahomed in Egypt, and he asked me to go with him to Mecca. In Egypt I was living with an acquaintance of mine. I came to Bombay, believing we were going to Mecca. I was born in Constantinople." His Lordship then discharged the rule, ordering that Aysa, Seeta and Suroor, not having been in custody at the time of the order, and Ameena having stated that Syed Mahomed was her husband, and she desired to return to him, they might go where they liked. Fullucksoor should go back to the house where she had been living.

After a preliminary enquiry into the charge of kidnapping, the Magistrate committed the accused to take his trial at the Criminal Sessions. The accused was defended by Mr. Mayhew and Mr. Inverarity. The case which created the greatest excitement at that time in the Mahomedan community ended in the conviction of the prisoner, who was sentenced to two years' rigorous imprisonment. The curiosity excited by this beauteous Circassian was great. In the Court she declined to remove the veil from her face; but the presiding Judge having intimated his inclination to have a glimpse of her beautiful face, the Advocate-General informed his Lordship that she would have no objection to unveil herself in Chambers, and by arrangement she did so in the presence of his Lordship, the Advocate-General, and other counsel engaged in the case.

After the disposal of the case every one enquired "What will be now the fate of the beauteous Circassian." One of the native papers chivalrously said, "It is not her fault that nature made her beautiful." The writer then enlarged upon the misfortune which may come upon ladies endowed with the fatal gift. "The fair girl could not live under the protection of the police for ever. There are no homes in India for deserving victims of vicious men. We have no Marquis Townsend to throw himself into the breach. She could not go out as a governess, even if she knew anything to teach, her beauty having placed her far out of the educational pale. And if she could not be a governess, to be an ayah she would be ashamed even were she not too beautiful for that. The difficulty would, however, be solved easily, if anybody came forward to marry her enchanted and enamoured by her beauty." Taking this hint Munshi Mirza Ismael, a Persian teacher in the Elphinstone College, came forward and married Fullucksoor. The couple lived together on very happy terms until poor Fullucksoor went mad and was sent to the Lunatic Asylum, where she died. The whole credit of saving this fair girl from degradation and ruin, by rescuing her from the hands of an unworthy creature, rightly belongs to Mir Abdul Ali and his father. The lady admitted in Court that she was very kindly looked after by the Khan Bahadurs. It might be mentioned that the task of the police in this case was rendered exceptionally difficult as the Memons had combined themselves to free the kidnapper at any cost. They and the Turkish Consul did all they could to save the kidnapper, but after all Justice triumphed.

THE CURRENCY NOTE FORGERIES AT MADRAS.

WHEN forgeries of Rs. 1,000 currency notes of the Madras Circle, on an almost unprecedented scale, came to light in June 1872, the news created great sensation throughout the whole of India. Rs. 54,000 worth of these spurious notes were seized at Benares, and there was good reason for believing that notes bearing a face value of upwards of four lakhs of rupees were in circulation in different Presidencies. They were lithographed on a set paper, bearing a colourable imitation of the water mark and belonged to the series B 1129. The numbers were between 30,000 and 31,000; the first two figures were printed from the stone, the rest impressed separately from type, not quite truly and in blacker ink. The Madras police had exhausted all their resources to get a clue of the gang of clever forgers, who seemed to have done their work in a very ingenious manner. Eighteen of the notes were presented for payment at the currency office, Madras. It was believed that twenty-two of these Rs. 1,000 notes were put in the Bombay market for circulation. The fraud was discovered at Benares. A native went there in the beginning of the year, and giving himself out to be the agent of a Madras Raja, he bought jewellery and other articles from various shop-keepers till he ran up bills amounting to Rs. 1,48,000. He paid this sum in Rs. 1,000 notes of the Madras Circle. Six of the spurious notes were at the same time discovered in Bombay by the police, who telegraphed to Benares describing them, and received answer from the authorities there that all the notes were of the same size and make. It was believed that there were no less than thirty-two notes in the Bombay market. The utterer of the notes, the so-called Madras Raja's agent, had disappeared in Calcutta, where also several notes were discovered. The authorities strove hard to bring the culprits to book. A clue to the forger-in-chief was at last found by the police, and advertisements describing his appearance and that of one or two others on whom suspicion fell, were inserted in all the leading papers. It was at one time believed that the notes had been printed in England, and that they were really a clever forgery, and people began to look suspiciously on all Rs. 1,000 notes that were tendered. But the forgery turned out to be a clumsy affair, and one which ought never to have imposed on anybody. In July of that year two natives were cleverly apprehended by the police in Bombay while dealing with a quantity of these notes, and fourteen more notes were recovered from them. A reward of Rs. 10,000 was offered for information leading to the arrest and conviction of Vancutta Chellummyab.

After great difficulties the forger Chellummyab was arrested at Madras, with an immense quantity of property in his possession. Chellummyab called at the Bank of Madras. He did not get cash in exchange for the notes advertised for, but a draft on a certain branch of the Bank in favour of another party. This draft had been pounced upon by the police, and had, of course, afforded a clue to the detection of the others. In addition Chellummyab had also 'peached,' and the case promised sensational disclosures. With the arrest of the leader of the gang of forgers, the labours of the Madras police seemed to end, though as it really turned out they were only on the threshold of their discoveries.

Curiously enough at this very time the minds of the Bombay police were also much exercised in regard to forged notes for one thousand rupees, which came from another nest of forgers in this Presidency. The fraud appeared to have originated at Ahmedabad, as that was the place where the notes came from. As the forged notes continued to make their appearance in the bazars, they created the greatest excitement in commercial circles. On the 11th of July a man was taken into custody for attempting to pass a forged Rs. 1,000 note as genuine. Most of the notes which had been seized before were such very clumsy imitations of the genuine note, as to be easily detected by any one. But the note, the genuine article, which came from Ahmedabad, was said to be a remarkably good imitation, but for one fault it would have passed muster for a long time without detection. The fault was that the forger had not succeeded in imitating the water mark.

In the last case the forgery was discovered through the absence of this mark, and information being given to the police, the man who attempted to pass it was taken into custody. It was a curious fact that all the forged notes with which Indian bazars were flooded, were of the old "black and white" pattern.

However, to return to Chellummyab. The property seized on him amounted to over Rs. 2,11,000, all of which was carried in a very old portmanteau. The joy of the Madras police was unbounded when they secured Master Vancutta Chellummyab, the leader, who was so much wanted, and on whose precious self a price far above the value of other mortals had been set. The particulars of his capture are not without interest.

It appeared Vancutta Chellummyab had been in Negapatam for the three days before his capture. On July 7 and again next day he honoured the Madras Bank with a visit; on the latter day cashing no fewer than twenty Rs. 1,000 notes at the same place! The extraordinary part of it is that on the man stating his business and presenting the notes to the Agent himself, the forgery business flashed through the latter's mind (as no doubt it would have done to the mind of any one with a thousand rupee note before him). The man after conversing in Telugu, took up a remark made in English by the Agent. The notes, however, were genuine, and Vancutta Chellummyab went off unmolested, the

Agent little thinking he was allowing the nice little sum of Rs. 10,000 to slip through his fingers. On Sunday morning a native, while conversing with the Inspector of Police, Kistnasawmy Moodelly, mentioned casually that a man was at a certain chuttrum, who appeared to be very flush of cash. The latter had only a few hours previously received a descriptive roll of Vancutta Chellummyab, and his suspicions being raised, he made off 'instanter' for the chuttrum. On arriving there, however, he was told that his man had left to proceed by the 8-30 train to Trivellore. There was yet time, and the Inspector made for the station sharp.

Here Vancutta Chellummyab was pointed out, and he proceeded in the most cool manner possible to enter into a conversation with him. Vancutta Chullummyab was not in the slightest degree disconcerted, and appeared as anxious to impart as the other was to obtain information. Presently Kistnasawmy said he was anxious to purchase certain jewellery. Vancutta Chellummyab thereupon pulled a heap from out the folds of his clothes, displaying at the same time a number of currency notes. This was the crisis, and Vancutta Chellummyab was marched off a prisoner. So far the principal offender and one of his accomplices were secured; but there were great surprises in store for the police and public, for they gave the police the slip in an unexpected manner. The "revelations" made by the chief prisoner had proved delusive ; but on July 13 he said that if he were taken to the Triputty Hill, he would then point out his correspondence and stock of forged notes. On Saturday evening the prisoners arrived at the railway station, some fifteen miles distant from the sacred hill, under charge of a native escort, the European officers not accompanying the party in order not to offend the prejudices of the Brahmins by ascending the holy hill. The police had to deal with criminals of no ordinary character. At the very outset two European gallant officers in charge of the case allowed themselves to be egregiously humbugged. They were first told that if they—the European officers—ascended the hill, their presence would tell that something was going on, and the house to which Vancutta Chellummyah was to lead the police could not be quietly pounced upon. When it was pointed out that their presence at the Triputty station would show as much, and prevent the thing being managed secretly, they pleaded that it would offend the feelings of the Brahmins. When the forger got the Europeans to remain behind, his next object was to delay the ascent, so as to reach the top of the hill after dark. He, consequently, managed to prolong the period of ascent from the usual four hours to eight hours, and so to delay the arrival of the party at the top of the hill till eight o'clock in the evening. Meanwhile a Hindu police officer, holding the post of Deputy Commissioner, had arrived at the foot of the hill shortly after they commenced the ascent, but, unfortunately, he could neither get bearers to carry him up the hill, nor make up his mind to walk (as the European gentlemen did next morning), and stayed at the foot of the hill till the morning.

Arrived at the top of the hill, Vancutta Chellummyab, the principal prisoner, became the leader of the detective party. His handcuffs had been taken off; but till this time a policeman walked by his side grasping his hand. To get rid of this close attendance was his next object, and most cleverly he accomplished it. He led them by the edge of the tank to a part where the buildings and trees came down so close to the water's edge that the party could walk in single file, and the attendant policeman let go his hold and walked before. This was the forger's opportunity, and in a moment he and his confederate suddenly plunged into the water and were lost to view, before the policemen had time to realise what had happened. A brave Bobby, who could not swim, jumped in after Vancutta Chellummyab, captured his turban and with difficulty got to shore again. A private servant of one of the Inspectors, who could swim, struck out and seized hold of Vancutta Chellummyab, but the forger's companion came to his assistance, and between them they half drowned the captor, who was glad to "make off." The escaped prisoners were not seen alive after that. The police said that they could not have escaped, because the tank was immediately surrounded by a crowd of people, who would have caught them or beaten them back, if they had any inclination to side with the police, and frustrate the designs of the prisoners. There was a great public clamour in regard to the fraud committed by the prisoners, with such daring and ingenuity.

It was at first thought that they had got out of the tank in the first confusion ; or that they might have swam to the little temple in the middle of the tank, and there rested until a favourable moment arrived for swimming to the shore. Two days later, however, the bodies were found, and an inquest was held. The witnesses all seemed to imply that the bodies were those of the escaped prisoners', but the *Madras Times*, a leading paper of the Presidency, considered that there was an absence of the direct testimony of identity to be expected in such cases. The journal added " the circumstances are such as to make it extremely improbable that the men who escaped should have been drowned."

In this matter the Sardar made enquiries in conjuction with Mr. Vincent, who worked with conspicuous zeal, and rendered very valuable assistance to Captain Weldon in the course of his investigation. A lottor signed by the Chief Secretary to the Government of Fort Saint George, Madras, dated 20th of March, was sent to the Bombay Government, together with the report of Captain Weldon on the "Great Note Forgery Case," requesting the conveyance of the thanks of the Government to Sir

Frank Souter, the Commissioner of Police, and to Mr. Vincent, his deputy, for the ready and valuable assistance they afforded to Captain Weldon in the course of his enquiries. As recommended by Captain Weldon, the Government authorised "a reward of Rs. 100 to be presented to Detective Inspector Abdul Ali, on behalf of the Madras Government, for his good services" in connection with the enquiries, and the gift was accordingly made.

THE DEPOSITION OF THE LATE MAHARAJAH MALHARRAO GAEKWAR.

In the beginning of seventies the Baroda State was reduced to the verge of anarchy. Numerous and serious were the complaints made as to the despotic character of the ruler, Malharrao Gaekwar, about whose villainy and depravity of heart, the most extraordinary stories were current. The culminating point was reached in 1874, when it was known that he had attempted to get rid of Colonel Phayre, the then Resident of Baroda. It was in connection with disclosing the circumstances of the attempted murder of the Resident that Mir Abdul Ali and his father rendered most signal services, not only to the Government and the Baroda State and its people, but to the country at large, for their labours resulted in the deposition of a despotic, heartless and ignorant ruler. Both the Khan Bahadhur detectives were the able lieutenants of Sir Frank Souter, who called them his "right-hand men," and it was due to their skilful and honest exertions that the guilt was brought home to the late Gaekwar.

Before narrating the facts of the case, something must be said respecting Malharrao's life. The despot's own life was attempted three or four times, and the means adopted were sorcery, human sacrifices, poison, &c. In former years he was strongly accused of an attempt upon the life of his brother, and was incarcerated for the offence, but when his case was taken up by Mr.

George Taylor, the evidence on which his guilt was held to be established was found to be so faulty, that he came to be looked upon as a very ill-used individual, and the Bombay Government pressed Khanderao to set him at liberty. The Gaekwar's family had been notorious for the implacable and rancorous animosity which its members had from time to time borne towards each other, and in the history of Baroda false accusations sustained by elaborate perjury has been as readily made use of as powdered arsenic for the removal of a detested relative. Ganpatrao, the eldest of the five sons of Sayajee, succeeded to the *gadi* in 1847. During his reign two of the brothers died early. In 1856 he himself died, as was generally believed, of poison administered by Khanderao.

Two attempts were then made upon the life of Malharrao. At first, Khanderao proceeded by sorcery, but the result not answering his expectations, he consulted a Brahmin who declared that the black art could have no influence upon the life of a prince, unless human sacrifices were freely resorted to. Khanderao was equal to the occasion, and proceeding to the prison in Baroda, selected thirty-five life-prisoners, and ordered them to be put to death at the rate of five daily for seven consecutive days. Twenty-five of the victims were duly sacrificed ; the remaining ten would have also met the same terrible fate, had not the remonstrances of the Dewan put an end to this butchery. As sorcery proved unavailing, Khanderao, at the instigation of the atrocious scoundrel Bhau Scindhia, resorted to poison. Two wretches were employed to administer powdered arsenic to the heir-presumptive. A quantity of the poison was given to Malharrao's cook with directions to mix it in his food—directions which were carefully obeyed. Malharrao and several of his family partook of the poisoned food, and were attacked with serious illness, escaping death solely through the promptitude with which remedies were applied. Malharrao setting an example which was subsequently imitated, immediately held an enquiry, and caused the whole of his servants to be brought before him. The cook confessed, and produced from the folds of his turban the remaining quantity of the powdered arsenic. The proofs were evident, but the Gaekwar refused to see their force.

The attention of the Bombay Government was called to the case, but the only result of the consequent enquiry appeared to have been that Bombay was honoured for a time with the presence of the two individuals who were employed to seduce the cook. After the failure of this attempt, Bhau Scindhia soon recovered his presence of mind. A European soldier was found, who consented to declare that one of Malharrao's agents asked him to shoot Khanderao when the latter had occasion to visit the Residency. The evidence of this soldier was not particularly reliable; it was shown that the alleged agent could not have met him on the day he specified, and Colonel Wallace, the Resident, told Khanderao that he believed

Malharrao was innocent. But Khanderao refused to believe in the innocence of his brother, and sent him to Cadra, where he was kept closely confined until the death of the Gaekwar transferred him from the prison to the throne. It is a circumstance curiously illustrative of the disposition of Khanderao—who knew how to secure support, if not sympathy, from quarters where it was denied to his brother, in every way the smaller least villain of the two—that in his jealous rage he seized the Patel of Cadra and three others on a charge, which happened to be false, of having held secret communication with the prisoner, and put them all to frightful deaths. One was hanged, another beheaded, a third was blown off the mouth of a cannon, and the fourth was cast under the feet of an elephant. It is well to remember that when the good hater Khanderao died, his hatred towards Malharrao did not die wholly with him. He had left representatives who pursued Malharrao with as much vindictiveness as he himself ever showed.

As for Malharrao personally he was the last person this peninsula capable of exciting any enthusiasm amongst his family or adherents. Wholly uneducated and of a very ordinary mind, he was never able to impress his companions with respect, though he was not deficient in certain astuteness, and his obstinacy was unlimited. In person he was the reverse of princely; he was undersized, of mean presence and coarse dark complexion. His eyes looked different ways, and his large sensual lips were kept asunder by black projecting teeth, supported by a band of gold visible when he spoke. Unlike his brother Khanderao he was averse to field sports, and he had converted the race-course of Baroda into a macadamised road for the ladies of his *Zenana*. Of his early days little is known, perhaps there is little to be known. He never went to school, and had no instruction in anything but vice. The result was that he could read little and write less. At a very early age means of debauchery were suggested to him, even by his parents. This should be remembered when Malharrao's vices are censured. They were probably as much the result of bending the twig as evidence of the natural inclination of the tree.

Malharrao was born in Baroda, and was about forty-two years of age when he was put on his trial. During his youth and early age he was considered mad or wild, and the court-physician was in constant attendance upon him. According to the statement of his enemies, he often used to attempt the lives of those who offended him, generally with the sword, and some people say that in a few instances he succeeded. In accordance with the customs of the people he was married in his infancy, his *Ranee* being the daughter of Nana Khanvolkar, who was also arrested in connection with the attempt upon Colonel Phayre's life. Khanderao and Malharrao had committed a whole host of crimes, but all the crimes of all the Gaekwars from Damaji downward, sink into insignificance when compared to the wild accounts which were heard from a real sincere hater of this man. According to these statements Blue Beard was a saint compared to Malharrao, while John Lockland or Richard Crookback would have trembled in his presence. His whole life, according to some, had been made up of poisonings and attempts to poison. The policy of putting to death the leaders of the hostile factions seemed to have actuated Malharrao as soon as he ascended the throne. Rowji Master, Mallarba, Ganoo Bagh, and Bhau Scindhia were despatched by having their mouths forced open and poison poured down their throats. Bhau Scindhia was put to death in a terrible manner. When Malharrao stepped from prison to the throne, he threw Bhau Scindhia into jail. Handcuffs were put upon him in addition to the chains already fastened upon him. The prison authorities then ordered him to swallow a pill of poison that had been prepared for him. On seeing the poison, Bhau Scindhia began to call out and cry for mercy and help. The pills were then forced into his mouth. But as he still refused to swallow them, he was squeezed to death by a machine known as *sikunja*, a kind of press for torturing a man to death. There was no reason for his execution beyond the fact that he was put in office by Khanderao. Govindrao was similarly treated because the despot suspected him of too close an intimacy with his wife. A couple of his accomplices in the Phayre affair also, it is said, died the same death, so that they could tell no tales, and had not Sir Lewis Pelly arrived in Baroda, some others would have followed them. On the very day Colonel Phayre arrived after his absence from the Residency, a man had been sent to his long account, causing the gallant Colonel to exclaim, "What, are they killing them every day?" Indeed not a man of note died, but it was at once concluded that Malharrao had been at work with his poison, and as he generally experimented upon a goat first, the sudden death of one of those animals was regarded with equal dread and suspicion.

Most, if not all, of this series of alleged murders were reported to the Resident and by him to the Government; but the informations were either unsupported or there were some other, doubtless, sufficient reasons, which induced Government not to interfere. One of the last poisoning freaks of this monster was, it is stated, that he ordered a pound of arsenic to be put in the ice which was to be used at the Residency. This was attempted only six months before the Commission was appointed. It was only on the representation of His Highness' *intimes* that the plan was abandoned. The 'Nazar Bag' or the new marble Palace was built on land occupied by cottages which were all destroyed, and the tenants or owners received no compensation. The foundation of the garden was laid by a grave stolen from the compound of Mir Bakerali, brother of the Nawab of Surat. This action completely destroyed a large tract of land, but no compensation was given for it. No woman was safe from his desire, and the wildest stories were extant of his villainy in this respect. Any girl passing in the street or the fame of whose beauty reached him, was 'puckrowed' by his minions with reckless audacity. On one occasion the victim being the sister of a Residency clerk, serious steps were being taken, when Damodar Pant confessed that he alone was guilty, and in a fit of over-zeal to win his master's approval, he had done it unknown to Malharrao.

It would not be out of place to state here the condition of the affairs of administration in Baroda, which will give the public the materials for forming a sound judgment as to the strong or weak points of Malharrao.

When Mr. Dadabhoy Naoroji and his officers first arrived at Baroda they found matters in the worst possible condition, the affairs of the State in every department were neglected—bribery and corruption reigned supreme. The Sirdars and Silladars were loud in their expressions of discontent, and but little was needed to set them in open defiance of the Gaekwari officials. Mr. Dadabhoy and his men set to work with a will to carry out the reforms with which they were charged. For two days they worked unceasingly (twelve hours being the average of each day's work), weeding, cutting, and clipping. The Dewan at first experienced much opposition from the Gaekwar's satellites, and not unfrequently from the Prince himself. Occasionally Mr. Dadabhoy would go to him and say that such and such a measure was necessary, perhaps one that affected the Gaekwar personally. Malharrao would protest—perhaps tell Mr. Dadabhoy that it was not his business—that he had no right to interfere, and address him with unprincely rudeness. "Well," Mr. Dadabhoy would say, "if you behave in that manner I shall simply resign." This threat invariably had the desired effect, and His Highness would frankly acknowledge his error, and beg the Dewan not to think of going away. Perhaps the most neglected of all departments was that of justice. It was openly sold to suitors—the man who had the longest purse always won his case. The Darbar used to accept bribes, entries were even made of the sums paid by various winning suitors. The cause used to be called on before the Darbar, and the Vakils on each side were allowed to make use of the vilest language towards each other and the suitor they were contending against, to the intense delight of Malharrao and his courtiers, who looked upon the whole business as a farce, knowing well beforehand who was to win—*i.e.*, the man who had paid most money. This state of things Mr. Dadabhoy very speedily put a stop to. Mr. Dadabhoy, with the assistance of Messrs. Pestonjee Jehangir, Appajee Ramchander, Laximon Jagannath, and others, effected most pressing reforms, but their labours were wasted for they could not reform the Maharaja himself.

But to return to the poisoning case. In November 1874 the attempt to poison Colonel Phayre was made. Instead of at once instituting an impartial enquiry, *i.e.*, appointing some one unconnected with the Residency to investigate the matter, Colonel Phayre set about it himself. Shortly after commencing his investigations his suspicions fell upon the havildar at the Residency. He was an old and to all appearances faithful servant, to whom Colonel Phayre had become rather attached. The havildar was taken into custody, but was not detained long, as Colonel Phayre did not think there was any evidence against him. In the meantime Colonel Phayre was transferred in consequence of a *kharita* written by Mr. Dadabhoy to Lord Northbrook, the then Viceroy of India, on behalf of the Gaekwar, and Sir Lewis Pelly came to Baroda as the Governor-General's Agent and Special Commissioner. He entrusted the inquiry into the poisoning case to Sir Frank Souter, the Bombay Commissioner of Police, whose services were placed at his disposal by the Government of Bombay. The havildar subsequently confessed, on the condition of being pardoned, to his share in the whole transaction.

A few days after that, the Jemadar went to Sir Lewis Pelly, and though warned by him that he had no chance of a pardon, persisted in confessing his share in the plot. His revelations were startling, and implicated the Gaekwar most seriously. He swore most positively that he had personal communication with, and received money from, the Gaekwar as a reward for the attempt on the Resident's life. In corroboration of his story, the police succeeded in tracing certain of the sums which, he said, were given him by the Gaekwar, and some had even been recovered. His confession also implicated Eshwantrao Jassood, a man attached to the Baroda Darbar, but who was always placed at the disposal of the Resident for the conveyance of messages between the Residency and the Palace, and he was usually to be found, when not on duty, at the Residency. Sallam, a sowar, was found also to be implicated. These four men were taken in custody at the Residency. The Jemadar, a few days after his confession, attempted to commit suicide. He asked his guards to allow him to visit the well in the courtyard for the purpose of drawing water for his personal use. They not suspecting his intention did so, but as soon as he got near the brink, he sprang forward and fairly jumped into the well. Ropes and appliances were procured, and he was fished out with some difficulty. Sir Lewis Pelly's attention was drawn to the commotion below, and he came down and enquired of the Jemadar his reason for attempting to commit suicide. The man answered that his life was of no value, he has been untrue to his salt and deserved to die. After obtaining the Jemadar's confession, Sir Lewis Pelly sent for Mr. Dadabhoy, and acquainted him with the serious turn the affair had taken as against the Gaekwar, and the latter was also made aware that the Jemadar accused him (Malharrao) of instigating the attempt to poison the Resident.

It was on the 6th of December 1874, that Sir Frank Souter, Kt., C.S.I., C.I.E., Commissioner of Police, Bombay, received official instructions directing him to proceed to Baroda to enquire into the charge of attempt to poison the Resident, Colonel Phayre. In two days, *i.e.*, on the 8th of December, the Commissioner left Bombay for Baroda, taking with him Khan Bahadur Akbar Ali and Khan Bahadur Abdul Ali. They were met at Baroda by Rao Bahadur Gajanand Vithal of the Ahmedabad Police, whose services were, at the request of Sir Frank Souter, placed at his disposal. The Khan Bahadurs and the Rao Bahadur were immediately associated together and ordered to work as one body. While prosecuting enquiries into the poison case, they obtained information on the 24th of December, which they reported to the Commissioner, that Wasudev Bhau, the head manager of all the Gaekwar's banks, in company with one Ganpatrao Atwale, had proceeded to Bombay, and that their going there was suspicious. The detective officers were ordered to make careful enquiries into the matter, and on the 26th of that month they obtained information, which they jointly reported to the Commissioner, that large sums in cash had been despatched to Baroda from the different Gaekwar's State banks at Bombay. The Gaekwar had two firms in Bombay—one conducted under the title of Narsidas Laxmidas, and the other under that of Parwattee Kank. These firms were attached, and seven lakhs of rupees were recovered, a large sum of money being already despatched secretly to Baroda. Enquiries into this matter were being carefully kept up, when on the 29th December the Commissioner came to Bombay, bringing with him Khan Bahadur Akbar Ali and Khan Bahadur Abdul Ali, with the object of following up the clue regarding the removal of treasure. Gajanand Vithal was left at Baroda to continue enquiries there in co-operation with the Khan Bahadurs at Bombay. Detective arrangements having been organised in Bombay, the Commissioner returned to Baroda on the 4th January, and the two Khan Bahadurs accompanied him. The Commissioner remained at Baroda, and during this time the Detective Police ascertained that a large sum of treasure had been removed from Bombay to Baroda, and this information was at once reported to the Commissioner. On the 8th of January the Commissioner left Baroda *en route* to Calcutta to lay the results of his labours personally before Lord Northbrook, the Viceroy and Governor General of India. In order that further searching enquiry might be made in Bombay regarding the transmission of treasure, the Khan Bahadurs were brought back to Bombay. On the 9th January the Commissioner left Bombay for Calcutta, but before starting directed the Khan Bahadurs to go on with their enquiries regarding the treasure, and to make their reports to, and take their orders from, Mr. Edgington, Acting Commissioner of Police.

On the 14th of January 1875 the Gaekwar was arrested, and on the same day the Khan Bahadurs brought information of so positive a nature in regard to the removal to Baroda of forty lakhs of treasure in Government currency notes of Rs. 1,000 each from the Gaekwar's branch bank in Bombay, that Mr. Edgington immediately proceeded to the Secretariat in person, where he reported the fact to the Under-Secretary to Government, Mr. W. Lee-Warner, and to Mr. P. Ryan, Assistant Secretary. The latter officer at once communicated the important intelligence by letter to Sir Lewis Pelly, who acknowledged its value by stating that it was this information which in large measure induced him to set on foot the machinery which in twelve hours resulted in the discovery and recovery of the notes.

On the 17th of January 1875 the Khan Bahadurs returned with the Commissioner of Police, on his way back from Calcutta to Baroda, and were present in the Residency during the interrogation of the Senapatee by Sir Lewis Pelly. The evidence was interpreted by the Commissioner of Police, and led to the despatch of Captain Jackson and Gajanand Vithal to recover the money which the Senapatee had then consented to give up. The Khan Bahadurs were thus the means of saving the treasure. Sir Richard Meade, in his letter to the Secretary to the Government of India, dated 10th May 1895, said : "There can be no question that the recovery of this large sum was wholly due to the intelligence and oxertion of the members of the Bombay Detective Police."

Besides the forty lakhs of rupees, the Bombay detectives found a box from the palace which from its appearance one would have thought held nothing valuable, but on being opened it was found full of canvas bags, each of which contained two thousand rupees. Altogether the box contained Rs. 70,000. Another box containing a similar sum of money was also found. Still another sum of one and a-half lakhs of rupees was found concealed in the palace. A body of sepoys were soon at hand, who shouldered the bags of wealth, and carried them to a crane, by which they were lowered into the street like so many bags of cotton. They were then conveyed to the treasury. Thousands of tolas of gold and silver and jewellery were also found. One diamond necklace alone was said to be worth about fifteen lakhs of rupees.

It must not, however, be imagined that the Police Commissionor and his assistants had nothing to do but to seek and find treasure. They had a most difficult task to perform in collecting evidence against the Maharaja. The police had occasionally a deal of trouble. One of the principal prisoners was Damodar Pant upon whose confessions the whole case turned.

Damodar Pant was a Brahmin endowed with an extraordinary amount of cunning. He was unscrupulous to a degree, and exercised so much control over the Gaekwar that the latter was absolutely not his own master when Damodar Pant was near. It was he who from the first used all his influence to thwart Mr. Dadabhoy's reforms often successfully—yet whenever he was not present, Mr. Dadabhoy always found the Gaekwar amenable to reason, and ready to withdraw any hasty remarks he might have made to him, and willing to promise anything Mr. Dadabhoy might choose to urge upon him.

This Damodar Pant, who was a secretary to Malharrao, and who fattened upon the Maharaja in his prosperity, but betrayed his master in his adversity, first gave a deal of trouble to the police. Once he refused all food, and seemed determined to pine himself to death. It was, however, subsequently found that he objected to receiving food at the hands of a soldier. He was humoured in this respect by being allowed to be served by his own servant. Every day the police discovered new treasures, accumulated additional pieces of evidence and raked up fresh crimes. The Commissioner and his assistants had considerable difficulty in obtaining the evidence which they did. Promises of safety were no inducement to the witnesses, who asked, "How can you guarantee us from molestation? If Malharrao had influence and power enough to have a British Resident removed, what can he not do to us?" But when their lord and master was in durance vile, these time-servers, who were reserved through fear, became communicative. In this respect Mir Abdul Ali's services were of incalculable value. For as Mr. Henry Cleveland, Government Solicitor, wrote to him subsequently, he (Mr. Cleveland) saw from the demeanour of the witnesses that they had confidence in Mir Abdul Ali, and were not afraid to speak the truth when he was present. Mr. Cleveland further said that the confidence was not extended to any other member of the police force. Mir Abdul Ali was a most valuable agent of the detection, for he had made himself thoroughly acquainted with the various books of accounts which were relied on by the prosecution, and on several occasions attended the consultations with counsel and gave explanations without which the then Advocate General Mr. Andrew Scoble (now Sir Andrew Scoble) and Mr. Inverarity, who were engaged for the Crown, could not have understood the accounts. In the words of Mr. Cleveland, "it was mainly owing to Mir Abdul Ali that some of the evidence which was produced at the enquiry was forthcoming." The police obtained the evidence of the purchase of diamond dust, which the Maharaja was led to believe was the most effective poison, with the additional property of leaving no trace.

Colonel Phayre was in the habit of drinking a glass of sugared water and fresh pummelo juice every morning after he came home from a walk. One day he swallowed a mouthful of sherbet, but then luckily for himself fancied there was something wrong with the taste. He was in the point of throwing the rest of the drink away, when he thought he noticed a peculiar sediment in the glass. When the poison administered to Colonel Phayre in sherbet was analysed, it was found to contain diamond dust as well as arsenic. The presence of the diamond dust with arsenic led one to guess that the cause of so atrocious an attempt at murder could not be the gratification of private malice on the part of Colonel Phayre's servant, as the poor people simply could not afford to purchase such an expensive agent of destruction. Dr. Wellington Gray, who analysed the poison, opined that if the Colonel had drank the whole draught, his death would have been certain, but as it was he had a providential escape. The most remarkable piece of evidence yet given was traced by Khan Bahadur Mir Akbar Ali and Khan Bahadur Mir Abdul Ali. The former having learnt that one of the prisoners, named Ravji, a Residency havaldâr, who was employed as a tool to do away with the Resident, had kept the powders which he had received from time to time in his belt, directed his attention to finding the belt. He soon discovered the belt. He saw what is called the "slide" through which a sword or truncheno would be passed, but he found no powder. As he was about to return the belt, his eyes fell upon a secret pocket. Akbar Ali introduced his fingers till he came in contact with a substance. That substance proved to be paper. He opened the packet or tore it open, and found the paper disclosed. He at once called the Commissioner, who came and took out the paper, and on examining it he found it not only to contain arsenic, but arsenic of the same physical characteristics as that found in the powder in Colonel Phayre's tumbler of sherbet. The finding of the poison in the belt of Ravji was relied upon by the prosecution as strong confirmatory evidence of the truth of the existence of a conspiracy to murder Colonel Phayre. It was admitted on all hands that were it not for the "indomitable perseverance of Mr. Souter and his detectives, there would have been but small chances of any case ever being made out against the Gaekwar and his courtiers."

As soon as strong evidence to establish a *prima facie* case had been obtained, the Government of India appointed a Commission to try Malharrao. The Commission consisted of the Chief Justice of the Calcutta High Court, Sir Richard Couch (President), His Highness Maharaja Scindhia, His Highness the Maharaja of Jeypore, General Sir Richard Meade, Raja Sir Dinker Rao, and Mr. P. S. Melville. The trial, which was the most important and sensational in the history of India, being the first in which a Native Prince was publicly tried on such grave charges, excited the greatest possible attention. Serjeant Ballantine, the eminent counsel, was specially called from England to defend the Maharaja. The *Bombay Gazette* established a branch printing office at Baroda, and issued extras of the full proceedings of the case every evening.

The counsel for the prosecution were Messrs. Scoble (now a Q. C. and a member of the House of Commons) and Inverarity, and were instructed by Mr. Hearn, Public Prosecutor. Serjeant Ballantine, who was assisted by Messrs. Purcell and Branson, and instructed by Messrs. Jefferson and Payne, received £5,000 as the amount of retainer only. He received £100 a day. The brief was forwarded to Aden, so that Serjeant Ballantine need no "coaching" on his arrival in Bombay. Serjeant Ballantine was one of the acutest lawyers at the English Bar. He had not only had great experience in regard to election, petitions and other similar enquiries, but he was retained for the defence in the great Overend Guerney case. He was counsel for the plaintiff in the celebrated Mordaunt case, in which he resisted the temptation of cross-examining the Prince of Wales. He also appeared for the claimant to the Tichborne estates in the case before Chief Justice Bowen, and, by electing to be non-suited, gave his client the opportunity of beginning *de novo* whenever he could find the means to do so. Serjeant Ballantine was considered to be the very best cross-examiner at the English Bar, and the natives were wonderfully pleased to hear that he was coming to defend Malharrao in whose favour the fickle mind of the populace was already turning. All the principal stations between Grant Road and Baroda were crowded by people anxious to have a glimpse of the

"Serjeant Saheb." When the train reached Baroda, the platform was literally crowded with native nobles and local magnates, and the concourse of people outside was very large. The eminent barrister was given a very hearty reception.

The enquiry commenced on the 23rd of February 1875 and the unique spectacle was witnessed of a reigning prince being placed in the dock and his erstwhile ministers and courtiers appearing in Court to give evidence against their former masters. The presence of His Highness the Maharaja Scindhia and His Highness the Maharaja of Jeypore tended to raise the proceedings above the level of a purely legal investigation. Though there was a little of oriental magnificence in or around the katchery, yet there was an unmistakable air about the whole scene of a Prince was being tried by Princes and representatives of a Sovereign greater than Princes. His Highness the Maharaja Scindhia was dressed in white muslin with gold embroidery around the edges. On his neck he wore two necklaces, one of large emeralds, partly concealed by the other which consisted of several rows of splendid pearls. Below these was a *plastron* of diamonds of immense value which flashed in the light. A very large emerald pendant from one of the necklaces hung over the *plastron* that partly covered his capacious chest. From his left ear hung a cluster of pearls of great price; one or two were considered sufficient for the right ear. On his wrists were bracelets studded with diamonds *en suite* with those on his chest, and a diamond, the size of a hazel-nut and brilliant as a star, added lustre to one of the fingers of his right hand, while a larger emerald gave value to the other. The sight of His Highness blazing with jewels of inestimable value might have made an Empress pale with envy. But the Maharaja wore them all in the way of business. His Highness looked every inch an Eastern Prince. The Maharaja of Jeypore, renowned for his enlightened policy and his excellent administration of the affairs of his kingdom, also looked very charming.

The Maharaja Gaekwar, who came in Court with Sir Lewis Pelly, seemed to be in great distress, and deeply impressed with the humiliation of his position. He looked askance at the chair, and it cost him an effort to seat himself in it. He looked pale and confused, and the expression of his countenance was one of weakness rather than evil.

Mr. A. Scoble (now Sir Andrew), the then Advocate General, and Mr. Inverarity, instructed by Messrs. Hearn, Cleveland and Lee-Warner, appeared for His Excellency the Viceroy and Governor General in Council; Serjeant Ballantine, Mr. Branson, Mr. Purcell and Mr. Shantaram Narayen, instructed by Messrs. Jefferson and Payne, appeared for the Gaekwar. Mr. Vasudev Jagannath, Pleader, High Court, watched the proceedings on behalf of His Highness the Gaekwar, while Mr. George Taylor and Mr. B. M. Wagle were present on behalf of the Ranees and the infant-child of His Highness the Gaekwar.

After a very lengthy and exhaustive inquiry, the Commissioners met to draw up their report for submission to the Government of India. The three European members (Sir R. Couch, Sir R. Meade, and Mr. P. S. Melville) were of one opinion, and sent in a detailed report, while the three Native Princes, who sat as Commissioners with them, dissented from the view taken by the English Commissioners. They had each written a separate minute differing from three European Commissioners, and wrote it as their opinion that the Gaekwar was not guilty of the offcncos charged. The joint report of the European Commissioners contained the following paragraph at the end :—

" Regarding the case from every point of view, we are unable to find any sufficient reason which would justify our declaring the Gaekwar not guilty of the offiences imputed to him. The Maharajas of Gwalior and Jeypore and Raja Sir Dinker Rao do not concur in the view we have taken of this case. We have considered the reasons for their opinions contained in the separate report which each of those members of the Commission has rendered. We believe that the evidence, after making every reasonable allowance on the score or character of the witnesses, proves :—(1) That an attempt to poison Colonel Phayre had been made by persons instigated thereto by Malharrao Gaekwar. (2) That the said Malharrao Gaekwar did by his agents and in person hold secret communications with some of the servants employed by Colonel Phayre, the Resident at Baroda, or attached to the Residency. (3) That the said Malharrao Gaekwar caused monies to be given to those servants. (4) That his purposes in holding such communications and causing such monies to be given were (*a*) to obtain information of what passed at the Residency relating to himself and his State; (*b*) and to cause injury to Colonel Phayre by means of poison."

Upon this report of the Commission the decision of Her Majesty's Government was announced by Lord Northbrook, Governor General of India. The Gaekwar was deposed and deported. He and his issue were debarred from all privileges, honors, and rights, and the one individual whom perhaps he detested more than Colonel Phayre himself—H. H. Jamnabai, widow of Khanderao, was allowed to adopt some member of the Gaekwari house as his successor, the Government of India reserving the right of either accepting or rejecting the choice. The resolution on the question distinctly stated that "the Commissioners being divided in opinion, Her Majesty's Government have not based their decision upon the enquiry or report of the Commission, * * * that the result of the enquiry has been to prove the truth of the imputation against His Highness." The deposition was expressly based upon "circumstances relating to the affairs of Baroda from the accession of His Highness Malharrao to the present time (of his deposition)." The circumstances being "his notorious misconduct, his gross misgovernment of the State, and his evident incapacity to carry into effect the necessary reforms." The choice of Rani Jamnabai fell upon the present Maharaja Sayajirao, whom the Bombay Police brought out from a corner of obscurity.

It may be mentioned that an attempt had been made by the Gaekwar's friends to corrupt the chief of the police and his officers. About 8th March Mr. Souter received a visit from two native chiefs. They told Sir Frank Souter that they appeared on behalf of Baldhri, sister-in-law of Gaekwar, and signified that if he used his best efforts to liberate Malharrao, the sum of ten lakhs would be at his disposal. Of course the worthy officer sent his tempters to do their business in all probability with little ceremony. The fact that an attempt was made to corrupt even the Commissioner of Police to contrive the liberation of Gaekwar showed that the police were exposed to considerable temptations in the execution of their duty, but their fidelity stood the severest test.

Serjeant Ballantine in his address to the Commission had remarked that it was a public case and got up by them. In summing up the evidence, and while alluding in particular to Sir Frank Souter and his detective, the Advocate-General remarked :—

" Mr. Souter is a man well known throughout this side of India. He has been an officer in the service of the Government for many years, and his services have been recognized by Government by conferring upon him the Star of India. He wears, though in a lesser rank, the same decoration that is so worthily worn by three of the members of the Commission ; and even if it were not the case that Mr. Souter is personally known to the members of the Commission, surely the fact that he is an English gentleman ought to have preserved him from the imputation which my learned friend was instructed to cast upon him. But Mr. Souter has a reputation as dear to him as mine is to me, and as my learned friend knows Mr. Souter better, he would find to be a gentleman of honour, and of honour as untarnished as that of any man in this place, and it does not recommend the case put forward by the defence to have it suggested here in open Court that gentleman of Mr. Souter's position and character is—I will not say—a puppet in the hands of his own police, but actively engaged with them in a vile conspiracy for the purpose of running His Highness the Gaekwar." * * * * *

"Of his three men it may be permitted to me to speak here one or two words. Mir Akbar Ali is an officer of forty-four years' service. He joined the service in 1831. He has received in recognition of his services the honourable distinction of Khan Bahadur—a distinction conferred by the Government of India, and a distinction not conferred lightly or without due consideration. During the whole forty-four years that he has been in the public service, there was not one event upon which my learned friend could cross-examine him. There is not one single instance in his career to which the research or the ingenuity of those who instruct my learned friend could point out attributing to him the slightest disgrace. He comes before the Commission as a man of unspotted character, whose services have been recognized by the State, and nothing whatever discreditable to him is on record.

" As to the Junior Khan Bahadur Abdul Ali—he of course has been for a less period of time in the service of the State than his father ; but he has also gained from the Government of India the honourable title of Khan Bahadur ; and when he was put in the witness-box for cross-examination not a single question was asked of him. If there had been anything in his career upon which he conld have been cross-examined, no doubt my learned friend would have been instructed to put questions showing he deserved the character which my learned friend has attributed to him. No such question was put to, and we must therefore presume that he, like his father, has a character untarnished, notwithstanding the difficulty and delicacy of the services he has had to perform."

The result of the enquiry into the charges against the Gaekwar has proved how skilfully and completely the police mastered these most serious obstacles with which they had to contend, and in the face of the extraordinary efforts made and temptations held out to induce them to betray their trust. The business of watching and guarding the witnesses from being tampered with was, if possible, even more difficult, certainly the duty was more responsible and anxious than the first working of tracing out and procuring the evidence.

THE AURANGABAD CURRENCY NOTE FORGERIES.

THE forgery of currency note in India is not an impossibility, and its detection is most difficult, for the simplicity and ignorance of the people afford favourable opportunities for the passing of forged notes in villages and small towns. In 1877 a forgery case which had about it all the elements of a romance, was tried at Aurangabad, in the Deccan, before a joint Commission appointed for the purpose by the Resident at Hyderabad and the Nizam's Government. The criminals, eight in number, were charged with forging and uttering bank notes, purporting to be those of the Government of India, of the value of Rs. 1,000 each. The principal witness, in the first instance, was chiefly concerned in attempting to utter the forged notes, and had received the promise of pardon under the usual conditions. This, however, he forfeited at an early date by making use of his position to threaten two innocent soukars to whom he and his uncle, another forger, were indebted. He asserted that unless he and his relative were fully acquitted, he would infallibly implicate them in the crime. His attempt was discovered and frustrated in time, and he received his just reward in a sentence of ten years' rigorous imprisonment. The interest of the case chiefly centred in one Chintamon Gangadhar, who also made a full confession. This man, who appeared to be a highly educated Brahmin of the better sort, speaking and writing English with fluency, had once held a prominent position under the Municipality of Bombay, and had amassed a large fortune during the time of the share mania of 1865 in the city. He seems to have first thrown up his position and then lost his fortune, and finding himself at a low ebb, he was tempted to resort to dishonest methods. Coming to Aurangabad, he connected himself with a gang of swindlers, of whom one after proposing to him participation in a murder, which was declined, suggested that the simplicity of the neighbouring inhabitants of Khandesh would make it easy to pass among them forged bank notes. Chintamon at once went to Poona, and procured from an artist, named Dhondoo Punt, fourteen bank notes for Rs. 1,000 each. The notes were made of ordinary overland paper, and were such exceedingly clumsy forgeries, judging from the specimens produced in Court, that it is perhaps not to be wondered at that even the simple Khandesh ryots refused to accept them. Eight months were spent in travelling about and attempting to pass these notes, and continued ill-success had at last the effect of making Chintamon quarrel with his confederates. They agreed to separate after burning the fourteen notes; eleven were given to Chintamon to be burnt, and his confederates solemnly assured him that the remaining three had also been destroyed.

As Chintamon said in his confession, he then thanked his gods that he had been preserved from crime, and determined to lead an honest life from thenceforth. Unfortunately, however, the remaining three notes had not been destroyed. Months afterwards two of the confederates took them to Hyderabad, and attempted to pass one of them at the Bank of Bengal at Chaderghat. The note was seized, and the clue carefully followed up. One of the men got alarmed and turned Queen's evidence. While this case was under enquiry at Aurangabad, the police in Bombay were actively co-operating with the authorities at that station, and on learning from Lieutenant LeQuesne, through Mir Abdul Ali, that Chintamon Gangadhar, one of the principal offenders, was probably to be found at or near Poona, the Commissioner sent an agent acquainted with the accused, in company with a picked policeman, in search. On reaching Poona they found that he had left that place, and his capture was deemed impossible, for he was a man of remarkable ingenuity and great resources. But promptly following up the information received they successfully traced him out. Just as Chintamon had succeeded in regaining a respectable position, and had gone to Secunderabad to take up an appointment in connection with the Nizam's Government, he found himself under arrest, and he was tried and sentenced to ten years' imprisonment in connection with a crime of which he firmly hoped that every trace had been destroyed many months before. The seven others were sentenced to various terms of imprisonment, ranging from two years and upwards. The Bombay Police, and particularly Sardar Mir Abdul Ali, rendered very valuable assistance to Lieutenant LeQuesne, the Police Master at Aurangabad, in bringing the culprits to book. Mr. C. B. Evan-Smith, First Assistant Resident, Hyderabad (Deccan), in his despatch to the Government of Bombay, said that the Resident Sir Richard Meade had expressed " a hope that this Government may deem the services of Khan Bahadur Mir Abdul Ali, Chief Detective of the Bombay Police, deserving of special recognition." He added that the great abilities of this valuable police officer were well known to Sir R. Meade, and he had well sustained his reputation in the present case. Lieutenant LeQuesne, the Superintendent of Police at Aurangabad, who most ably conducted the prosecution of these criminals to a successful issue brought to the notice of the Resident the great assistance received in connection with the case from Sir Frank Souter, K.C.S.I., and the valuable and important services rendered to him by Khan Bahadur Mir Abdul Ali. In his report to the Resident at Hyderabad Lieutenant LeQuesne said :—" I would bring to notice the unremitting labour and energy which Khan Bahadur Mir Abdul Ali has displayed in the most complicated and intricate case from beginning to end. I feel convinced that had it not been for his unweary efforts and his knowledge of criminal cases of this character, that with the limited means I have here at my disposal that the case would never have been brought to its present satisfactory conclusion. Excepting the three or four days he was in Bombay where he had proceeded in connection with this case, he has been at work with me without cessation, frequently ten hours a day, from the 10th June to this date; and in bringing his services to the notice of the Resident I would ask that in addition to the thanks I consider him entitled to the Resident to be good enough to interest himself in him and recommend a most faithful, worthy and indefatigable servant of the Government of India for advancement. I need not enter into any lengthened eulogy of him as his services and merits are well known to Sir Richard Meade, K.C.S.I., personally in the late Baroda case."

The Government thereupon issued a resolution, dated 22nd August 1877, in which the services of Mir Abdul Ali were highly eulogised. It stated, "Government consider that great credit is due to Police Inspector Khan Bahadur Mir Abdul Ali for the zeal, acumen and ability displayed by him in connection with this important, complicated and difficult case. To his efforts when working with and under Lieutenant LeQuesne the successful conduct of the enquiry, and the conviction of this gang of forgers and utterers of false notes would appear to be in great measure attributable. His Excellency the Governor in Council concurs with the Resident in considering Khan Bahadur Mir Abdul Ali's services to be deserving of special recognition." The Commissioner of Police was then asked to report what reward he would recommend should be bestowed upon Abdul Ali.

In pursuance of this resolution, the Commissioner, in his official report to Government, dated 12th December 1877, said, "As regards the important service rendered by Khan Bahadur Mir Abdul Ali at Aurangabad, which has been so warmly acknowledged by the Resident at Hyderabad, I would beg to attach copy of the certificate granted to him by Colonel Dowker, Commanding at Aurangabad, who sat as President on the Commission for the trial of the forgers and utterers of the currency notes, and from which it will be seen that in the opinion of that officer the successful termination of this case was entirely due to the skilful and laborious efforts of Khan Bahadur Mir Abdul Ali. Before submitting any recommendation for a reward to this meritorious police officer, I consider it but due to him that I should briefly recall to the notice of Government a few of the exceptionally good and important services which he has from time to time rendered, many of which are of considerable political significance." The Commissioner then described the "excellent service" rendered by Abdul Ali in connection with the trial of the State offender Moulvi Liakat Ali. After reviewing various other important, mysterious and complicated cases which he successfully and skilfully detected, the Commissioner said, "Viewing therefore the past extraordinary services of Khan Bahadur Mir Abdul Ali, and taking them in connection with the admirable and important work which he has now rendered at Aurangabad, I feel bound to strongly recommend that in lieu of his money pension already enjoyed he may now receive in recognition of his eminent services a permanent grant of land, rent free, of assessed value of not less than Rs. 500 per annum." To this recommendation, Sir Frank Souter attached the copy of letter sent to Abdul Ali by Messrs. R. Hearn and H. Cleveland, the then Government Solicitors, which, he said, "will show the high opinion the law officers of Government entertain of Khan Bahadur Mir Abdul Ali's ability, and of the most valuable assistance which he has from time to time rendered them in the preparation of criminal cases for trial at the High Court."

As regards the suggestion of the grant of land the Government, however, did not consider that the proposals could then be entertained, and called upon the Commissioner for an opinion as to the reward which should be granted to Mir Abdul Ali for his special service. The Commissioner, who appreciated the great value of the aid rendered by Mir Abdul Ali in the case, said that he had hoped that Mir Abdul Ali's claim to a grant of land would be favourably considered from the fact that Government had already recommended in their letter to the Secretary, Government of India, Foreign Department, dated 21st February 1876, that his services at Baroda and those prior to that should be so recognized. The Commissioner in his report strongly recommended "substantial means of acknowledging the very valuable services" of Mir Abdul Ali, adding that if Government did not see their way to reconsider his original recommendation, he would venture to suggest that "such personal monthly allowance may be granted to the Khan Bahadur as Government may consider his services to deserve, or that he receive a money reward." Should the latter be determined on, then he would beg respectfully to recommend that Rs. 2,000 be granted for the special and very important service which Khan Bahadur Mir Abdul Ali rendered at Aurangabad.

The Government thereupon issued a resolution, dated 23rd April 1878, granting a reward of Rs. 2,000 to Khan Bahadur Mir Abdul Ali, who was instrumental in laying open all the details resulting in the conviction and punishment of eight offenders, for the forging and uttering Government notes within H. H. the Nizam's dominions. Colonel H. Dowker, the President of the Commission, wrote in the following eulogistic terms about Mir Abdul Ali's services: "I became acquainted with Khan Bahadur Mir Abdul Ali at Aurangabad in June and July 1877. He has been engaged in a very complicated forgery case, and by his detective ability the whole nest of forgers were brought before a Commission and were sentenced to different periods of imprisonment. I feel convinced had it not been for the important labours of this admirable detective, the plot would never have been unravelled, and this gang of forgers would have been abroad to work their evil will. I wish Khan Bahadur Abdul Ali all success, and trust that in all cases on which he may be engaged, the same termination may be brought about as in the Aurangabad Forgery Case."

FORGED GOVERNMENT CURRENCY NOTES.

In 1877 Bombay was again infested by currency note forgers, whose operations were conducted on an extensive scale. The forged notes were freely but carefully circulated, and every precaution was taken by the forgers to baffle the best detective skill to trace them. The forged notes were nearly perfect in design and were well executed. The task of detection was rendered still more difficult by the fact that to all appearance the parties concerned in the notorious fraud seemed to hold a respectable standing in their community, and nobody suspected them of the swindle which they were perpetrating on the public with impunity. They had, as a blind to their real profession, set up certain respectable avocations. While the police were making enquiries into the matter, information was given by a broker, named Motichand Bhimji, that certain Hindus, residing at Vithalwadi, had offered him a commission, if he undertook to exchange Government currency notes for Rs. 1,000 each, which he suspected were forged, for a sum of Rs. 250 each. He estimated that the parties had in their possession seventy or eighty forged notes of that value, besides other counterfeit notes of a lesser value, to what amount he could not tell. In September 1876, Motichand had first a conversation with one Mulji Rameshwar, who informed him that he had a plan by which thousands of rupees could be made, and particularly asked for assistance in carrying out that plan. He at the same time produced a document purporting to be a forged Government of India currency note for Rs. 100, on which he asked to be advanced Rs. 15, saying that he would shortly show to Motichand a Rs. 1,000 note, which he assured them no one would be able to detect as false.

Motichand pretended to fall in with Mulji's plans, but placed himself in communication with Mr. Edgington, the then Deputy Commissioner of Police, and by his means the whole of the persons implicated in the offence were detected and run down. A trap was laid for the arrest of the unsuspecting forgers, who in their greed to realise as much money as possible fell blindly into it. After a number of interviews had taken place between Mulji and Motichand, a false note for Rs. 1,000 was handed by Mulji to the informer with instructions to find a purchaser for it. Motichand produced a person named Lakhmidas, who was also acting in concert with the police, and the two went with them to Motichand's house, and were shown into a room where everything that was said and done could be heard and witnessed by members of the police force stationed in an adjoining room. It was arranged there that Lakhmidas should purchase the Rs. 1,000 note, and also that he should become the purchaser of other notes of the same values. This having been agreed upon, Mulji said he would go out and bring the person whom he represented to be the owner of the notes, and he did go, and returned after a short absence in company with one Mehepa Vijianand. The negotiations between the parties were then further continued, and Mehepa produced three or four forged notes for Rs. 1,000 each. The police then entered the room in which the culprits were seated. Hameer Mehepa, one of the forgers, snatched up the notes, and realising what had happened, attempted to swallow them, but they were extracted from his mouth by Inspector Sweeney. Three of the forgers were arrested on the spot. The principal forger Umbeer Mapa managed to escape, but he was subsequently arrested. He was found concealed in a house on the Kalbadevi Road.

When search was made in the houses of the prisoners, there were found in various shops occupied by the second prisoner, a large number of dyes, plates, and other instruments that could be used for the manufacture of false notes and counterfeiting coin. Plates for making the water mark on the notes were found in Motichand's possession, and the ashes and remainder of a quantity of forged notes which had been burned by him or his friends to avoid detection were also discovered. It was also found that for a considerable period he had been engaged in engraving the plates on which the notes were to be impressed. It was further discovered that he purchased from a Borah a bottle of green ink for the purpose of making the green marks upon the notes. In the house of the prisoner there were found also a considerable number of tools, such as would be used for engraving plates for the manufacture of notes, and instruments for making counterfeit Australian sovereigns, and half anna, quarter anna, and pie pieces of the East India Company, besides various coins of Foreign States. Further implements, such as dyes, moulds, and stamps that were used for the manufacture of these forged notes were discovered in possession of a man named Depah, a servant in the employ of one Jessmal, a moonim of a respectable native firm, while he was conveying them in a box from his master's residence to that of the prisoner Umbeer Mapa. Thereupon Jessmal, moonim, and Parsuram, moonim, who resided together in the same house, as well as the servant that was conveying these articles, were all three arrested by the police. The men were placed before the Commissioner of Police, Sir Frank Souter, who, after hearing the facts of the case, admitted the three last prisoners to bail, and ordered the first four prisoners to be kept in custody, directing a further investigation to be made by the detectives into the matter. The stamps and dyes were for several amounts, and were each made separate in detached forms, constituting the several parts of Government currency notes. The first prisoner, Umbeer Mapa, was known as an expert in workmanship of this sort, and had been frequently employed by banks and houses of agency in this

Presidency to execute cheque forms, &c., for them. The detection of this forgery of Government currency notes caused such a great commotion that for some time several petty dealers in the native town declined to take in exchange a single currency note unless it was guaranteed to their satisfaction.

At the Fort Police Court, before Mr. Nana Morojee, Ameer Mehpa, Mehpa Vijianand, Mulji Rameshwar and Nathoo Irjee, were charged as follows :—Prisoners Nos. 1 and 2 with having in their possession certain seals, plates and other instruments and materials, with intention that the same should be used for the purpose of forging valuable securities, to wit, Government currency notes, with abetting the commission of the said offence, and also with forging such valuable securities as aforesaid ; and prisoners Nos. 2, 3 and 4 with fraudulently using as genuine five forged documents purporting to be Government currency notes for Rs. 1,000 each, knowing the same to have been forged, and with abetting the said offence.

Sardar Mir Abdul Ali took a very diligent part in getting together the threads of evidence against the prisoners. He exerted himself day and night to bring to justice the organised band of forgers, and he was ably assisted by Mr. Sweeney and other officers. When he had obtained sufficient evidence to secure their conviction, certain confessions were made by prisoners Nos. 1 and 2 to the effect that the prisoner No. 1 handed to prisoner No. 2 twenty-five notes for Rs. 1,000 each, five of which had already been recovered by the police. The remainder, prisoner No. 2 said, he had placed in a box which he left for the purpose in a house adjoining the house of the moonim named Jessmal, at Vithalwadi, in a Multani firm. A party of detectives, with Mr. Inspector Sweeney, repaired to the house in question. On arrival the three Multanis, constituting the firm to whom the box containing the twenty forged notes had been entrusted, denied all knowledge of the box. Prisoner No. 2, on being asked by the police, pointed out where the box generally stood in the house, from which place it had since been removed. This spot also still bore the mark as if a box had been freshly taken away. Consequently a minute search was instituted through every part of the house on all the three storeys, but nothing could be found, until it was discovered that the house had a fourth storey, which was not inhabited, but used for rubbish and useless articles. In searching this place the box was found, which corresponded in size to the marked place where it once stood in the lower storey of the house, which prisoner No. 2 had previously pointed out. The box was found broken open and the notes extracted. It was afterwards admitted by the Multanis that they had been burnt. The box was also found to contain stamps and dyes of every description of foreign and native coin, and also several coins which were counterfeit made of brass and other inferior metal. Certain other stamps and materials were also missing according to the statements of the 1st and 2nd prisoners. The articles were recovered by the police from a well in the compound of the house.

The case was, after preliminary enquiry by the Magistrate, committed to the Sessions, which were presided over by Mr. Justice Green. The prisoners had retracted their confessions and secured the best available legal talent to defend them, Mr. Inverarity appearing for the first prisoner, and Mr. Starling representing the second accused. The third was undefended, while the fourth had already been discharged by the Magistrate, as he was not in any way an accomplice in the affair, but was merely acting under the directions of his masters. The jury found the three prisoners guilty. Mehepa Vijianand, who was the principal offender, was sentenced to ten years' rigorous imprisonment; Hameer Mehepa was sentenced to seven years' rigorous imprisonment, while Mulji Rameshwar was sentenced to a term of four years' imprisonment, with hard labour.

The valuable services rendered by Sardar Abdul Ali and others in this most important case were brought to the notice of the Government by Sir Frank Souter in his report, dated 5th May 1877, and Government were pleased to sanction a reward of Rs. 2,000, Sardar Mir Abdul Ali received Rs. 400 of this amount as his share.

THE GREAT BANK FRAUDS.

It is now many years since the public mind in this Presidency was exercised and agitated over a remarkable case of forgery of currency notes, valuable securities and bank documents. The case was an extraordinary one from beginning to end, and the adventures of the culprit, who was styled the "Prince of Forgers," reads like a transcript from the pages of some sensational detective story rather than like sober fact. In September 1867 fourteen persons were charged with having committed frauds on the Bank of Bombay (Poona branch), some of them being more implicated than the rest. The charges against them were forgery and abetment of forgery and cheating and criminal breach of trust. The case was tried before the Sessions Judge at Poona. The chief witness in the case was Pestonji Fardunji, the arch-conspirator and the primemover of the whole plot. From his confidential position in the Bank as a shroff he had peculiar facilities for his nefarious deeds, and peculiar opportunities of judging whether the frauds he projected and carried out were or were not likely to succeed. In the words of Mr. Hayllar, a barrister-at-law, who prosecuted the gang, Pestonji Fardunji was probably one of the "greatest scoundrels who ever breathed," and the counsel said that "it is very much against the grain" to be compelled to rely upon him as a witness to establish the case. But from the peculiar circumstances of the fraud, it became absolutely necessary to make him Queen's evidence—to allow him to turn approver—in order to bring home the offence to the rest of the forgers and swindlers.

Govind Narayen Davria was the man of most marvellous powers of forgery—which is not surprising in view of the fact that he was the son and grandson of forgers. He obtained his living entirely by the practice of the nefarious art, and had attained such skill that if provided him with a single specimen of handwriting intended to be forged, he would copy it so exactly that the actual writer would not be able to detect any difference. He was no ordinary forger. He had obtained a chemical knowledge which enabled him by applying some valuable liquid to paper written over to erase all traces of the original, and then his mechanical skill came into play, and enabled him to produce an entirely new document. Bottles of the liquid, which was his own manufacture, were found in his house. He went about his work too with caution, always having a *segrie* of charcoal by his side ready to destroy the paper he may be engaged upon, if disturbed. Such wonderful proficiency had he obtained that a Government promissory note originally for Rs. 5,000 which was bought from Mr. Bomanji Jijibhoy, was after undergoing the necessary manipulation at Davria's hands, actually re-sold to Mr. Bomanji Jijibhoy for Rs. 10,000. It was impossible to estimate the extent of Davria's crimes. He employed one Balla Munday as the go-between to carry the documents to be forged to him and when forged, to take them back to Pestonji. The frauds commenced as far back as 1863, and were not discovered until 1867 owing to the complicity between Davria and Pestonji.

It appeared from the documents discovered that a grand coup was intended by which the entire assests of the Bank would have been cleared out. This was to have been the last scene in the drama, when all the actors appeared on the stage, but luckily their plan was discovered. Davria had on the 16th of April 1866 forged two hoondies for Rs. 5,000 and Rs. 3,000, purporting to be drawn by one Khooshaldas's firm in favour of the Bank and signed by Shivram, a shroff in the Bank, who was also implicated in the fraud. This shroff used to freely lend money to his friends, the cash balance then being entirely under his control, and as he always received one day's notice before the accounts were examined by the English accountant, he was always able to make things apparently correct by means of various devices. The favourite plan was to borrow money from sowcars for a day or two, and placing it to make up the deficiency in the cash balance (which was chiefly operated upon), and returning the monies again the next day when the danger was over.

In April 1866 Chimanlal, a clerk, came to know of these frauds, and threatened a disclosure unless silenced. Accordingly Hanmunta, one of the prisoners, who was a moonim in the employ of one

Khooshaldas's firm, was induced to accept hoondies drawn in the firm for Rs. 5,000, which was given to Chimanlal on a stamp paper as the hush-money. The acceptance was a forgery, because Hanmanta had no authority to sign. On the 13th of April a hoondi was forged to make up the deficiency in the cash balance, when these hoondies fell due and were dishonoured. A suit was filed by the Bank against the firm of Khooshaldas, when Hanmanta confessed that the documents were forgeries, and this led to the whole plot being subsequently revealed. It was also discovered that Davria had forged a cheque for Rs. 15,000 in Major Ethbridge's name, and that he was the perpetrator of the fraud known as the Hyderabad fraud. Davria was ably defended by Mr. Branson of the Bombay Bar, and on various technical grounds he and the whole members of his gang, after a trial extending over a month, were found not guilty and discharged.

FURTHER EXPLOITS OF DAVRIA.

HAVING obtained a fresh lease of professional life Davria was free to further life and display his exceptional talents ; and without fear of detection or arrest he plied his nefarious trade of forgery freely, and swindled not only the people but Government also by forging Government promissory and currency notes. In 1872 Narayen Davria forged about a hundred currency notes of the value of Rs. 1,000 each and sent them to Bombay through his confidential agents for sale, while he himself remained at Poona in hiding. On the 28th of June 1872 there came to Bombay three persons, who represented themselves to be the agents of a firm in Poona. In consequence of certain information which the police had obtained, a strict watch was put upon the movements of these three men, and a little plan was arranged for the discovery of the object of their visit to Bombay, and for their punishment when the object (then tolerably well suspected) was discovered. An European Inspector disguised himself as a Parsee gentleman, and he had his attendants the "well-known detective" Khan Bahadur as coachman and another Mahomedan detective as ghorawalla. The "Parsee gentleman" throw himself in the way of the agents and bought of them fourteen currency notes of Rs. 1,000 each at a reduced price. The agents were, however, considerably astonished when the Parsee Shet turned upon them, and was so base as not only to refuse payment for the notes but to arrest the seller of them.

Two of the men became desperate and managed to escape, but they were arrested the following day, and since it was discovered that the notes originally came from Davria, whose agents they were, Mr. Vincent, the then acting Deputy Commissioner of Police, and Colonel Henderson, Superintendent of Police at Poona, at once started for Poona and sought out the house of the head of the firm named by the agents under arrest in Bombay. But the telegraph had been set at work, and when Mr. Vincent and the Colonel entered the house they found that Messrs. So-and-So of the firm had got the hint and taken it so that none of the plates of which the notes had been taken could be found. The manager of the bogus firm was all indignation at the search, and threatened his visitors with legal proceedings. Notwithstanding these protestations of innocence, Mr. Vincent knew pretty well where the wind blew, but since the chief actor in the drama having got the scent had made himself scarce, he had to return to Bombay. The three agents were, however, convicted at the Sessions and sentenced to a long term of imprisonment. Several other members of his gang were arrested by the police and brought to book on different occasions.

These are not the only exploits of Davria. But since his adventures alone would fill a volume, suffice it to say that he continued to give trouble to the police and the people until the year 1879 when his career was cut short by the Sardar, who was sent to Poona under Government orders with the ostensible purpose of assisting Major Daniel in the arrest of Wasudeo Balwant Fadke, the notorious dacoit of the Deccan, although his real purpose was to assist Colonel Gunthorpe of the Berar Police and his Inspector Mr. Stevens in arresting Davria. The forger was to some extent popular, as he freely gave money to the poor people who would not betray him. The Sardar engaged a sodagar at first, and through some agents he arranged to buy the spurious notes. A trap was laid to entice Davria to a house, where he was told a sodagar had come to buy notes. Having made all the arrangements for laying the trap, the Sardar returned to Bombay, his presence being urgently required in some important case, leaving the matter in the hands of Colonel Gunthorpe, who succeeded in trapping Davria to the bait. Davria was placed in the Poona Jail, but he determined not to be put on his trial. In the cell a kerosine-oil lamp was kept burning. Davria poured the oil on his body, and lighting a match, set fire to his clothes and burnt himself, thus put an end to his romantic career. The Sardar earned the thanks of the public for relieving them from the annoyance of having at large a dangerous character, who had defied the police so long and with such singular success.

DOUBLE MURDER AT OOMERKHADI.

BRUTAL REVENGE OF A DISAPPOINTED LOVER.

In June 1884, a singularly brutal case of double murder claimed the attention of Sardar Mir Abdul Ali, through whose exertions the perpetrator of the horrible deed was brought to justice. The victims were Mahomed Safar Shoostri, a Mogul merchant, residing in Moonshee Ali Akbar Lane, Oomerkhadi, and his young wife Haji Bebee, who was only eighteen or nineteen years of age. The Oomerkhadi house, where the crime was perpetrated, was situated in the middle of a compound of some extent, surrounded by a wall seven-and-a-half feet in height. There was one large gate in the wall. The house consisted of four rooms, the largest of which was used as the bed-room, while another room was used as an office. The 25th of June was the first day of Ramzan. It is usual for Mahomedans to turn out into the streets in large numbers on the night preceding the day of the fast, and hence there were a number of persons in the street on that night. Shoostri returned home at midnight and awoke his wife, and having taken some food, they both retired to bed at one o'clock on the morning of the 25th of June. About two o'clock a man entered the bed-room of Shoostri, extinguished the light, and cut the mosquito curtains with a knife. Haji Bebee awoke from sleep by feeling a hand touch her body. She called out to her husband. But no sooner did she arouse her husband than she heard a scuffle between her husband and a stranger, whom she could not see as the room was in total darkness. She saw her husband fall down from tho cot, and screamed for assistance. She called out "Thief, thief!" The stranger turned to her and said in Persian پدر سوخته تو هم صدا میکنی ("Father is burnt, *you also* raise cries").

These words, though quite insignificant in themselves, subsequently put the Sardar on the right track in the pursuit of his inquiry on the assumption that the murderer must have been familiar with the deceased woman and that he must be a Persian since he spoke in that language. Fortunately the head of the Bombay Detectives had come back to Bombay from Poona, and he arrived just in time to unravel a crime which if the case had rested in the hands of an officer of only ordinary capacity and intelligence would never have been traced. According to the depositions of the victims the murderer, after first stabbing Shoostri, turned towards the girl and threw her down on the floor. He then allowed his knife to mercilessly run into her tender heart, saying "You also called out 'Thief, thief!'" On hearing her screams, two other persons, and a female cook, who slept in an adjoining room, ran up to her succour. A servant in the employ of Mr. Mirza Hoosein Khan, solicitor, Fateh Ali by name, living in the next house, was also aroused, and on going out into the street, observed a man rush out of the gate of Shoostri's house and run down the street. On going to Shoostri's room they found him lying on the floor of the bedroom bleeding, while his wife was sitting in an upright posture, leaning against the wall, and also bleeding. They were removed to the J. J. Hospital, where their dying declarations were taken down by the late Mr. Ryan, the then Second Presidency Magistrate. Their depositions, however, did not give any clue to the assailant. They described how they were stabbed, but they could not say by whom it was done. They had no enemies, and being quiet and respectable people, were generally popular. They were kept in the hospital and treated, but they died the next day within a few hours of each other.

The police now directed their attention to the search of the murderer. Sardar Abdul Ali and Mr. Sweeney, who were on the spot immediately after the occurrence, lost no time in collecting information which might lead to the detection and capture of the murderer. As the dying persons had said that the doors of the gate were fastened from inside, the Sardar concluded that the man must have climbed up the wall, and found an entrance into the compound. A close scrutiny resulted in the discovery of a cloak and skull-cap left by the murderer close to the scene of the murder under a table. His conjecture was that Haji Bebee knew the murderer, as he expressed a disagreeable surprise at her raising an alarm, for which she was stabbed. He, therefore, made enquiries of her relations about her acquaintances, and ultimately discovered that a certain Mogul was deeply smitten with her beauty and loved her passionately. The Sardar at once set to discover her lover. On enquiry he ascertained that early on the morning of the murder, a Mogul returned to the dharamsalla near the Null Bazar, and one of the inmates noticed that his clothes were torn, and that he was without the cloak and skull-cap which he had been wearing the previous evening. The Sardar pursued his enquiry, and ultimately ascertained from Haji Bebee's brother that the name of her lover, who was on hostile terms with him, was Haji Mirza Aga. He had declined to marry his sister Haji Bebee to him, and hence the hostility. The Sardar succeeded in finding and arresting Haji Mirza Secunder, who, it was ascertained, used to frequently visit at the house of Haji Bebee's mother, but he was afterwards prohibited from going there. He then went on a pilgrimage to Kerbella, and was said to have entertained a hope that, on his return to Bombay, he would be able to obtain Haji Bebee's hand in marriage. In this hope, however, he was doomed to bitter disappointment; for she was married to Shoostri when he was away in Arabia. It was also ascertained that two months prior to the murder, the prisoner made the acquaintance of a Persian named Mahomed Tucki and his wife. The latter was in the habit of visiting the houses of several Persians, and among them that of Haji Bebee, for the purpose of receiving alms. The prisoner asked her to take a message to Shoostri's wife, which she refused to do. It was in such terms as these—" Whether Haji Bebee, now that she is married, would recognise old friends." Subsequently the prisoner asked Mahomed Tucki to join him in committing a theft in Shoostri's house; and it was arranged that they should meet on the evening of the 23rd June and carry the design into execution. Mahomed Tucki did not go that evening; and on the following day the prisoner questioned him why he had not kept his appointment? He at the same time said he had attempted to get over the wall of the deceased's house, but had failed; and showed Tucki green stains on his clothes, caused by the moss on the top of the wall. He said he only wanted Tucki to help him to get over the wall. Tucki consented to go on the following evening. The prisoner lived in a dharamsalla near the Null Bazar. On the evening of the 24th June, as he and Tucki were standing near the mosque at Baboola Tank, Mahomed Hassam, Hajee Bebee's brother, passed by. He observed and heard that the prisoner pointed him out to Tucki as Haji Bebee's brother. This occurred at 11 p.m. Later on the same night Tucki helped the prisoner over the wall of Shoostri's compound. On the prisoner returning to his room early the following morning, some of the inmates of the dharamsalla noticed that his clothes were torn, and that he was without the cap and cloak, which he had been wearing the previous evening. His clothes were very dirty and wet. He borrowed a shirt of another person, took off the clothes he had been wearing, tied them up into a bundle, and went out. He afterwards returned home without the bundle; and from what transpired subsequently, it appeared that he had gone out to bury the clothes. After his arrest, he pointed out the place where the clothes had been buried, not far from his residence. Sardar Mir Abdul Ali himself dug up the place in the presence of Mr. Gell, the Deputy Commissioner, Mr. Mirza Hoosein Khan, Superintendent Sweeney and several other respectable persons who bore witness to the fact, and also to the statement of the prisoner that the clothes belonged to another person from whom he had borrowed them and were buried there by him. Mahomed Tucki, the accomplice, who had helped him to climb over the wall, only then came forward and made a confession, stating that he had lent the clothes to the accused.

The case was tried before Mr. Justice Hart and a Special Jury at the Fourth Criminal Sessions of the High Court. The prosecution was conducted by Mr. Farran (now Sir Charles Farran, the Chief Justice), while the prisoner was defended by Mr. Kirkpatrick. The prisoner retracted his former admission and pleaded not guilty. But the evidence against him was overwhelming. Mr. Justice Hart, in summing up the case to the jury, remarked that the chief witness was Mahomed Tucki, an accomplice, whose evidence could not be accepted without corroboration. In his Lordship's opinion, there was abundance of corroborative evidence ; and the only question was as to whether it was reliable or not. There was material corroboration supplied by the prisoner himself ; for he took the police to the spot where the clothes were buried, and in pointing them out said, "Here are the bloody clothes." The suggestion made by the prisoner's counsel that the case had been got up by the police could not, his Lordship remarked, be sustained. The jury found the prisoner guilty by a majority of eight to one ; and the prisoner was sentenced to death.

After the capital sentence was passed upon Secunder, he continued to preserve wonderfully cheerful disposition. In his cell in the jail he preserved calmness, and he did not seem to be affected by the fate he was doomed to meet in a short time. He took his food regularly and without hesitation, and unlike prisoners awaiting the capital punishment he seemed to be enjoying very good health—in fact, his weight actually increased, a very rare occurrence in the case of a prisoner awaiting the gallows. He remained unconcerned until the last moment, and when it arrived he unhesitatingly allowed the rope to be adjusted round his neck with marked pleasure, which he ascribed to the prospect of his shortly meeting his beloved girl in the other world, where he himself had despatched her. His last words, as he climbed up the gallows, were the following lines from Saadi :—

عاشقان کشتگان معشوق اند
بر نیاید ز کشتگان آواز

" Lovers are the slain ones of their beloved ;
From the slain ones no voice proceeds."

This he spoke in the most audible tone, and very soon he was launched into eternity.

THE PAREL MURDER CASE.

A MOST shocking and brutal murder was perpetrated in Bombay on the night of the 21st of November 1887, the victim being a young Mahomedan woman of prepossessing appearance. The mystery with which the affair was at first surrounded, the brutality with which the crime was committed, and the ingenious methods adopted to baffle the detective skill of the police, created quite a sensation and excited deep and melancholy interest on the part of the public. No trace of the offender was left behind, and it was at first supposed that the dark mystery would remain an everlasting secret. But to the superior skill, inexhaustible energy and remarkable police acumen of Sirdar Mir Abdul Ali the offender was eventually traced, tried at the Criminal Sessions of the High Court, convicted and sentenced. On the morning of the 24th of November 1887 a small dealwood box with a counterpane close to it was observed on an open piece of marshy ground close to the Elphinstone station at Parel. It was at first thought that the box contained goods which had perhaps been stolen, and a report was at once made to the police, who, on examination, found the box to be locked and a very offensive smell issuing from it. A European police officer was at once sent for, and when he caused the box to be forced open the body of a woman in an advanced state of decomposition was found coiled up and jammed into it. Her face was mangled beyond recognition, but it was hoped that the unfortunate Mahomedan girl would be recognised by her clothes, and the police by beat of *battaki* and other means got together thousands of people in the hope of her being identified, but without success. What was still more strange was that no woman was then reported to be missing from any house in Bombay. Sir Frank Souter placed the case in the hands of Mir Abdul Ali.

The detective police were greatly puzzled, and began to think that the girl could not have belonged to Bombay, but that she had perhaps been murdered in some other place and brought to the city with the object of evading detection. Failing to get any clue at the spot where the body was found, Mir Abdul Ali came to the conclusion that the deceased must have been a stranger to Bombay, and acting under this belief he at once instituted enquiries at the rest-houses or "Moosafarkhanas." Three days later he succeeded in very cleverly obtaining a clue to the box in which the dead body had been found. It was ascertained that it had belonged to a Pathan named Syed Gool, who had recently married by *nicka* a strange woman residing at Ismael Habib's Moosafarkhana. Prosecuting his inquiries further Mir Abdul Ali obtained information that Syed Gool had very suddenly taken steamer to Aden, and that he was accompanied by his daughter and a friend; but strange to say that he had not taken with him the woman he had so recently married by *nicka.* Further investigations resulted in the discovery of the fact that the clothes found on the deceased woman were very similar to those usually worn by the woman who married Syed Gool. As these and other circumstances pointed to the man as the likely offender, and Mir Abdul Ali applied to the Commissioner to instructions to Aden for the arrest of Syed Gool, but the evidence was of such a meagre character that naturally Sir Frank Souter felt some hesitation. But he had such a thorough confidence in the judgment of Mir Abdul Ali that he at once telegraphed to the Resident at Aden for the apprehension of Syed Gool on his arrival at that port. How very high was the opinion entertained by Sir F. Souter of Mir Abdul Ali's ability could be judged from the following passage found in his despatch to the Government of Bombay: "I must admit that at this stage I considered the evidence as scarcely sufficient to justify the arrest of the suspected person, but instinctively the Khan Bahadur seemed to fix on Syed Gool as the perpetrator of the crime, and having, from long experience, learnt to place much confidence in his sound judgment, I, acting on his advice, wired, through Government, on the 28th November, to the Resident at Aden to apprehend Syed Gool, his daughter and his companion Noor Mahomed, who were passengers by the steamer 'Wave' and send them to Bombay."

In accordance with this request the trio were arrested and brought back to Bombay under a guard of the Aden Police on the 10th December. Soon after arrival Noor Mahomed, the accomplice, made a clean breast of the whole affair before Mir Abdul Ali, and was eventually admitted as an approver, as it would have been impossible to bring home the offence to Syed Gool without his evidence. This confession went to show that Syed Gool arrived in Bombay from Karachi, accompanied by his daughter, about nine years of age, in the beginning of September and put up at Ismail Habib's Musaferkhana. His friend Noor Mahomed (the witness) also joined him from Karachi a few days later. On the 24th October a woman, calling herself Sherif Khatum, came to the same Musaferkhana, situated at Pakmodia Street, and on the 26th Syed Gool married her by *nicka*, and went to live in a house in the same street, his friend and daughter also residing in the same house. A few days after the marriage quarrels ensued between Syed Gool and his wife on account of his taking possession and disposing of her jewels. Each day seemed to bring fresh troubles in the house, and at last Syed Gool seems to have made up his mind to take her life. It would appear that several plans were thought of to carry out his objects, and ultimately he purchased a pair of long iron pincers, with which, assisted by Noor Mahomed, he got hold of and pressed the wind pipe of her throat, till he successfully strangled her.

Afterwards Syed Gool, with the aid of Noor Mahomed, packed the dead body in a wooden box, which they wrapped in gunny bags and tied up with coir rope. At 2 o'clok in the afternoon of the day in the early hours of which the ghastly crime was committed Syed Gool and Noor Mahomed placed the box and a counterpane, purchased at the time of marriage, into a bullock cart and drove to the Elphinstone Road railway station, outside of which on the main road they caused the box and counterpane to be placed and there discharged the driver. Here they engaged a man named Rama, residing in a chawl close to where the box had been put down, to watch it and the counterpane, and paid him one anna, saying they were going away, but would be back immediately. It was afterwards ascertained that on this same morning Syed Gool disposed of the remaining ornaments he had removed from his wife's body, and later on purchased passage tickets for himself, daughter and Noor Mahomed, and embarked for Aden in the s.s. 'Wave' on the 24th idem. As Syed Gool and Noor Mahomed failed to return to the Elphinstone station, the man Rama, after waiting a considerable period, removed the box and counterpane into his room for safety, and kept them there till the 23rd, when in consequence of the bad smell which began to issue from the box, he became alarmed, and at night quietly moved it and the counterpane out on to the spot where they were discovered by the police the following morning. The Sardar thought that the box must have been purchased from the neighbourhood, and so he made enquiries, and had ascertained actually, before the arrest of the murderer at Aden, that the box was made by a carpenter for Syed Gool.

The trial of Syed Gool at the Criminal Sessions lasted five days, at the end of which time he was unanimously found guilty by the jury and condemned to suffer death. The Honourable the Advocate-General, who conducted the prosecution in this case, remarked in his address to the jury that great credit was due to the detective police for the detection of the case. In his address to the jury the Honourable Acting Chief Justice Mr. Bayley, who tried the case, remarked: "The police deserve very great credit for the way in which they presented the case. I cannot agree with the suggestion that they have exercised any undue influence on the witnesses to get them to give the evidence they did. It is quite impossible to believe that all these twenty-four witnesses could have been engaged in a conspiracy against the accused. It is most probable that the accomplice made a clean breast of everything, and upon his statement the Khan Bahadur very clearly and carefully collected the evidence of the various parties concerned." His Lordship in passing sentence stated as follows: "Syed Gool Khairullakhan, after a long and protracted trial by a most intelligent jury, you have been found guilty of a most cruel and horrible murder, and no one who has heard the evidence can doubt for a moment that you took that woman's life as described by your accomplice. There is not the slightest reason to assume that the police have improperly dealt with the witnesses in the case, and in the course of a long experience I have scarcely ever seen a case so clearly proved against a prisoner as this one."

Mr. F. A. Little, Public Prosecutor, who instructed Mr. Farran in the case, gave a willing testimony to the worth of Sardar Abdul Ali. He wrote, "I have often heard both Mr. Hearn and Mr. Cleveland speak of Khan Bahadur Mir Abdul Ali in the very highest terms of praise * * * * * Khan Bahadur Mir Abdul Ali has instructed me in a number of cases—amongst them being three very notable cases—which created great public interest. The Mogul murder case in 1884, Mirza Aga Secunder having murdered, whilst sleeping in their house at Oomerkhadi, a well-known Persian merchant, Haji Mahomed Safer Shoostri, and his wife, Haji Bebee. (2) The Khoja murder case in November 1895, Shamji *alias* Shanker bin Rahim, having murdered, on the premises of H. H. Aga Khan in the Love Lane, His Highness's head cashier; and (3) the recent Parel murder case, Syed Gool having murdered his wife, deposited her body in a box at Parel, and sailed for Aden. In each of the cases I believe it was owing in a great measure to the Khan Saheb's great judgment, tact, and skill that the offenders were brought to justice and hanged." * * * * *

TRIPLE MURDER AT DADAR.

One of the most atrocious cases of murder ever known in the criminal annals of the city and in which three persons were ruthlessly murdered, was committed in Bombay on the 18th October 1888. The scene of this horrible tragedy was a bungalow situated a short distance from the Dadar station of the B. B. and C. I. Railway Company. The crime was committed in broad daylight, and the brutality and ferocity with which it was perpetrated and the mysterious circumstances connected with it created quite a panic. The discovery of the offender taxed the utmost energy of Mir Abdul Ali, who displayed remarkable skill and tact in the detection of the crime. The victims belonged to a most respectable Parsee family, who, though once very rich, had been for some years in reduced circumstances. One of the victims, Bai Rattanbai, was a widow of Mr. Framji Cowasji Mehta, and was fifty-eight years of age. Another victim was her unmarried daughter, Bai Banoobai, aged twenty years, while the third was a child of the tender age of five or six. Rattanbai lived in a house at Lady Jamsetji Road, near Dadar, with her two sons, three daughters, and a grandson, named Aspandiar, about six years old. Her two daughters and sons used to go to their respective callings during the day, while Rattanbai and her daughter Banoobai remained at home, and sometimes Aspandiar also when he did not go to school. On the morning of the 18th October 1888, Rattanbai's two sons and two daughters went out as usual to attend to their business, leaving Rattanbai, Banoobai, and Aspandiar and a servant in the house. The servant, who was only nineteen years of age, was taken in their employment only a few days previously. On the 3rd of the month he introduced himself to the family as a malee, and inquired whether they needed his services. He represented that he was formerly in the Wadia family at Mazagon, in which locality he resided. He gave his name as Crishna Laximon, but he was commonly called "Rama," and was said to be a native of Alibaugh. He was eventually taken as a domestic servant on a salary of Rs. 4 per mensem, and it was stipulated that he should work in the house from 6 a.m. to 6 p.m. every day. Up to the date of the tragedy, Rama was very regular in attendance, and did his work to the satisfaction of the lady of the house.

On the morning of the fatal day when Rattanbai's two sons and two daughters left home, nothing exceptional was noticed. But in the afternoon a lady friend of the family, who came to pay a visit, opened the front door which had been closed, and entered the house. She called the names of her friends, but on receiving no reply, she went into the cook-room at the rear of the house, where, to her horror, she observed corpses of the mother and her grandchild lying in a pool of blood. She ran out in a fright and shouted for help. Two Parsees and a policeman promptly arrived, and besides the two corpses in the cook-room, they discovered Banoobai lying in a side-room, a stream of blood running out of the wounds which had been inflicted upon her. The unfortunate victims had their heads frightfully broken and mangled, in all probability by means of a pestle, which, stained with fresh blood, was lying on the floor. As soon as the tragedy was reported at the police station, which is very near the bungalow, Superintendent Grennan went to the house, and was followed after some time by Mr. Gell, Deputy Commissioner, and the Khan Bàhadur. An inspection of the house gave the clearest evidence of the motive for this terrible crime. Almost all the chests and cupboards, both on the ground-floor and on the upper-floor, had been broken open and all the articles abstracted. The rooms were littered over with clothes and papers and broken and empty boxes, and the murderer had taken away whatever article of any value he could lay hands upon, including a silver tea-set, silk and gold embroidered sarees, diamond ear-rings and brooches and gold bangles. To all appearance, it seemed that the foul deed must be the work of at least several persons.

The head of the Criminal Investigation Department first of all tried to find a clue on the spot. To him—as to every body else—it was a matter for wonder that the horrible deed was done without any of the neighbours being in the least aware of the ghastly tragedy that was being enacted within a few feet of them. The bungalow certainly could not be said to be situated in an isolated place. It stood in the middle of a small compound, a couple of yards from the public road. Adjacent to it and situated in the same compound was another bungalow occupied by a Hindu family. The boundary was marked by a very low wall, scarcely four feet in height, and quite close to the wall by the side of the road was the hut of a native workman. At the back were the huts of dyers, and, as stated above, the police station was not far from the scene. The Khan Bahadur fixed the probable hour of the horrible deed at noon, because they were certainly committed before the unfortunate persons had taken their meal. As the tragedy was not discovered until the evening, the murderer or murderers had a full start of several hours to clear away. The plan seemed to have been carried out with such an atrocious thoroughness that it left no chance for the victims to cry for help, or else the loud noise which must have attended the hammering of the chests and cupboards would have attracted the attention of the neighbours. The general belief was that if the servant was guilty of the crime, he must have been assisted by several others. The whole district was largely populated by Bhandaries, who are not a very peaceful or law abiding class of people. The task of capturing the offenders seemed to be most difficult, if not quite impossible, as nobody knew the servant's real name or his whereabouts. The surviving members of the family gave the police the name and address of the servant which they had learnt from him, and they estimated that property worth about Rs. 2,000 had been stolen from the house. Mr. Gell, who was Acting Commissioner during the absence of Colonel Wilson, gave instructions to Inspector Cobb to make inquiries regarding the missing servant Rama, and to take him into custody, if found. The same night Inspector Cobb found a man named Rama, who was in the service of the Wadia family at Mazagon, but he was not the individual wanted. Further inquiries were made, but no trace of the man could be obtained.

As the detection of the crime was important, and the anxiety of the townspeople very great, a reward of Rs. 300 was offered, in anticipation of Government sanction, to any person or persons, other than policemen, who would furnish information leading to the arrest and conviction of the person or persons who had committed the atrocious crime. Mir Abdul Ali guessed that as the missing servant knew the name and address of the man Rama, brought by Mr. Cobb, they must have known one another. On this theory Mir Abdul Ali and other officers working with him inquired of Rama, whether he had known any person answering the description of the missing servant, and if so, who and where he was. Rama after a great deal of deliberation said that some time ago he had mentioned his master's name and residence to one Dhanji, the brother of Nanoo Narayen, *alias* Crishna *alias* Rama in his presence, and that the description of the absconding servant tallied with that of Dhanji Nana Dalvi's brother residing at Mount Road, Mazagon. Two days passed, but no trace of Nanoo Narayen could be found. Information was then received by the police that the murderer was a native of Kaswan Taluka, in the Savantwadi Estate. Search was made all night for him, but without success. At last on the next Sunday afternoon the police received information that the supposed murderer had gone to the house of his brother, who was in the service of Dr. D. Rozario at Mazagon. He was promptly followed and apprehended in an out-building attached to that gentleman's bungalow. He stoutly denied at first having ever been in the service of a Parsee family at Dadar. His clothes were found to bear clear marks of blood upon them, although an attempt appeared to have been made to wash them away. In general appearance he was the same that he was before, except that he had shaved and cut short his hair, evidently to change his appearance with a view to avoid detection. He was taken in custody to the bungalow of the Mehta family, and there identified by the surviving members of the family and the neighbours as the missing servant.

When the members of the family and their friends saw the man, their excitement became intense, and they would undoubtedly have wreaked their vengeance on him, had it not been for the intervention of the police. He was then removed to the Byculla police office, and after giving several evasive answers, he eventually stated to Mir Abdul Ali that he was sleeping on the afternoon in question at the shop of two goldsmiths immediately after the murders.

This aroused the suspicion of Mir Abdul Ali, who consequently deputed a smart detective Jamadar Tatia Laximan to fetch the goldsmiths after placing a police guard at their shop. At midnight the two goldsmiths were brought to the police office, and being interrogated by Mir Abdul Ali, they told him that Narayen had given them five articles of jewellery on the afternoon of the 18th October and that they paid him one rupee on account. Mir Abdul Ali then confronted the goldsmiths with Narayen, who on seeing them became pale and confused, and eventually admitted the delivery of the jewellery to the goldsmiths. He then made a clean breast of the whole crime.

Next morning he took the police officers and some members of the bereaved family to Mahim, and explained the manner and order in which Rattanbai, her daughter and grandson had been murdered. He showed the different boxes and cupboards in the house which he had forced open. He denied that he had any accomplice with him, and took the whole responsibility of the crime upon his own shoulders. He stood the ordeal of interrogations before the relatives of the persons he had slaughtered with unabashed face. He preserved all along a remarkably cool and collected demeanour, and throughout the examination he carefully said as little as possible, in order to avoid committing himself to anything. Why he had done the terrible deed he could not say. No feeling of animosity or vengeance had prompted him to the deed, since he had been kindly treated. In the course of his confession he said that about 11 o'clock in the fore-noon he was cleaning some utensils, when, all of a sudden, something came into his head. He rose from his work, took up the iron pestle, and with that he first felled down the little boy Aspandiar, who had a toy pistol in his hand, and was playing with a rocking horse. The fiend next turned upon the old lady Bai Rattanbai, who was in the cook-room engaged in cooking food. He believed that the one blow on the head killed her outright, but in order to make sure of his work, he dealt her several additional blows. He then went into the room where the young lady Banoobai, who was suffering from a head-ache, was asleep. She, too, was taken unawares, and stunned by the very first blow that was dealt to her. He denied that she had offered any resistance, and this is extremely probable since the poor lady was murder-ed in her bed, before she had time to realise who her assailant was.

Banoobai was a courageous and well-built lady, and her relatives stated that if she could have met her antagonist face to face she would have most certainly got the better of the thin slightly built man who was opposed to her. The victims had all died without raising any cry for help, almost without a groan. Their murderer then went upstairs, and with a pickaxe broke open chests and cupboards. From a chest, which he had been suspected a few days before of trying to tamper with, he took out a sandalwood box and broke it open. It contained a bundle of rubies, but he did not know that they were valuable. He put them, he said, for what they were worth in his pocket, as well as a bangle or two of coral. He pointed out some glass beads, which he had thrown away as being of no value. The wretched man was placed before the late Mr. Ryan, the then Second Presidency Magistrate, and the case was remanded for a fortnight in order to enable the police to prosecute further inquiries. During the interval Mir Abdul Ali succeeded in tracing the antecedents of the villain. The inquiry led him to suspect that two years before Narayon had murdered with a knife a Hindu boy of the tender age of nine years for the sake of Rs. 5 only, and thrown the body into a gutter in the compound of a cotton mill at Tank Bunder. During the investigation it was further ascertained that Narayen had previously committed two thefts, one in the bungalow of Lady Sassoon, where he was employed as a pankhaboy, and the other in the house of a Parsee doctor, in whose service he was for three days under a false name of Rama. Lady Sassoon's property was partly recovered, and the receiver was prosecuted and convicted. The receiver of the doctor's property was left unmolested, as it had been broken up and disposed of.

At his trial in the Sessions Court Narayen withdrew the confession he had made before the police. But the majority of the jury returned a verdict of guilty, and the presiding Judge, in passing sentence upon the accused, remarked that the jury could not possibly have come to any other conclusion. The principal member of the Parsee family stated in cross-examination that it was impossible for one person to carry away the property. This statement naturally led the judge and the jury to believe that Narayen had accomplices in the crime ; and the impression of the public was also strengthened on this point. The police were placed in a peculiar position, for if they had adduced evidence to rebut the allegation about the loss of so much property, the case would have been weakened, this person being the principal witness for the prosecution. Colonel Wilson naturally considered it very desirable to clear up this matter, and therefore directed the Khan Bahadur, accompanied by Rao Bahadur Daji Gangaji, to interview Narayen with his consent on the 21st February (that is two days before his execution). After an ordinary conversation, they turned to the subject of the murders. Narayen solemnly assured the police officers that he was the only murderer, and that the property found with the goldsmiths was the only property stolen by him. After this he expressed great repentance for what he had done, and requested the officers to send a Brahmin to assist him in his prayers to the Almighty for the forgiveness of his sins. A Brahmin was accordingly sent to Narayen the next day, and the culprit, after bathing himself, offered formal prayers, assisted by the Brahmin, for the forgiveness of the murders of Rattanbai, Banoobai, and Aspandiar. Narayen also prayed to be pardoned for one more murder of the boy who was killed in the compound of the mill at Tank Bunder.

WHOLESALE SMUGGLING OF ARMS AND AMMUNITION.

As Mr. H. G. Gell, who was then Acting Commissioner of Police, remarked in the official annual report to Government for 1887, " Khan Bahadur Mir Abdul Ali, Superintendent of Police, Detective Branch, after four months' incessant attention and patient enquiries, succeeded in apprehending and bringing to justice an organised gang of Pathans, who had for a long time carried on an illicit trade in arms and ammunition with the trans-frontier outlaws." The Government of India took a special interest in the case as the outlaws were said to belong to the party of Umra Khan, whose name so recently was much in the mouth of everybody, when an expedition was sent to Chitral against him.

In the beginning of 1887, and subsequently information was received from the Peshawar Police to the effect that a Pathan, named Sandalah Khan, of the village of Bandi in Bajour, was in the habit of purchasing guns and ammunition from Haji Shamsuddin, a blacksmith and gun repairer at Bhendy Bazaar in Bombay, and taking them up-country packed as cotton bales. Enquiries were made for the man Sandalah, but as his description and particulars were not supplied by the Peshawar Police, no information regarding him could be obtained.

In the month of May 1888, a Pathan Havildar, named Amanatkhan, of the Bombay Police Detective Branch, received by post two letters from a Pathan sodagar, stating that five Pathans, named Suleman-shah, Feroze Khan, Sandalah Khan, Gulam Hasan Khan, and Amir Khan, had arrived in Lahore, and were residing near Sarai Sultan, and that they would shortly come to Bombay to purchase guns and catridges from Haji Shamshuddin. The letters further stated that on the 15th Rajab last (29th March 1888) Sandalah Khan had obtained from Haji Shamshuddin certain breech-loading guns and cartridges and taking them to Lahore.

On receipt of the letters Khan Bahadur Mir Abdul Ali set inquiries on foot, and found that three Pathans were in the habit of visiting Haji Shamshuddin and holding secret conversations with him. The Khan Bahadur consequently employed two co-tenants in Haji Shamshuddin's shop, and made arrangements with them to watch in co-operation with the detectives the movements of Haji Shamshuddin and the said three Pathans. The men thus employed found that these three Pathans had rented through Haji Shamshuddin two rooms on the first floor of a vacant house in a street near Haji Shamshuddin's shop, and saw Haji Shamshuddin giving at his house in a secret and suspicious manner to the Pathans on different occasions some guns and cartridges. They also saw Haji Shamshuddin two or three times take to the rooms of the Pathans some bundles containing cartridges. In the afternoon of the 23rd August 1887 the three Pathans placed 4 bales in a labour cart at the house in which they resided, and two of the Pathans took them to the B. B. and C. I. Railway goods station at Grant Road, where they booked them to Peshawar City to the address of one Hazrat Gul. The Pathans declared that the bales contained piece-goods, and one of them signed a consignment note to that effect. The bales were so packed that they appeared to be exactly like those of piece-goods which merchants generally despatch by rail. Immediately after this Khan Bahadur Mir Abdul Ali, Inspector Framji Bhicaji and other detective officers arrested the Pathans and seized the bales, which were opened in the presence of the railway authorities, and were found to contain very cleverly arranged in separate pieces in straw two military Martini-Henry rifles, one ordinary Martini-Henry rifle, one B.-L. carbine and 3,290 military ball cartridges. The cartridges bore marks of being manufactured at the Kirkee Factory. The names of the two Pathans were then ascertained to be Feroze Khan and Sandalah Khan. The third Pathan was also apprehended. His name, Feroze Khan said, was Hazrat Gul, the man named in the consignment note, but the latter said his name was Shaik Wali; his proper name, however, was eventually ascertained to be Sulemanshah. They were subsequently ascertained to be the agents of Umra Khan.

The detective officers then proceeded to the rooms in the occupation of the said three Pathans, and on searching them found one military Schneider rifle and 522 military cartridges of the aforesaid description. A Persian letter was also found in the rooms. This letter contained some allusions to a transaction in arms. Haji Shamshuddin was also arrested the same day, and his shop was searched under magistrate's warrant on the 25th August last, when the detectives found 42 guns, 17 revolvers, 2 pistols, 7 country swords, 121 ball cartridges, out of these Haji Shamshuddin failed to account for 21 guns, 14 revolvers, 2 pistols, 121 ball cartridges. The Pathans, who were also natives of Afghanistan, and Shamshuddin were charged before the Second Presidency Magistrate, Mr. P. Ryan, under the provisions of Sections 14 and 19 of the Indian Arms Act of 1878, with possessing the rifles and cartridges found with the former, and the latter was further charged with possessing other fire arms and cartridges. The prosecution was conducted by Mr. Frere, the officiating Public Prosecutor, assisted by Khan Bahadur Mir Abdul Ali, while Haji Shamshuddin was defended by Mr. Brown, a well-known solicitor. After several hearings the magistrate convicted all the offenders on the 2nd October, and sentenced them to undergo rigorous imprisonment for a term of two years each, and ordered the arms and ammunition to be confiscated. After the expiry of the sentence the men were allowed to go back to Afghanistan, at the intercession of Umra Khan. It was ascertained during the course of the enquiry that these Pathan agents were systematically sending arms and ammunition into Afghanistan, and that in consequence of the demand, exceptionally large consignments had arrived in Bombay in 1887 and 1888.

EXTENSIVE FORGERY OF POSTAGE STAMPS.

One of the most daring and clever forgeries that ever came within the experience of the Bombay Police was discovered in September 1890, a man having succeeded in printing forged postage stamps, and selling them to the public without detection. The story of the discovery of the forgery is rather a curious one. For a considerable time previously the detective police in Bombay, under Sardar Mir Ali, had been at work trying to discover the perpetrator, and it was only by carrying on their inquiries in a quiet and secret manner that they at last managed to hunt him down. That such a thing was going on somewhere in India was first found out by a collector of old and used stamps in London, who noticed on careful examination that a forged stamp had by some means got into his possession. He at once reported the discovery to the police, and in turn the Postmaster General in Bombay was communicated with. The matter was placed in the hands of the Commissioner of Police, and the detectives were set to work at once. Their task was, as may be imagined, no light one, but in the end their perseverance was rewarded, and they succeeded in tracing a forged postage stamp similar to the one found in London to a young Portuguese clerk, in the employ of Messrs. Gaddum Bythell and Co., merchants, Church Gate Street. This lad was taken into custody on suspicion, but he soon cleared himself of the charge. He, it was evident, had no idea that the stamps he had been using were forged, but referred the police to a licensed stamp vendor, a Bania Hindu, named Ramdas Lakhmidas, from whom he purchased the stamps. Ramdas was promptly honoured by a visit from the detectives, who surprised him at his father-in-law's house at Tanna and arrested him. He, as a matter of course, denied all knowledge of the offence, and said he was under the impression they were genuine, although that seemed strange from the manner in which he procured them. He referred the police next to a man at Girgaum, who, it would appear, had been in the habit of supplying Ramdas with stamps.

This man was called on at his place of abode in Girgaum by the Khan Bahadur in disguise; and he was rather surprised to find that he was a Brahmin called Shrida, *alias* Khundo Sakaram. He belonged to the Davria gang, the members of which, belonging to Poona, had been known as a famous tribe of forgers, all or nearly all of them having been at various times sentenced to a long term of imprisonment. Shrida was arrested, and a key was found concealed in his turban with which his room was opened. A search of the premises revealed the fact that the police had at last succeeded in hunting down their man, for over two hundred of the fictitious postage stamps *for one rupee* were found in his possession. With all the appliances found in the room for manufacturing the stamps, Shrida was taken to Byculla. The demeanour of the prisoner on finding he was caught was most cool, and even impudent. He made a clean breast of the whole affair, and even went the length of illustrating to Colonel Wilson, the Commissioner of Police, and to Mr. Gell, his deputy, how he printed the stamps.

The water-marks on the stamps were so cleverly imitated that even the best experienced connoisseur would have found difficulty on closest examination in discovering the trick. Shrida's mode of printing so successfully as to reproduce the stamps was quite a clumsy one. He had the impression of the stamp on a stone, much after the same style as a lithographer would have. Then, after applying the ink, he put on the paper, and deftly ran his thumb over the surface of the paper, thus taking the impression on to it. It was difficult to ascertain how far the revenue had been defrauded, and how many people in Bombay had innocently affixed those forged stamps on letters which they despatched to England, because it would seem Shrida had been carrying on his illegal trade for seven months at least. One of the most remarkable features of the case was that the postal authorities in Bombay declared the workmanship of this Hindu to be superior from an artistic point of view to the stamps supplied to the Government of India.

Khan Bahadur Abdul Ali went to inspect the stock of forged stamps and the implements used in their production. The prisoner was present under escort. He explained in greater detail how the work was done. His first step was to polish an oblong piece of stone bearing the stamp, set in a block of wood, with an admixture of *cocum*, similar in quality and color to ordinary tamarind. His next process was to lightly touch the cut stamp, delicately finished with a tint of light grey. He then adjusted a piece of paper upon it, which he carefully rubbed with the concave side of a shell, so as to ensure the application of full pressure on its surface. The paper was then removed with a clear and distinct impression upon it, and was placed on a square piece of copper, drilled with holes and perforated. The water-mark was next impressed, and the production was a piece of work which almost approached the finish of the genuine article. The only difference noticeable in the process of lithography was that some of the lines across the stamp were somewhat coarser than the impression on the original. Another difficulty to be encountered was to prevent the ink from filling in the reliefs. These defects were scarcely discernible to the naked eye, but could be easily perceived through a magnifying glass. The highest credit was due, without doubt, to the Khan Saheb and his energetic subordinates, who had by their patient investigations suceeded in running the culprit to earth and recovering the entire apparatus by means of which he had carried on the fraudulent practice. The prisoner was convicted, and was sentenced to a long term of rigorous imprisonment. One of his accomplices was also convicted and sentenced.

For his most valuable services in this case Khan Bahadur Mir Abdul Ali was highly complimented by Colonel Wilson, who brought his services to the notice of the Government.

MYSTERIOUS MURDER AT CLERKE ROAD.

A BRUTAL murder was perpetrated at Clerke Road in May 1890 under the most mysterious circumstances. The case affords striking illustration of the little worth attached in some quarters to human life. The circumstances under which this heinous crime was committed were most revolting. It is too terrible even to think of that a man should come forward to commit a murder for the paltry sum of Rs. 25. In this case two persons were hired for Rs. 50 to kill an innocent man by his own uncle for the sake of property worth Rs. 300, which was claimed by the deceased. It was a highly enigmatic murder, and its detection seemed most difficult, but thanks to the great abilities of Mir Abdul Ali what seemed to be a profound mystery difficult of being solved, was unravelled in a highly creditable manner. Colonel Wilson related the case in his official report to Government in the following terms:—

This was a highly mysterious murder perpetrated by three persons for the trifling sum of Rs. 50. On the morning of the 26th May the dead body of a Hindu youth was found lying near a tree on the footpath of Clerke Road. Round the neck was tightly tied a long piece of coir rope, the two ends of which were fastened to two uprights of the tree guard. The body had only two *bundies* on. Battaki was beaten all over the town, but no one came forward to identify the body. A photograph of the deceased was then taken, hand bills were distributed all over the city, and to prevent decomposition the body was kept in ice till the 28th May, when it was at length recognized as that of a Hindu carpenter named Raghunath Moroba *alias* Rogia, who used to reside alone in a room of a house in Mugbhat. On enquiry the police discovered that the deceased had gone to Uran to see his sister on the 24th May, and had returned to Bombay on the 25th May; that the same afternoon a Mahomedan had called to see the deceased; that in the evening the deceased had left some mangoes with the Mahomedan, and that the deceased had not afterwards returned home. Searching enquiries were made, but no information could be obtained regarding the Mahomedan. The police further ascertained that the deceased had not been on good terms with his uncle Pandu Mankoji who resided at Uran. With this clue the police went to Uran for enquiry, and it then came out that Rogia's father was dead, and that his uncle had refused to give him his share in the ancestral property. Rogia about two months before the murder had convened a caste meeting at which Pandu was directed to let him have either his share or Rs. 300 in cash, but Pandu rejected the decision and threatened Rogia's life. The police further learnt that a Mahomedan named Kassim Kutbuddin *alias* Pangia, residing in the compound of Pandu, had suddenly left for Bombay the same day they had arrived. Pangia had a brother by name Mahomed Hussein. On returning to Bombay the following morning and on going to the room of Mahomed Hussein the police found him and his kept mistress Aisha just on the point of going out. On their searching the room the dhotur of Rogia was found with some money. The skull-cap of Rogia was recovered from a Marwari's shop, where it had been pledged by Mahomed Hussein the day after the murder. Mahomed Hussein and Aisha then confessed that they and Pangia had killed Rogia at the instigation of Pandu, who had offered them Rs. 50 for the perpetration of the deed. That sum Pangia had obtained from Pandu the previous evening and given them Rs. 25 as their share. Pangia was arrested at the Carnac Bandar before he could get a ticket to go back to Uran, and his share of money was found on his person. Mahomed Hussein proved to be the man who had gone to call Rogia in the afternoon of the 25th May, and it appeared that the same evening Mahomed Hussein and Aisha had met Rogia at Nul Bazar, had given him liquor at several shops until he became drunk, had then led him to Clerke Road and brutally strangled him to death, and had placed his body in the position in which it was found. The woman was made an approver, and the two murderers and the uncle Pandu were convicted at the third Sessions of the High Court, condemned to death, and all three executed. Great credit is due to Khan Bahadur Mir Abdul Ali for the tact displayed in this case and the skill in joining together each link in the evidence, also to Superintendent Grennan and Inspectors Grayhurst and Roshan Ali for their hearty co-operation and assistance throughout the investigation.

WILFUL DESTRUCTION OF HOUSES IN BOMBAY BY FIRE.

In the year 1889 there were two cases of incendiarism, and they were both traced by the vigilance and zeal of Mir Abdul Ali. Both the cases were reported in the annual report of the Police for 1889 by Colonel Wilson in the following terms :—

In the first case of mischief by fire one Morarji Pitamber, a Kutchi Bania, purchased a house at Patakwadi in 1888 for Rs. 3,500, obtaining a deed of sale for Rs. 5,000 and mortgaging the house for the amount paid. He then insured the house for Rs. 6,000. In order to defraud the Insurance Company, Morarji instigated two persons, named Khimji Hirji and Jhala Ahmia, to destroy the house by fire, promising them a reward of Rs. 500 out of the insurance money.

Accordingly they stocked a vacant room of the house with inflammable materials saturated with kerosine oil, and set fire to it on the night of the 23rd January 1889. The fire was put out after a little damage had been done without any injury to the tenants. Consequent on certain information received by Khan Bahadur Mir Abdul Ali, Superintendent of the Detective Branch, all the offenders were apprehended and charged before Mr. Hamilton, the Third Presidency Magistrate, and Jhala was made an approver at the instance of the Public Prosecutor. . . . .
Morarji was let off by the magistrate, while Khimji was committed to take his trial at the Sessions. His Lordship the presiding Judge in his summing up to the jury, praised them for their diligence and care in the case. . . . . .
I cannot here refrain from remarking that this case was brought to a not altogether unsatisfactory conclusion entirely through the efforts and persistence of the detectives and Public Prosecutor.

In the second case, a fire was discovered on the evening of the 27th July 1889 in an uninhabited two-storied house in Elphinstone Road, Parel. On hearing the alarm a police sepoy promptly ran to the spot, and with the assistance of others managed to extinguish the fire before serious damage had been caused. On inquiries being made it was found that the landlord of the bungalow who was in pecuniary difficulties, had some time before purchased it and the plot of ground attached for Rs. 11,000, and had then insured the bungalow for Rs. 20,000. The bungalow had been mortgaged, and in consequence of being pressed by the mortgagee for the amount of the mortgage, the landlord, after making elaborate preparations, instigated a Parsi carpenter, who was working under him, on the promise of a handsome reward to set fire to the house. Shavaksha the landlord and Jivanji the carpenter were arrested, and before the magistrate Jivanji was made an approver. The case was committed to the Sessions, and Shavaksha was sentenced to transportation for life. The case was an important one, and presented several difficulties, and praise is due to the police and detectives concerned for its detection. I have mentioned these two cases somewhat at length as they are the only ones, with the exception of one in 1870, in which the ship "Aurora" was scuttled and set fire to off the Prongs Lighthouse, which have ever been brought to light in Bombay: and as it is only when the crime is frustrated by the extinction of the fire that such cases can be proved, it is impossible to say how many fires, where there has been a question of insurance, have not been the work of incendiaries.

THE KEMBEKAR STREET POISONING CASE.

DEATH OF FIVE PERSONS.

ONE of the most tragic and at the same time most atrocious and mysterious cases on record in the annals of Bombay crime, occurred early on the morning of Thursday the 22nd of January 1891, when no fewer than five persons, belonging to a Mahomedan family, died suddenly within a couple of hours of each other. It was at first hard to say to what the deaths could be attributed, for all the five persons were quite healthy and had taken their meals as usual the night previous ; but looking at all the circumstances surrounding the mysterious occurrence, there appeared to be some grounds for supposing that the deceased persons had been the victims of foul play.

To come to details, it seems that Abdulla Noor Mahomed, aged about 56 years, a retired Cutchi Memon merchant, lived with one of his sons named Bachoo, a young man of some 27 years of age, and Bachoo's wife, on the third floor of a large house in Kembekar Street, lying off the Parel Road, and not far from the Pydhowni Police Station ; while the fourth floor, which was also rented by Abdulla, was occupied by Abdulla's brother Molidina, a man of 70 years of age, Halemabai, his wife, a woman of 50, Karimabai, his step-mother, an old woman of some 80 years or more, and Molidina's grandson, a lad about 9 years of age. There were also living on the floor occupied by Abdulla a female servant, Fatmabai by name, and a youth named Dawood, who also assisted in the house work, while a woman named Mariam was engaged as a servant by the occupants of the fourth floor, but she did not reside on the premises.

On Wednesday Abdulla and his son Bachoo took their evening meal at about 7-30, and after dinner Abdulla, as he was wont to do, went out to visit a friend, Hajee Sahboo Sidick, who lived close by. After he had been talking some time with Sidick, Molidina came to him in a somewhat excited state, and having said that Halemabai had been taken seriously ill, asked Abdulla to go with him for a doctor. Abdulla and Molidina then went to the house of Pir Ahmed Shah, a priest and native practitioner, who accompanied Molidina to his wife's room, while Abdulla remained on the *otla* (verandah) on the ground floor of the *hakim's* residence. While the *hakim* and Molidina were in the latter's room, a messenger arrived, and conveyed the intelligence that Abdulla had been taken very ill while sitting on the *otla* at the doctor's house. In the meantime Sidick having also been informed of Abdula's illness went to his assistance, but the man died shortly after his arrival. The doctor arrived a few minutes later, and then Sidick, assisted by some other Mahomedans, removed the body to Abdulla's room, and placed it on a cot.

Molidina, who was sitting by the side of his wife's bed, on hearing sounds of weeping in his brother's room, proceeded thither, and seeing Abdulla lying dead on the bed fell in a heap on the floor and gasped for breath. He was speedily placed on a couch in the same room, and died almost immediately. About this time Fatima, the servant, rushed into the room, and on noticing the dead bodies became greatly distressed, and showed signs of sickness. She was quickly taken by her brother and his daughter, who had been sent for, to their home, where she expired shortly afterwards. Karimabai, who was attending on Halimabai on the floor above, on being told of what had happened, went downstairs, and when the poor old woman saw the bodies of her two sons, her grief became insupportable ; indeed, despite her extreme weakness, she had to be literally torn from the sad scene and borne upstairs. But her troubles, great as they were, were not yet at an end, for on reaching the top of the stairs she was told, that during her short absence, Halimabai had also breathed her last. The poor old woman, quite heart-broken, sank, sobbing on the floor, and on being lifted up was placed on a cot, on which she died within half an hour.

The information of the tragic occurrence being conveyed to the police, the interment of the bodies was stopped by the order of Mir Abdul Ali, who instinctively suspected that there had been foul play. The bodies were conveyed to the morgue in Kamatipura, where a *post mortem* examination was conducted by Doctor N. H. Choksy on behalf of Dr. Sydney-Smith, Surgeon to the Coroner, but strange to say, he found no traces of poison, and moreover opined that all the deceased had suffered from was heart disease. Mir Abdul Ali, who was ably assisted by Inspectors Nolan, Cobb, and Greyhurst, was, however, firmly of opinion that strychnia or some vegetable poison may have been administered, which in many cases it is quite difficult to discover. The case was thus rendered most mysterious, and at one time it was apprehended that it would remain enshrouded in mystery. A suggestion was made that the deaths were occasioned by the deceased having partaken of food cooked in uncleaned cooking pots, but Mir Abdul Ali discountenanced that suggestion as absurd. Small quantities of viscera were placed in sealed bottles and were forwarded to Dr. Barry, the Chemical Analyser to Government, whose report threw some light on the problem. The report said that all five persons had died of strychnia poisoning.

About three months prior to this tragedy Asubai, a young Mahomedan woman, wife of Haji Abdulla, one of the five victims, died at the house of her husband in Kembekar Street, and was then buried at theMemon burial-ground at Mangalwadi, Girgaum. A few days after the tragedy occurred, a nephew of the woman, who had been away, arrived in

Bombay, and having learnt that the five members of Asubai's family had died under very suspicious circumstances, he communicated certain information to Mir Abdul Ali, and it resulted in the body of Asubai being exhumed. The contents of the stomach were extracted, and forwarded to the Government Chemical Analyser for examination; and it was ascertained that the viscera contained strychnia poisoning. The suspicion pointed to Bachoo, one of the surviving members of the family, as the murderer, and it was suggested that his success as a poisoner and his escape from detection in his first attempt encouraged him to make the second.

Accordingly Bachoo Hajee Abdulla and his wife, who were the surviving members of the family, were arrested by the police on suspicion. They also arrested Dawood Abbaji, a servant of Bachoo. The servant on being turned Queen's evidence, made a clean breast of the whole affair. His confession went to show that about ten days before the occurrence he decided to go to his native country. He asked Bachoo, who owed him some money, to repay the debt. Bachoo was hard up, and he told the servant to wait for a few days, and also postpone his departure to his native country as he had to get some important work done by him. Afterwards Bachoo administered an oath to Dawood and bound him to keep secrecy. Being assured by Dawood that the secret would be quite safe with him, Bachoo said that he would bring some medicine and give it to

Dawood for the purpose of killing the five members of the family. Dawood asked Bachoo why he wished the five persons to be killed. The accused replied that he was hard up and wanted money, promising to pay Rs. 400 or Rs. 500 to Dawood if he carried out his instructions. Dawood, who was naturally an avaricious person, at once closed with the offer. Bachoo then gave him some white powder, and asked him to administer it to the five persons at one and the same time. Dawood divided the powder in five parts, and waited for a favourable opportunity, it being left to him to administer it either in milk, food, or tea. It would be tedious to describe how skilfully the cook carried out the plan, which resulted in the death of five persons, who died after excruciating pain within a few hours of each other. Bachoo afterwards asked Dawood to abscond from Bombay, and as he was about to do so he was arrested by the police. Bachoo's wife was discharged in the absence of sufficient evidence to connect her with the guilt; but Bachoo was committed to take his trial at the Second Criminal Sessions of the Bombay High Court, which was presided over by Sir Charles Sargent, the Chief Justice. The best legal talent available was procured for the defence of Bachoo, who was proved to be a fast young man of about 27 years of age with spendthrift habits. It was said that though the extent of his extravagance was not very great, being probably not more than a couple of thousand rupees, yet it was sufficient to bring him into pecuniary difficulties, and that his creditors had threatened to take action against him to recover their money. Instead of trusting to the generosity of his father who was of rather a frugal mind to settle the debts, Bachoo conceived the horrible idea of putting him out of the way, and thus securing the money he wanted. But his scheme for enriching himself did not end with compassing the death of his father, but it embraced the murder of the whole household except Bachoo, his wife, and the cook Dawood, who was used as the agent for administering the poison. After the poison had been administered by Dawood, he quietly sat down and calmly waited for the result of the diabolical plot. They even made preparations for the expected deaths by placing pot of water on the fire to boil, with the intention of afterwards performing certain rites over the bodies. While police visited the house, biers had been provided for conveying the bodies away, and *Moolahs* were busily engaged in making shrouds for the corpses. In a most praiseworthy manner the police obtained possession of the bottle of poison and carefully following up the clue, discovered the vendors, who were druggists, having their shops near Pydhowni. The druggists deposed to having sold twenty-five grains of strychnine (sufficient to kill twice as many men) to Bachoo. Mir Abdul Ali and other officers furnished links in the chain of evidence. After a careful enquiry the jury found the prisoner guilty of murder by a majority of seven to two. His Lordship agreeing with the majority of the jury, passed capital sentence upon Bachoo, who appealed to Government of Lord Harris, but a reply was received to the effect that "the offence, which was brought home to him, was of a diabolical character, and that any leniency in the case would be misplaced. The law must, therefore, take its course." Bachoo appealed with similar unsuccessful result to Government of India, and he paid the extreme penalty of law on the Saturday the 6th of June 1891. In this case the police had to labour under a great difficulty as monies were flying like anything to get evidence in favour of the culprit. The Memons made a common cause and left no stone unturned to save Bachoo, but fortunately justice could not be tampered with.

THE DUARTE POISONING CASE.

A MOST cruel and heartless murder was committed in May 1895, so planned and executed that nobody suspected foul play. A more infamous and more dastardly crime could scarcely be imagined. The agency employed to kill the man being poison, the crime would have passed off as a natural death and it would never have been discovered but for the zeal and perseverance of Mr. Brewin (who has distinguished himself in many intricate cases) and Sardar Mir Abdul Ali, who rendered very able assistance to the former officer in bringing the criminal to justice. On the 17th of May one Anacleto Duarte, an East Indian, whose life had been insured in the Sun Life Assurance Company of Canada, died suddenly, and as there was not the least foundation for entertaining a suspicion as to the death being caused by foul means, he was buried quietly, and as he was practically a pauper, the funeral expenses were defrayed by one Francis Xavier Fonseca, a bailiff in the Small Causes Court.

The evidence in the case was wholly of a circumstantial nature, but it was of such strength as to practically amount to positive proof. The police supplied step by step every link in the chain of circumstancial evidence, and wove it round Fonseca until its cumulative force amounted to the direct testimony of eye-witness. But to begin at the beginning. Duarte, who was 39 years of age at the time of his death, appeared to be a man of weak intellect, and could be led astray easily. He had taken too much to drinking. His wife used to complain that Fonseca led him into bad habits. Duarte was in the habit of borrowing small sums of money from Fonseca. On the 21st of May Fonseca called at the office of the Sun Life Assurance Company and reported Duarte's death, which he then attributed to sun-stroke. Mr. Ellis, the Agent of the Assurance Company, asked him why he had not reported the death when it occurred four days before, and Fonseca said that he had only heard of the death himself that morning. As a matter of fact, though this did not transpire till afterwards, there was ample evidence that Fonseca not only knew of the death on the day it occurred, but actually lent fifty rupees to Duarte's brother for the funeral expenses. Mr. Ellis told Fonseca that he must prove his claim before the money could be paid over to him; and on the following day, on a full consideration of the peculiar circumstances of the case, and the somewhat curious nature of the death certificate, he decided to contest the claim.

A long correspondence ensued between Mr. Ellis and Mr. Hemming, Fonseca's solicitor, and eventually, early in July, Mr. Ellis's suspicions having been aroused, he decided to communicate with the Commissioner of Police. The evidence at this stage was *nil*, but the circumstances pointed to Fonseca as being the only person who could have a motive in compassing Duarte's death, and he was ac cordingly arrested on suspicion. He was first charged with cheating the insurance company, but as the police soon obtained evidence sufficient to warrant them to charge Fonseca with murder, the charge of cheating was withdrawn, and the grave charge of murder was preferred against Fonseca. It was shown he had established a very strong influence over Duarte at a period anterior to the application for the policy, and that both at that time and during the earlier months of the year he constantly sought Duarte's company and supplied him with drink. That there was some object in all this was clear enough; and that object was found in the policy on Duarte's life, an assignment of which to Fonseca offered no difficulties in view of the latter's ascendancy over a naturally weak mind. It was clear that Fonseca hoped to encompass Duarte's death by supplying him with liquor, but he was in serious pecuniary difficulties which could not permit him to wait until Duarte was consumed to death by liquor, and as his creditors pressed him for money, he, with a view to get himself possessed of the insurance money, administered Durate a poisonous pill in a glassful of rum, which resulted in his death. (Fonseca boastfully talked of his luck in anticipation of getting the amount of insurance, but when the police exhumed the body of Duarte his joy flew, and he exclaimed, '*Aj apna varghoda hogaya,*' which when freely translated meant that 'I am done for to-day.')

Mr. Vincent in his annual report of the working of the Police for 1895 related the case in the following terms :—

On the 3rd of July 1895, Mr. Ellis, the Agent of the Sun Life Assurance Company of Canada, made a report to the police that one Anacleto Duarte, an East Indian, whose life had been insured in his Company for Rs. 10,000, had died suddenly on the 17th May 1895 under circumstances which appeared suspicious. After a few preliminary inquiries had been made, the widow of Duarte and others, who were present at Duarte's death, were interviewed on the 6th of July, and from the information given by these persons it was thought advisable to exhume Duarte's body with a view to an inquest being held upon it. On the 7th July Duarte's body was therefore exhumed, and shortly after the Coroner with his jury and Surgeon viewed the body, the Coroner subsequently directing his Surgeon to make an autopsy and to forward to the Chemical Analyser to Government the viscera for analysis.

During the investigations which followed the exhumation, it transpired that one Francis Xavier Fonseca (also an East Indian), a bailiff of the Court of Small Causes, induced Duarte in May 1894 to consent to his life being insured. Fonseca, fearing that Duarte's usual medical attendant would not give a satisfactory certificate, took him to one Dr. DeMonte at Bandora and succeeded in obtaining from Dr. DeMonte the necessary medical certificate, which was subsequently sent to the Insurance office. In this proposal it was contemplated to insure Duarte's life for Rs. 7,000; but after the papers had reached the Sub-Agent's office and before they were submitted to Mr. Ellis, Fonseca got the Sub-Agent to alter the amount of the insurance from Rs. 7,000 to Rs. 10,000 without Duarte's knowledge or consent. Fonseca was named as the beneficiary in this proposal, and it was he who undertook to pay the premia as they became due. In forwarding the papers to Mr. Ellis these facts were stated and in consquence Mr. Ellis declined to entertain the proposal, as he said it amounted to a speculation on human life. Owing to this objection, Fonseca's name was struck out as the beneficiary and the object of the insurance was then stated to be "business purposes." The proposal having reached Mr. Ellis in this shape, he forwarded the papers to his head office in Canada, and in due time a policy of Rs. 10,000 arrived in Bombay, which Fonseca having declined to take up, as he said it was not in his favour. In November 1894, Fonseca having learned that a policy issued for "business purposes" could be assigned to him, he induced Duarte to submit to a second medical examination by the same doctor, with the view of submitting a second proposal for an insurance of Rs. 10,000 upon his life. Having had duly filed up all the necessary papers with regard to this second proposal, which it was alleged was being obtained for "business purposes," Fonseca forwarded them to the Agent of the Company and forthwith obtained from that Agent an interim receipt for the first premium due on the policy, promising to pay the amount of the premium on the following day. Immediately upon his obtaining the interim receipt, Fonseca took Duarte to his Solicitor, and there got Duarte to assign to him on a printed form, which had been obtained from the Insurance Agent, all his right, title and interest in the policy covered by the interim receipt. Having obtained this assignment, Fonseca was desirous of learning whether the Insurance Company would recognize it, and with this object in view he continued in correspondence with the Insurance Agent. These second proposal papers having in the meantime reached Mr. Ellis, he declined to entertain the second proposal on the life of Duarte unless a cancellation fee was paid for the first policy which had been issued and which had lapsed owing to

Fonseca omitting to pay the premium upon it. Fonseca, learning of this decision of Mr. Ellis, paid the cancellation fee and continued in correspondence with the Company with a view of ascertaining whether the assignment made to him could be recognised by the Company, and during this period he omitted to pay any premium although repeatedly urged to do so.

On the 2nd February 1895 Fonseca appears to have been satisfied that his interests in the policy were secured to him as far as the Bombay office of the Company was concerned, and consequently on that day he paid the first premium which ought to have been paid in November 1894. On the 28th February Fonseca paid the second premium, which kept the policy alive until the 30th April. By the terms of the policy, 30 days' grace were allowed at the end of each quarter for the payment of the premium on the next quarter, during which period the policy held good even in the event of the death of the insured. On the 15th May 1895, Fonseca was informed that the second proposal had been accepted by the Company's head office, and that the policy would arrive in a few days. Fonseca at this time was sorely pressed by his numerous creditors for money. He had borrowed the amounts to pay the two premia and the days of grace were fast going by. Unless he could secure the Rs. 10,000 on the policy, he was a ruined man. On the morning of the 17th May 1895, Fonseca, in company with a Mahomedan servant of his, called at Duarte's house and took Duarte with him to a liquor shop. The Mahomedan servant remained in the street, whilst Fonseca and Duarte passed into the shop and into the back room. Fonseca called for two glasses of rum, which were served him, and which he and Duarte appear to have drunk. Fonseca and his servant then drove off home, Duarte returning to his own house. Shortly after Duarte's return home, he complained of a bitter taste in his mouth, and in answer to his wife informed her that Fonseca had given him a pill and some rum. Within a few minutes of his returning home, Duarte was seized with convulsions, which resulted in his death almost immediately. The relations of Duarte not suspecting any foul play, induced one Dr. Ferreira, their usual medical attendant, to give them a death-certificate, which enabled them to get the body buried without a Coroner's inquest being held upon it.

On the day following the burial of Duarte, Fonseca set about taking the necessary steps to establish his claim to the Rs. 10,000, the amount of the insurance policy, and in doing so he endeavoured to bribe the Agent of the Insurance Company with the view to bring about an early settlemnt. He also went about from doctor to doctor, endeavouring to get one of them to sign the "Attending physician's statement," which had to accompany his claim papers. On the 16th July the Chemical Analyser to Government reported that he had detected strychnia in Duarte's viscera, and in consequence Fonseca was arrested for the murder of Duarte. During the investigations which followed this step, it transpired that Fonseca had early in May obtained from Mr. Tom Farrell, an Assistant at Stephen's stables, some white powder, which was to be used to kill rats, but which appears to have been used for the purpose of poisoning Duarte. Fonseca had no difficulty in administering the poison to Duarte, who was of weak intellect, and who was completely under his control. Fonseca appears to have acquired his ascendancy by constantly supplying Duarte with liquor. In fact, Duarte was reduced to such a miserable state by the constant state of drunkenness he was in, that it is more than probable he would have died at an early date from the effects of his heavy drinking. Fonseca's necessities, however, were pressing, andwould admit of no delay, hence he was driven to hasten with poison the result he wished for. The Corouer's proceedings in this case were protracted to a length which evidenced its importance. Quite 19 days were occupied in recording the evidence when the jurors committed Fonseca for trial on a charge of murder. The magisterial enquiry also occupied several days, and the trial at the Sessions Court lasted a week and resulted in a unanimous verdict of guilty against Fonseca. The investigation of this most difficult and extraordinary case was entrusted by me to Mr. Superintendent Brewin, who, with the able assistance of Sardar Khan Bhadur Mir Abdul Ali, accomplished the task set him in a manner, which earned for him the encomiums of both the Bench and the Bar.

In October last, the Political Secretary to Government wrote to Mr. Vincent that H. E. the Governor-in-Council had perused with satisfaction his account of the services rendered by Mr. Superintendent Brewin and Sardar Khan Bahadur Mir Abdul Ali in the investigation of the case. The Commissioner was requested to convey to the officers the appreciation of Government of the valuable work done by them.

TESTIMONIALS.

BOMBAY, 19*th January* 1876.

DEAR ABDUL ALI,

You asked me the other day to write to you a letter stating what I thought of your conduct in the Baroda case, I have much pleasure in saying that I was greatly struck by the close attention you paid to the case during all the time that I was with you at Baroda, namely, for about two months.

You were living in the same compound that my tent was in, and I had occasion to see you at all hours of the day and night. I always found you at your post (looking after the witnesses) whatever time it was I wanted to see you.

It was part of my duty to take down the statements of the witnesses.

There were gentlemen at Baroda who were desired to act as interpreters for me, but I found them unable to do this work satisfactorily, and I was obliged to ask Sir Frank Souter to allow you to interpret for me.

I have no hesitation in saying that you were of the greatest possible service to me in enabling me to take down the statements of witnesses correctly.

I saw from the demeanour of some of the witnesses that they had confidence in you, and were not afraid to speak the truth to me while you were present. I believe that this confidence was not extended to any other member of the Police Force.

I can also testify to your having made yourself thoroughly acquainted with the various books of accounts which were relied on by the prosecution, and I well remember that on more than one occasion you attended the consultations with counsel and gave explanations, without which the Advocate-General and Mr. Inverarity could not have understood the accounts.

If it is not presumption in me to express an opinion on the subject, I should say that it was mainly owing to you that some of the evidence, which was produced at the enquiry, was forthcoming.

Yours truly,

HENRY CLEVELAND.

BOMBAY, 20*th January* 1876.

I HAVE much pleasure in testifying to the very high opinion which I entertain of Khan Bahadur Mir Abdul Ali of the Bombay Police. My acquaintance with him dates from August 1866, when, on the day after I landed in Bombay, I found him in charge of an important Forgery case then pending before the Senior Magistrate, and which I was called upon to prosecute for Government. I had not had time to get either a clerk or an office, but owing to the intelligence and facility with which Abdul Ali put the case before me, and with which I was greatly struck at the time, I found myself at no disadvantage, and the prisoner, who was ably defended, was eventually convicted by the High Court.

From that time to this—a term of now nearly ten years—I have had many and frequent opportunities of maturing my opinion of Mir Abdul Ali, who has been engaged in a large number of the prosecutions which I have conducted for Government, including almost all the more important cases, and I consider him a most valuable officer. As a Police officer I have never known an instance of his exceeding his duty or neglecting it, and I have always found him thoroughly acquainted with every detail of the cases he has been engaged in, while his knowledge of English and his clear and retentive memory make him a first-rate witness. I have never known him give the prosecution a fall by any omission or by any want of tact or temper in the witness-box, nor have I ever known him to be censured by the Court for displaying any animus against a prisoner.

I have much pleasure in saying that the high opinion which I formed of Mir Abdul Ali in 1866 has been amply sustained ever since.

R. V. HEARN,

Government Solicitor and Public Prosecutor.

BOMBAY, 19*th April* 1884.

ON the 19th January 1876 I wrote Khan Bahadur Mir Abdul Ali a letter expressing the very high opinion I entertained of the services which he had rendered in the Baroda Poisoning case. As I am now about to leave India, I have great pleasure in speaking of Khan Bahadur Mir Abdul Ali in regard to the business I have had with him since I became Government Solicitor and Public Prosecutor, and while I was acting in those capacities.

I have had to do with Khan Bahadur Mir Abdul Ali off and on for the last 18 years, during all which time I have been in the office of the Solicitor to Government. In almost every important case of murder or forgery, I have found Khan Bahadur Mir Abdul Ali has been the officer selected by the Commissioner of Police for its management, and he has generally instructed me in the proceedings in the Police Court, and also in the High Court, when those cases have been sent to it.

I have much pleasure in stating that, in my opinion, Khan Bahadur Mir Abdul Ali is a remarkably efficient man.

I always feel I can rely upon what he says, and I believe that his zeal does not make him do unfair things to prisoners. I have so high an opinion of him and of the useful influence which he possesses and exercises over some members of the criminal class that I think if he were to leave the Police Force his loss would be a great one to Bombay.

If I could say more in his praise I would do so, as I have the greatest regard for him, and am really an admirer of his character.

I fully endorse all that Mr. Hearn has said of the Khan Bahadur in his certificate of 20th January 1876.

HENRY CLEVELAND,
Government Solicitor and Public Prosecutor.

BOMBAY, 26*th March* 1888.

I HAVE often heard both Mr. Hearn and Mr. Cleveland speak of Khan Bahadur Mir Adul Ali in the very highest terms of praise, and have now read the testimonials they have given him in January 1876, and Mr. Cleveland in April 1884.

Khan Bahadur Mir Abdul Ali has instructed me in a number of cases, amongst them three very notable cases which created great public interest—(1) The Mogul Murder Case in September 1884. Mirza Aga Secunder having murdered, whilst sleeping in their house at Oomercarry, a well-known Persian merchant Hajee Mahomed Shuffer Shoostri and his wife Hajee Bebee. (2) The Khoja Murder Case in November 1885. Shamjee *alias* Shunker bin Rahim having murdered on the premises of H. H. Aga Khan in Love Lane His Highness' head cashier; and (3) The recent Parel Murder Case. Sayed Gool having murdered his wife, deposited her body in a box at Parel, and sailed for Aden. In each of these cases, I believe, it was owing in a very great measure to the Khan Saheb's great judgment, tact, and skill that the offenders were brought to justice and hanged. I know of no officer of Police upon whom I can place more reliance, and from whom I would rather receive instructions, than the Khan Saheb, and I fully concur with Mr. Hearn and Mr. Cleveland in the very high opinion formed of him.

F. A. LITTLE,

Government Solicitor and Public Prosecutor.

PART II.

CRIMINAL LIFE IN BOMBAY.

OUR island is the gateway of all sorts of adventurous people who visit this country. The police have to deal with various sorts of people, who in daring and cleverness are equal to the first-class professional sharpers in Europe and America. It has been acknowledged that criminals of India are by no means less dangerous character. They give to the police no end of trouble, and their exploits savour of rather a romance than a real tale.

As we pass through the busy bazars of Bombay, and look upon its teeming masses of people of every nation, we little dream of the crime that exists, of the various kinds of villainy that are continually being practised there. We know, perhaps, of the swindler and the cheat, on a small scale at least. What stranger to Bombay, or, indeed, any other Indian town, has not discovered after, perhaps, he has gone home, chuckling with the idea that he has driven an excellent bargain, that he has after all been tricked by some wily Borah, who, sleepy though he may appear as he lazily smokes his hooka by his shop door, serenely indifferent to all that is going around him, is much more wide-awake than he looks? But that is not the crime of any great consequence. One of the worst features of low life in Bombay will be found described in the next chapter. There are many more forms of crime as terrible and as revolting. We hear now and again of brutal murders, and there are many more we know that never come to light. In the year 1891 when six persons, belonging to a respectable Memon family, were murdered by strychnia poisoning in Kambekar Street, some excitement was created in Bombay by a report of the wholsale importation of strychnine, much more than was required for medicinal or even manufacturing purposes, and the Health Officer expressed the opinion that many deaths put down to cholera were due to strychnia poisoning, murder being easily committed in this way. Natives have a great horror of *post mortem* examinations, and death from strychnia poisoning, as in cholera, resulting after a short illness, is often attributed to the latter cause, and interment or cremation follow immediately. The Kambekar Street murders, which were committed for the sake of monetary gain, would never have been discovered had the police not stopped the burials before the bodies could be hurried away. There are many other crimes, which when analysed all point to the desire for gain, the greed of riches, as the motive. We see nearly every day in the columns of the newspapers containing local news, paragraphs with such headings as "A Gang of Swindlers," "Raid on a Gambling Den," "Burglary," "Child enticed away and robbed," and many others. They are common, and the reader, perhaps, pays little heed to them. Little do they know of the tremendous amount of thought, of strategy, of labour, of exciting pursuits, the actors in those little every-day dramas have had before the criminals referred to therein have been brought to justice. The police are sometimes charged with laxity in attending to their duties; all sorts of harsh things are said of them when they fail to prove a case, or bring a delinquent to justice. But there are almost insurmountable difficulties in their way. In more violent offences, an assault for instance, unless a policeman actually sees an assault committed he cannot apprehend. A man may come to him, with his face all cut and bleeding; and the policeman may see the man who committed the deed running up the street with a blood-stained knife in his hand, but he cannot go after him. The sepoy must first report the matter to his superior, and a warrant must be obtained for the apprehension of the offender. So says the law. But by the time all that process has been gone through, where is the offender? Different criminals and their crimes described in the following pages show how poor dupes are inveigled to the dens and there robbed and swindled; how professional thieves go about their work; how they have different lines of business, just as honest tradesmen have; how cunning they are in evading detection, and how the police have to resort to all kinds of strategy to capture them.

A BOMBAY SLAVE MARKET.

SOME years ago attention was called in the newspapers to the flagrant outrage on public morals perpetrated in certain quarters of Bombay. The police had, from time to time, endeavoured to cope with the evil or, at least, to keep it out of sight; but without any great measure of success. The failure was, no doubt, in part due to defects in the law, which enable offenders to slip through its meshes. But in still greater measure it was due to the organisation which obtained amongst those who profit by the infamy which enable them to terrorise their victims and to set the police at defiance. In every large city there will be found haunts of vice which it is practically impossible to eradicate. Experience in Bombay has shown in a very disagreeable way that nothing is gained by closing particular streets to an infamous traffic—the evil spreading throughout quarters until then uninfected. Without sharing the optimism of those who hope to succeed in wholly eradicating the evil, we may say there is room and, indeed, a crying need for strong measures to put an end to certain forms of it, which is founded and maintained by a combination of scoundrels, the dregs of continental cities, who had some time ago established themselves in a notorious locality, where they made enormous gains out of the ruin and misery of the dupes, whom they had lured to destruction. Emboldened by their success in baffling the police authorities whenever an endeavour has been made to bring them to justice, these traffickers in vice make not the slightest pretence at secrecy. They flaunt their villainy, and making large gains, they rely on the immunity secured by imposing silence on those alone who could give conclusive evidence against them. The women whom they buy and treat and speak of as their slaves, dare not for their lives give information to the police and appeal to the law for protection. Happily, now-a-days there appears to be a prospect of obtaining a body of evidence which, when laid before the Government, results in application to a drastic remedy, to deliver Bombay once and for all from the presence of the pests who batten on the shame and misery in which they traffic. The evil is nearly extinct now in Bombay owing to the exertions of our indefatigable Commissioner, Mr. R. H. Vincent, C.I.E., and his able Deputy Mr. Gell, because if any suspicious characters are found, they are expelled as soon as sufficient evidence is available against them. Only last year a number of foreigners were driven away from Bombay by the Police, under orders from Government.

A certain Canadian Missionary, Mr. Robert H. Madon, with a few others, entered on a campaign against the "slave-dealers," who had established themselves and their market in the tainted district. They were labouring to effect what the police were unable to do—gain the confidence of the victims of the infamous system, and in due time they were in a position to place a strong representation before Government, based on facts which warrant unhesitating and decisive action. The system is one of practical slavery—slavery more hopeless, more ruinous to body and soul than that of negroes on a plantation.

It will be remembered that some years ago a case came before the Magistrate, in which a man was charged with importing two Russian girls for immoral purposes. Though that case was not proved against the accused, such cases, if evidence could be obtained, would be very numerous. There was a club composed entirely of men whose sole business was to entice to Bombay young girls, but it has now been suppressed by the vigilance of the Detective Police. There is certainly a legal penalty for crimes of the kind, but the difficulty is to get evidence to bring home a charge made against the offenders. They were a strong body, and were bound together by a pledge, or an oath not to reveal any of the secrets of their trade, and their "slaves" (for they referred to those they had in their power as their slaves) were so cowed by threats of the worst of punishments should they dare to utter a word of complaint to the police, that it was practically impossible to carry a criminal case to conviction against any of those ruffians. These bondwomen, whenever the police approached them, evaded their questions through fear of their brutal masters, but the missionaries working amongst them succeeded in eliciting some startling evidence. The world looks down with contempt and horror upon those unfortunates who live such terrible lives—nights of the wildest dissipation, and days of misery—yet they are more to be pitied than blamed. The majority of them have been brought to their present state through the trickery and deception of arrant scoundrels. From the facts ascertained it appears to be a common practice of those procurers to go at stated times to Europe (for they are not unprovided with money and can afford to take frequent voyages home), and by various devices attain their end. They sometimes go through a mock marriage with a girl, bring her out to Bombay and sell her to another man, who becomes her master and calls her his "slave"—which, indeed, she is, having bought her with his money. Forced by her brutal proprietor to submission, she is utterly powerless, and, surrounded by vice as she is, she yields in despair to her fate, and becomes what she is. As an example, the story of a young Italian girl, who was ruined by a villain, may be briefly related.

She came, she said, from Rome, where she led a good life, until she met a certain man, who courted and married her. Then he brought her to Bombay, where they took up their abode. After a few days her husband disappeared, and that first night she was left alone, a strange man, without any warning, appeared in her room. She roused the house, and called for assistance, when another man appeared, who turned out to be her new master. "Don't create any more bother," he said, "you know very well what you are here for; and if not, you know now. I paid Rs. 300 for you; so you had better do what you are told." The girl was helpless; escape she could not; there were too many watching her; and so she drifted down with the stream of others as unfortunate as herself. Here she threw up her arms and laughed bitterly as if reckless of what further became of her.

"Do you never think," she was asked, "what the end of all this will be?"

"I know well enough," she answered, "but what does it matter?"

"Three or four years is the longest this can go on; and what then?"

"I cannot help it; what can I do!"

"Why do you not run away? Go forth from the place; get away."

"I cannot run away. How can I?"

"Can you not go home?"

"I have no money. My 'man' comes and takes away all I get."

"Then why do you not go to the Italian Consul? He would send you home."

"He can do nothing. He won't send me home."

"He would if you told him your story, and said you wanted to get back to Rome, and lead a proper life."

"How am I to go to him? Ah, you do not know anything," the girl said, shaking her head significantly, and moving away as if disinclined for further conversation.

It was, no doubt, quite true, as that poor girl said, that her 'man,' as she called him, who owned her, took all her money from her, for it is the custom of those wretches. They meet nightly at their club, smoke, drink, play cards, and concoct plans for securing more "slaves" for their market. About three o'colck each morning, when the dissipation of the night is usually over, they go round and collect all the money they may have obtained during the night; and woe to those unfortunates if their purses, or boxes, wherever they keep their money, are empty; for if they do not get it by one means they are expected to steal, pick pockets—in short to obtain money anyhow; but no money means a volley of oaths, kicks, and blows. No wonder, then, those girls are so active, endeavouring to inveigle passers-by inside, knowing what to expect if no money is forthcoming at 3 a.m.

A very favourite method of kidnapping for the Bombay white-slave market is as was told by another girl. She was a native of Germany, and was enticed abroad with the promise of high pay as a bar-maid. She was first taken to Port Said, and in that lawless place she fell a victim to the wiles of a man who paid court to her. Thence she was brought to Bombay, and in Cursetjee Suklajee Street she had remained ever since. She was quite reckless, and cared nothing for the future.

THE STRANGE EXPERIENCE IN BOMBAY.

THE PATHETIC SIDE OF THE STORY.

In December 1892 a London paper reported the proceedings, then pending in the Thames Police Court, against a man described as a well-dressed foreigner, named Alexander Kahn, aged 34 years. Mr. C. F. Gill appeared on the part of the National Vigilance Society, to prosecute Kahn for the abduction of Frances Epstein, a girl under 18, by taking her out of the protection and against the will of her father for an immoral purpose. The girl herself gave evidence, which was to the effect that she made the aquaintance of Kahn in the previous spring,and in April he told her that he was going to leave London for Paris on Sunday the 21st May. She agreed to accompany him, and conveyed her clothes to the station, where she met a man named Sterling, and a girl named Gould, whom she had already seen in Kahn's company. They all four proceeded to Paris, and after staying there a week, proceeded *via* Marseilles to Alexandria, Port Said, Karachi, and finally to Bombay. In this city Kahn took a drinking saloon at Byculla in the girl's name, and paid through her £210 for it. There were women in the bar and gentlemen visited them. Colonel Wilson, the late Commissioner of Police, sent for Epstein, who passed throughout as Kahn's wife, although she was aware that he had a wife living. She believed what he told her—that he was about to obtain a divorce and would then marry her. When interrogated she did her best to screen Kahn; the bar was sold, Epstein receiving the money as the ostensible vendor. Kahn and Epstein then returned to Marseilles, the latter travelling as Miss Kahn, and pretending not to be connected with the accused. He was arrested on landing by the French police, and the girl Epstein was met by her father and taken to London.

This sad and typical story is contained in two letters, one written by Victor Epstein, the father of the girl Frances, and the second by Mark Epstein, her brother, adjuring her to get out of the "claws of the tiger Kahn" and to return to her family, broken-hearted by her disappearance and well-nigh ruined in the endeavour to trace and deliver her. More pathetic letters have seldom been written. They are given below *verbatim et literatim.* It may be mentioned that the father of the girl was a respectable tradesman in the East End of London. As will be seen by the tenor of his letters all his means and the resources of his friends and relations were freely spent in the endeavour, happily ultimately crowned with success, to get tidings of the missing girl and rescue her from the fate prepared for her.

The following is the letter of the father, written from London to Frances Epstein on the 25th September 1891, upon hearing that she was in Bombay :—

"My dear Daughter,—I thank God, because I hear that you are alive, because till now we were thinking day and night where you could be. It is true that what you did without letting me know, you thought would be for your own benefit, but unfortunately it proved not so. You have already found out your mistake by following your own mind. I hope that you also know now that advice of parents is best. All those people whom you listened to have turned out false against you, as you have proved yourself. Now you see who is a better friend to you, a stranger or your parent? Since you left London, I have tried as much as I could, even more than was in my power, to get you out of the hands of those that robbed you from your home. You sent me a letter bearing no address as to your whereabouts. That letter came from Port Said. You wrote that you were married to Kahn. I went to Paris with the hope of finding you there. In Paris I found out who Kahn and Sterling were. Kahn and Sterling were both engaged in this disgraceful business for years, and have already been convicted for it. Kahn is a married man, and his wife is living in Buenos Ayres, where she keeps an ill-famed house. He is not divorced from her, and if she will get to know where he is she will follow him. We received a long letter from Wolf Singer (Reisel Schlafeike's son), who is now in Buenos Ayres, and he informs us of all those facts. Kahn is also wanted at Monte Video, where he was caught and put to prison, from whence he managed to escape. They told you that they were respectable gentlemen from Paris; but you are in the hands of wild tigers. They showed you some jewellery, which belongs to his wife, and is now pawned in London. This was to make you blind in the matter; at the same time putting masks over their faces, pretending to be gentlemen, and also carrying a hope to make you unfortunate all your life-time. Yet, dear daughter, do not think you are forgotton!

"When I was in France, I watched day after day for eight days from early in the morning till late at night at the places where the ships start from, for different countries. During that time I neither ate, nor drank, nor even sat down to rest. Knowing I would not be able to speak the language, I took a gentleman from London with me who could speak French. Everything was at my own cost. But unfortunately I found nothing there. From Paris I went to Havre, and from Havre to Dieppe. I searched for you without tasting any food, thinking nothing of myself but to recover you. At the same time Abraham went to Antwerp at my cost and searched, but could find nothing. Mark stopped work for two weeks, and only tried to find money to recover you. It has cost me all I could get and Mark's money, and Abraham's health and all our strength. When I had no more money I would pawn anything possible to get some. We have tried and are still trying for you. It has cost me so much that I could not afford to keep

Moses at College. How could you bear to hear the sighs and the tears of your old father and mother who are putting their lives down for you!

"Our house is desolate, and every step is drenched with tears. But we are keeping the matter as secret as possible. Dear daughter, have pity on your aged father and mother, who are going from the world because of you. You are bringing your poor father and mother to the grave before their time. Dear daughter, think of what you have done; see how you are tearing limb by limb from us. Abraham's life is worth nothing; since you left he is ill from being grieved because of you. You are now as an animal, who is kept and fed well. The animal thinks that it is for its good that it is kept so, but it is only to please the owners who slay it for their own benefit. Dear daughter, do not be so hard-hearted against us; but come home. Do not think that because you have made a fault you are forgotten; but your parents still love you, and will love if you will prove worthy of it. The only way you can stop our fast flowing tears is by coming home. Abraham would go for you, but he has business of his own, which he cannot leave. He is putting his life down in trying to find you. Dear daughter, keep to the truth. Kahn robbed you from your home. If you want to be out of trouble, and you are married to Kahn, say that. You thought he married you to be your true husband; but in his thoughts he married you for immoral purposes, and he has a wife from whom he is not divorced (as we were told by Kahn's brother in Paris). Such a marriage is not legal, so try your best to be divorced from him. I am naturalised, and you are a British subject, so you obtain the protection from the English Government in any part of the world.

"Since you left we have been telegraphing to all parts of the globe, till, thank God, we received a letter that you are in Bombay. The letter bears no signature as to who sent it. I also inform you that the Marquis of Salisbury, Her Majesty's Secretary of State for Foreign Affairs, has been informed of the matter, and takes great steps in the case. His Lordship is now informed that you are in Bombay; no doubt there will be some instructions to the police of Bombay about the matter. Hoping that you will take to heart all that is in this letter."

Mark Epstein also wrote his lost sister a letter of passionate entreaty, promising forgiveness, and imploring her to return to her father and mother, and telling her what a villain Kahn is. The picture of the bereaved mother going "to all the witches, fortune-tellers, and sorcerers in London and coming back to us every day broken-hearted with a different story," is weird beyond the pencil of fiction:—

"Dear Sister Fanny,—With great pain and sorrow I write to you this letter, and before I go any further I beg of you to listen attentively, so that you may understand me rightly.

"The trouble you have given us is without end, and has absolutely taken our life away. On Thursday the 21st May—the day which we will never forget in our life—as soon as you left, we waited impatiently to receive a telegram to invite us to your wedding, but without result. Abraham got to know the next day when he came up to our place, and he at once said what the end will be. This gave us no rest, and we at once communicated with the police to see what can be done in the matter. Abraham walked about with detectives to find the cabman that you and Kahn went to the station with, and after a search of three days and three nights he found a cabman, and he told us he took you to Cannon Street Station. We directly found the porter to whom Sterling gave the key, and then we got to know you went to Paris. Our old grey-headed father went to Paris, but could not find you.

"We made sure that the vagabonds will take you to Buenos Ayres, so father, with the assistance of police, went to Havre and to Dieppe to watch the boats leaving for Buenos Ayres. Abraham went to Antwerp and to Bordeaux, and father and Abraham returned with nothing. Abraham got ill, and I lost my senses, and could not stop a minute in the workshop. Mother did not have a night's rest since you left; she went to all the witches and the sorcerers and fortune-tellers in London, and every day she came to us broken-hearted with a different story. In Paris father was informed by Kahn's own brother and by Karkon who Kahn was; would he be found there he would get killed. This is what father got to know of Kahn. He is the greatest villain God created. He is not divorced from his wife. She is in Buenos Ayres, and the jewellery which you have seen, and which is now pawned here, belongs to his wife, and as soon as she will know where he is, she will follow him. He has been in Buenos Ayres six times, and the last time he was found in Monte Video with women, he was arrested, but managed to run away. The news broke our hearts, and our eyes did not dry for a moment. Abraham tried his best to get some clue where you are. He telegraphed to Buenos Ayres and to other places, but without any satisfactory result. When we received your letter from Port Said, Abraham at once went to Lord Salisbury's office, and he telegraphed to all the boats that arrived about that date in Port Said, if they had such names as Epstein, Kahn, Sterling and Annie Gould on board. They spent about £60 in telegrams, and we could not find anything. We got yours and Annie Gould's photographs, and with letters together, we sent them to Port Said, Alexandria, Cairo, Bombay, Constantinople, Calcutta, Buenos Ayres, Monte Video and to a good many of the places, and we received hundreds of letters during the time, and where there was a girl by this name, she was kept and her photograph sent to us to see if it was you. All this trouble was for nothing, till yesterday when we received a letter that you were in Bombay, for which we thank and praise the Almighty that you are alive.

"Now, my dear sister Fanny, do not think of the past. Think of the future, try and save yourself and our poor parents from ruin. Do not fear anything. Be sure that we know your position. It does not matter if you are married to Kahn, or if even you are in a worse position than that fear nothing; say only you want to come home, and everything will be done and arranged for you in the best possible way. We are ready to do everything for you, and that we are not in a position to do, we have good gentlemen who will help us. You cannot imagine what Abraham is doing for you. You will be welcomed by all of us, and we will receive you with open arms, and we will even leave London for your sake, only we should see you and be together again.

"Dear sister Fanny, where is your heart, and where is your sense? You, our dearest, allow yourself to be mastered by a vagabond like Kahn! Awake your courage, and stand up face to face against him, and have your revenge on him who robbed you of your liberty.

"I and father and mother and all others send our best respects to you. We all kiss you from the distance. Our best wishes to you. I beg of you, you should soften your heart and write to us without delay. Be grateful to the gentleman Samuel, and to all good people that take an earnest interest in you, and demand justice from your enemies."

The man Sterling and the girl Annie Gould remained for a long time in Bombay, where they were abandoned by Kahn, whose tools they were. He fled to Europe.' Kahn appeared to have been well supplied with money, and to have paid the expenses of all four from the time they left London until the inquiries of the police in Bombay caused Kahn to return with the girl Epstein to Europe. Sterling and Annie Gould were, however, subsequently sent to London to give evidence against Kahn, who was convicted and sentenced to a long term of imprisonment.

A RETROSPECT OF GAMBLING IN BOMBAY.

THE remark made by Mr. Justice Manisty on one occasion, that his experience on the Bench had shown that "there is no greater evil in society, and none which causes more misery in families than that of gambling," can be aptly applied to the pursuit of that pleasure in certain native circles in Bombay. The vice is mainly confined to the lower strata of the labouring classes and to badmashes, and is productive of much mischief. It is true that gambling is not carried on now to such an extent as formerly, for the police have succeeded in greatly abating the nuisance, but it is still practised to such an extent as to be an incentive to the commission of crime. John Chinaman is a notorious gambler in his way; but it is doubtful whether he can surpass a native of Bombay in this direction. The recent decisions of the two Presidency Magistrates who have made the game of "Lal-sufed" and "Ekibeki" penal offences, and inflicted heavy fines on the gamblers, will, it is believed, have a salutary effect in doing away with this latest phase of the mania.

A brief history of gambling in this city for the last fifty years will, perhaps, be read with interest. Half a century ago the powers of the police were limited, and they had great difficulty in putting down gambling. Hence the vice prevailed to an alarming extent. The outcry against it was great, but nothing could be done since no preventative law was in existence. Throughout Bombay and its suburbs whole streets of houses were wholly given over to gamblers; and the keepers were often rich men, living in luxury, and reaping a rich harvest by way of *san* (commission). They laid by an especially large sum of money when the yearly Walkeshwar and Mahim fairs come round. Instead of lasting a few days, as now, the fairs were prolonged for weeks at a time, simply on account of the gambling that was carried on. The keepers of these houses decorated and illuminated their rooms, and engaged musicians and dancing girls to attract customers. Thither hosts of visitors from up-country flocked. They were no match for the sharpers they met in play, and were often robbed of all they possessed. It was a terrible time for the public of Bombay while the fairs lasted. People fought with each other, and stole money and jewellery to a great extent, and in some instance men were murdered by gamblers in order to rob the victims of the wherewithal to satisfy the cravings of their passion. In 1855 and 1856 several murders were committed, and a large amount of stolen property was traced to gaming-houses.

The evil had reached a climax, and the excitement in Bombay was at its height, when the Government stepped in and passed Act 13 of 1856, which forbade certain forms of gambling in the Presidency town. The police now got some power in their hands to deal with the gambling dens, but they found suppression a difficult task. Play in the open streets was checked to a great extent, though not entirely put down, and it was carried on secretly for a very long time without being disturbed by the authorities. Detection was well nigh impossible except when a member, who had been ruined in play and cast aside, informed on his companions, when a trap would be laid and the gamblers arrested. This went on for several years. The gamblers then removed to Coorla and other places, and freely and fearlessly carried on their business. In the neighbourhood of Coorla they were a terror, and reports of respectable people being robbed were made almost daily.

In 1865 a Bill was introduced by the late Mr. Jagannath Shankershet having for its object the prevention of gambling in the whole of the Presidency of Bombay, but as the Government of India disapproved the measure, it was abandoned. The Bill was brought in an amended form in the following year, and aimed at the abolition of gambling in certain places only in the Presidency. The Hon'ble Mr. Ellis, who was in charge of the Bill, urged the necessity for giving effect to the Act of 1856 in the neighbourhood of railway stations. He said: "The Council was aware that in Bombay the Police Act made gambling punishable. The consequence was that persons were disposed to gamble, and finding they could not do so in Bombay, went to the nearest railway station, and there set up a gambling house. A row of such gambling houses had been established at Coorla, and to these gamblers resorted, to the great annoyance of all respectable people. It was not merely that gambling was carried on but quarrels and disturbances broke out, and thefts were committed to make up for losses which had been incurred, and the consequence of this was that respectable persons who were accustomed to go in second-class carriages to Coorla frequently got their pockets picked by gamblers, and were quite unwilling to travel by rail. The nuisance had become so great that it was quite time to put it down, and a petition had already been presented to Government signed by several influential native gentlemen, praying that this nuisance be suppressed." The Hon'ble Sir Mangaldas Nathubhoy said that "he had heard several times of people being robbed and assaulted in the train by gamblers." The Bill was passed, but was made non-applicable to places beyond three miles of the railway stations and containing populations not exceeding five thousand.

THE GAMBLING DENS OF CHIMBOOR.

The result was that the evil was only transferred from one district of Thana to another, where law was made inoperative. Since Bombay and Coorla were getting a little too hot for the promoters of this business, and their trade was carried on under great risk of discovery and punishment, the extension of the railway brought a fresh chance to the keepers of these houses. There lies a village called Chimboor in the Thana district, a little more than three miles from the railway station, and, therefore, beyond the scope of the Act. This place being found most convenient for the setting up of shops or clubs, the gamblers made it the scene of their labours. At first a small beginning was made. The gamblers went to the place on a picnic and indulged in their favourite pursuit, returning to Bombay in the evening. There were no bungalows there, but some old-fashioned houses, which the enterprising gamblers hired by the month. In the short space of a year or two bungalows were built, and were well furnished. Every comfort was provided for visitors. People from Bombay flocked to the place; and so alluring did it become, that men journeyed from all parts of the Presidency to Chimboor. In the words of the Superintendent of Police, Thana, "strings of tongas belonging to gamblers awaited the arrival of trains at Coorla, to take their disreputable cargo of gamblers from that place with all haste to Chimboor, and bring them back to Coorla for Bombay in a similar manner. No hire was charged by the owners of the conveyances, as they all belonged to the chief gambling establishments, where raw youths and old men (apparently respectable) daily resorted." In the opinion of the officer, it had a most demoralising effect on the people, and he attributed "most cases of house-breaking and theft at Thana to the vice of gambling." As the "business" increased, the bungalows were extended, rooms being added where visitors could remain as long as they chose, receiving food and lodging gratis, and gambling till all their money was exhausted. The gambling house-keepers did all they could to render their dens attractive for customers with dancing girls and music, and even were so generous as to lend money to those unfortunate men who had spent their all, so as to enable them to pay their way home again. The profit of the house-keepers increased daily. There was a constant stream of people going and coming between Bombay and Chimboor, and matters became worse than ever before. Crimes of a violent nature increased. Thefts, assaults, robberies, and even murders, were committed, and on investigation were found to have been committed or instigated by men infatuated with the gambling mania, or who were in desperation for money, jewels—anything whereby they might satiate their cravings for this dissipation.

The excitement reached its height when some Chinamen took up their abode in the village. They started a game which became extraordinarily popular, and by which they drew in enormous sums of money. They had a board, which was divided into thirty-six squares, each bearing a number. Tickets with like numbers were sold for certain sums, or, as in many of the race lotteries of to-day, one ticket would be divided by a certain number of persons amongst themselves. Those tickets were even sold and bought in the bazars in Bombay, and the lotteries were drawn in the evening at Chimboor. This went on everyday, but credulous people did not detect the fraud that was openly perpetrated on them, although the winning ticket always went to the Chinamen or some accomplice who shared with them the ill-gotten gain. The stupid populace being blind to this trickery, day after day bought up the tickets as they were offered in the bazar, in the vain hope of some day getting a lucky card that would bring them a few hundred rupees. Young men spent their salaries before they earned them, and embezzled money to go to Chimboor or buy a ticket. When their theft was discovered, the prison, and even sometimes suicide, followed. The operations of the Chinamen soon excited the jealousy of the keepers of other gambling houses, and this resulted in the exposure and the expulsion of the Celestials from the village of Chimboor. The keepers of the gambling houses were little or no better than the men they expelled. They first lured their victim by giving him a chance or two to win in order to induce him to entangle himself further in their trap, only to dispossess him of everything that he had. For about ten years this gambling was allowed to go on, until, as crime increased, and Chimboor was pointed to as the cause, Government again stepped in.

In 1887 the Hon'ble Sir M. Melville introduced a Bill in the Legislative Council to remove the limitations imposed by the Act of 1866. The honourable member said that "the attention of Government was directed to the subject last year by an article in a native newspaper; and upon enquiry we were informed by the Commissioner of Police in Bombay, and the District Magistrate of Thana, that the mischief was one which had attained very serious dimensions, and which required to be promptly dealt with." The Commissioner of Police reported as follows: "Most professional gamblers find they cannot successfully carry on their occupation in Bombay, and resort to places outside in Salsette, and especially to Chimboor, where for years past regular gaming-houses have been established. These houses are notorious, and are almost daily visited by large numbers of bad characters from Bombay and other towns and villages in Salsette." The Superintendent of Police, Thana, in his report said that the "evil had not been eradicated . . . Chimboor was infested with gamblers to such an alarming extent, that Parsis, Hindus, Mahomedans, and Chinamen have for their separate use erected sheds, in gardens, where they carry on their nefarious practice in an open manner. The Chinamen have also coupled a lottery with gambling." The Mofussil Gambling Act was accordingly amended. But this did little good to Bombay. The proprietors of gaming-houses were determined not to give up their lucrative business without a struggle. Instead of going further away, they calmly returned to Bombay, and their ingenuity stood them in good stead to defy and baffle the efforts of the police. By the new method of gambling, which was known as '*Barsat-ka-satta*,' more mischief was wrought, and it created more excitement than anything that had been tried before. For years they played under the very eyes of the police, but were effectually checkmated once more.

THE RAIN SPECULATION IN BOMBAY.

Old residents of Bombay must be well aware of the excitement caused in years gone by of the *barsat-ka-satta* or rain-speculation in Bombay. The game itself was a novel and exciting one. Since the police invaded the Chimboor dens of gamblers and effectually put a stop to their trade in that village, it was anticipated that there would be no more trouble with this class of people. The Act of 1887 was passed in terms which were at the time thought sufficient to deal effectively with the gamblers, but in the words of Sir Raymond West, the Judicial Member of Lord Reay's Government, "the ingenuity of a certain class of gamblers found means of evading the law." The new form of gambling proved more pernicious to the public morals and public welfare. During the four months of the monsoon Bombay was made the hot-bed of speculators and gamblers, and the harm they did to the city was simply incalculable. For four months people simply went mad. Servants and clerks left their employment, artisans gave up their callings, shroffs and merchants deserted their lawful trade, to pursue this vice of gambling, which was the cause of ruin of many a family. It requires the facile pen of Dickens, the well-known novelist, to give a graphic picture of the horrors and evils wrought by rain speculation. In these days of sensational romance novelists in search of a plot would find ample food for their purpose. The plain and simple definition of the game of *barsat-ka-satta* is "a betting on whether rain would descend at all in a given time." Books were made up just as at the race-meetings. When clouds were hovering about betting became lively. A man would say perhaps "now it is two o'clock. Before half-past two the rain will fall." Another man might say "rain will fall between half-past two and three," and so on. The idea of the extent this passion of gambling had taken hold on the people could be judged from the enormous amount of money that changed hands every day.

It was estimated that more than twenty thousand rupees changed hands on a single wet day. The keepers of the gambling stalls pocketed enormous sums of money by way of commission. Out of a shed which ordinarily cost a rental of Rs. 50 a month, about a lakh of rupees was the average for the season accruing to those who lived by this nefarious traffic.

The rain-gambling was carried on in the heart of the native town, near the Mombadevi Tank. There were about one hundred and thirty stalls. In each compartment was a clerk with books before him, registering the bets made by a partner in trade, with the people who came thither to gamble. Bets ranged from one to a thousand rupees, and the time of betting on rainfall from a half to twelve hours. Very exact were the appliances for showing how much rain had fallen and very particular were they as to what constituted a fall of rain and what did not. Upon four posts with a firm foundation, rested a small square masonry structure, the surface of which was smooth and flat. At one end, not far from the edge, was a little cup-shaped hollow in the stone, from which a little tube led over the edge of the table. The rain that fell upon the stone found its way into the cup, and from the cup through the tube to the ground. This prevented any dispute; otherwise, on a cloud passing and discharging a few drops which could hardly be perceived, a person might have argued some rain had fallen; but the rule in this rain gambling was that water must run from the tube. If the water only dropped it meant nothing. The rain had to run in a steady flow, no matter how slowly, nor for how short a space of time, but it had to run. This proved a difficult matter sometimes, but there was a referee whose decision was final. The referee was no less a personage than the "worthy proprietor" of the shed in which the stalls were. The lessee had no voice at all in the matter. There was another kind of speculation, originated in Calcutta and latterly adopted in

Bombay, which was called "Calcutta mori." Two men could bet on that, one would say rain would fall within a certain period, and the other that it would not. They would then stand in front of a house, and looking up at the roof select one of those pipe-shaped tiles peculiar to this country, then watch the passing clouds, and for the rain to rush through tho tile. In the Calcutta mori it required a stiffer downfall of rain to win a bet than in the *barsat-ka-satta,* but by indulging in this the winner escaped paying the fees charged by the keeper of the gambling stall. This was in short the form in which the game was carried on without the least interference or annoyance from the police, who were powerless to deal with the gamblers.

The effect of this rain gambling can be better imagined than described. Much was written and said about it during the time of agitation to put a stop to it, but no one, unless he had paid a visit to Mombadevi on an unsettled day, when clouds were hovering about, could have imagined that such a stupid thing as betting on the rainfall could have created so much consternation, as it then did in Bombay. To many the four months of monsoon were a godsend, to others it was the advent of ruin and disaster. People flocked in from the mofussil to gamble with the clouds. If during these years, the census had been taken in Bombay between June and October, it is quite possible that a considerable increase in the population in Bombay and a corresponding decrease in the mofussil towns would have been found. This is not a mere figure of speech. It is a matter of fact to which testimony can bo borne by the police, who had exceptionally trying work to do consequent upon the increase of crimes of various sorts resulting from ill-regulated passion or depravity of heart which was traceable to this dangerous and seductive pastime. The place presented an appearance of an annual fair or a *tamasha.* It was lively enough with moving masses of people, looking nervously and eagerly upwards (even when the sky was clear), anxiously watching for signs of rain, or on the other hand, if they had a bet on no rain, descending for a given period, they remained trembling with emotion and fear, lest a cloud should be seen drifting their way. If the sky did give signs of rain, excitement would be roused, and would go on increasing and increasing as the cloud approached, the people rushing about, hustling and jostling each other, and shouting like maniacs. For a stranger to have attempted to pass down the street at these times was a physical impossibility; the road in fact was closed to traffic; and every morning cases of "disorderly behaviour on a public road and obstructing the traffic" had to be disposed off by the magistrates.

But the worst feature of this gambling was that it was not conducted fairly, and the consequence was frequently a fight and a serious assault on one or other of the parties concerned. This gave no end of trouble to the police and the public. The roguery was practised in this wise. Supposing a man who had bet on with another that rain would fall before a certain period, perceived that there was a possibility of his losing by a minute or two, he would go to the stall lessee with whom the stakes were lodged, and would bargain with him that if he put back the hands of his watch a few minutes, and thus helped him to win the bet, he would be willing to share the gain with him besides giving him the customary percentage allowed to the gambling agent. This trick often succeeded; since every game was to be decided only by the watch of the gambling agent.

This state of things could not, however, last long. The matter becoming serious, great clamour was made against it in the newspapers, correspondents writing columns and columns to rouse the public indignation against the vice. Thefts and embezzlements became matters of every day occurrence during the rains. Young boys stole money from their parents or ornaments which they pledged with or sold to Marwarees. Clerks robbed their employers in order to carry on speculation. Bill collectors misappropriated their takings; and they were a source of great annoyance and trouble. A common trick among the bill-collectors was to go to their masters saying that as they were returning to office with a large sum of money collected from the customers, they were set upon by budmashes and robbed of everything they possessed. In some cases, to carry out the ruse effectively, they actually got accomplices to assault them, and steal their money-bags from them, not objecting even to being bruised and cut in order that suspicion, were any entertained, might be allayed. The people in the tram-cars or trains discussed nothing but rain-speculation; and it would seem that the speculators dreamt nothing but the pouring and ceasing of rain. Rain was on their brain all day and night. When cries arose on all sides at the effects of this rain-gambling, the late Sir Frank Souter, the then Commissioner of Police, consulted the Government law officers as to whether the rain speculation did not come within the penalties leviable on persons conducting lotteries. They said no; and even opined that it could not be termed gaming as defined by the Act. The next thing to be done was to make a representation to Government to have the Act amended. Nothing effectual was done, however, until in 1889 a test case was brought before Mr. Crawley-Bovey, the then Acting Chief Presidency Magistrate. But it was decided that since in conducting *barsat-ka-satta*, no instruments were used as defined in the Act, the offenders could not come within the power of the law. The High Court was appealed to, but the gamblers procured the best legal-talent available to fight their cause, and the High Court upheld the decision of the magistrate, the judges declaring that until a change was made in the wording of the Act, the law was powerless to do anything. Thus baffled the police once more appealed to Government who took up the matter. The same year a bill was introduced by Sir Raymond West for the necessary amendment in the gambling Act in order to bring the rain-speculation within its scope. Sir Raymond West, in introducing the Bill in the Council, remarked that the object of the amendment in the Act was to prevent people from being tempted to public and reckless wagering, which became a fascinating pursuit, took people from their ordinary avocations, induced them to risk larger sums of money than they could afford to lose and demoralise those who took part in it and frequently led to disastrous results in the case of those who lost money. The Hon'ble Mr. Latham, the then Advocate-General, said that a very high authority in the English church had said that "gambling in moderation is no moral offence at all; but we in the Council can have no hesitation in saying that where a temptation is held out to people to indulge in conduct which if pernicious or extravagant, and which might lead to large losses of money, it should put down; and I am in a position to say that this rain-betting establishment is a gaming-house on a very large scale, which leads not only to people losing their own money, but to clerks and other employés risking the money they had been entrusted with by their masters."

At the second reading of the Bill, the Hon'ble Sir Raymond West remarked: "It will be within the recollection of the Council how the Gambling Act was evaded on the ground that wagering did not fall within the range or meaning of gambling in the legal sense, and immediately wagering on a large scale, and of the most injurious shape, was introduced and spread its evil effects throughout Bombay. The Bill to amend the Gambling Act was introduced to suppress that nuisance, and the means to carry that out is to make gambling include wagering. There has been a good deal of discussion on the fragmentary character of the provision of the Bill, but it is the same in all Bills of this kind which have to deal with what may be called slight violations of morality, leading to serious general mischief in practice. The evil that the present Bill aims at is a considerable violation of public convenience, and a remedy for the particular case has been felt by society to be necessary, and recognised as necessary, by all interested in our general welfare." The Act did not go beyond that end, and as was expected it proved effective, for at any rate until 1892 there had had been no rain-gambling sheds at Mombadevi; there was not that excitement which transformed the otherwise quiet and business locality into a boisterous one. There were no hosts of visitors to Bombay from all parts of the mofussil, to swell the ranks of rain-speculators, nor were there frequent reports of the bill-collectors being robbed of their masters' money in the monsoon.

For once the gamblers were effectually checkmated, but their restless spirit which seemed to be entirely conquered for a time by the penalty of law, was not to remain long in subjection. In two years' time they again commenced *barsat-ka-satta* in a somewhat different form to the great annoyance of the public; and this was only brought to an end by the infliction of heavy fine imposed upon the keeper of the house by Mr. C. P. Cooper, the late Chief Presidency Magistrate.

After the suppression of the *barsat-ka-satta*, very little was heard of gambling in Bombay for some time; but nevertheless it was carried on secretly, though not so extensively as before. It was a notorious fact that many persons had been depending for their living on it; and it was, therefore, very unlikely that they would take their defeat silently and not find means to defy the law. They kept houses in unfrequented localities of Bombay, and there secretly carried on gambling with dice and cards. These cunning men kept many spies to watch the movements of the police, whose detective powers were put to the severest test in discovering the haunts of the gamblers. In order to catch them red-handed, the police had to use various ingenious stratagems. Sometimes, a policeman in plain clothes would try to join in their company as an accomplice, and thus learn their secrets and eventually bring them to justice. Sometimes the gamblers hired a boat, went out on the water, and while enjoying a sail indulged in their vice freely without the least fear of being detected, much less caught. It was not unfrequently that complaints of quarrels between themselves on water were heard. The boatwallas, however, did not care whether the gamblers attacked or even murdered one of their associates so long as they were paid a handsome fare for their services.

In Parel and other out-of-the-way places, several gaming-houses were opened, but gambling was carried on with great care and secrecy. A nautch or dinner party was sometimes got up, but only as a pretext for gamblers carrying on their trade and as a blind to the police and the neighbours. They first took care to keep spies on the watch round the house, and in the vicinity of the police-stations, so that any suspicious movement on the part of the police to get a clue to their haunts might be known, and the alarm given at once. Often times, however, the police succeeded in reaching the house and gaining entrance, but only to find the men they pounced upon pretending to be deeply absorbed in the nautch or sitting comfortably at dinner, their cards and dice having suddenly and mysteriously disappeared. Finding from experience that the police are sometimes successful, notwithstanding all their precautions against surprise in getting at them, and being aware that all money found on the floor was confiscated, professional gamblers took to using counters, which were known to them by the name of *bunds*. These not only secured them against losing money, but made no noise, and this was a very great safeguard against detection, since gamblers have sometimes been betrayed by the clink of the coin passing from one hand to the other. The methods of gaming are simple. The dice are not square, but oblong in shape, and are numbered only on four sides: 6, 4, 3, and 2. One party will say, "I play *jitu*," which means they play for a couple of 6's, a couple of 4's, or a 6 and a 4; and the other will say, "I play *haru*," or "I play to lose," which means they play to turn up a couple of 3's, a couple of 2's, or a couple of 3 and 2. The dice are then tossed, and the one getting *jitu* in a required number of throws before the other gets *haru*, of course, wins. But cheating is often practised, and this is termed *nagan*. It is a strange yet most appropriate name, the theory being that, as no one is known to recover from the poisonous bite of the female cobra or *nagan*, the most deadly of reptiles, so the victim of the game *nagan* is sure to meet ruin at the hands of the sharpers he plays against.

The ways in which the professional gamester sets to work to secure victims for the *nagan* are not particularly ingenious. Anyone having a strong will or even common-sense need not fall into the trap. The gamester, well-practised in the wiles of his unlawful profession, and quick at discovering strangers to city life, first seeks the acquaintance of a probable victim, makes himself agreeable, and having won the confidence of the credulous and unsuspecting man, invites him to his house. His friends, or rather accomplices, drop in one by one, the party becomes merry, and ultimately a game is proposed. The stranger generally complies, since it would not be polite to refuse after the kind treatment he has received. Sides are chosen, and the game begins, but the dice are loaded. The stranger's side, as may well be supposed, wins at first. This makes him blind to the trick. When he begins to lose, he imagines that his partners (whom he does not suspect to be accomplices of his opponents) are also sharing his misfortune. To encourage the victim at intervals, when he becomes downcast with losses, the real dice are by clever sleight-of-hand transferred to the table, and the fortune changes for a few throws; but in the end the poor victim is robbed of all he has with him.

Sardar Mir Abdul Ali, Head of the Detective Police, can tell many exciting tales of clever and daring captures of gamblers in their dens. They are all of a like character. It would fill a decent volume if half the tales were told, and they would be uninteresting by reason of repetition. However, a few instances may be read with interest. An European police officer, well known for his promptitude and coolness in action, once discovered a haunt of gamblers, who had defied the police for eighteen months. Superintendent Brewin, for he was the police officer in question, one night received information that some Bannias were gaming in a house previously "spotted" by him. Knowing the difficulty of arresting the man, Mr. Brewin disguised himself as a Bannia, and went to the house at midnight in company with other officers. The task of reaching the man was by no means an easy one. The gamblers, it was known, were seated on the fourth storey of the house, every door of which was carefully barred, and all ingress or egress from one floor to another was further cut off by means of trap-doors. The only chance of reaching the gamblers without alarming them was through one of the surrounding buildings, which, as is usual in the native town, stand in close proximity to one another, being merely separated by narrow sweepers' gullies. A cordon of native policemen was first placed round the suspected premises. Mr. Brewin then entered the house on the right, while another officer went in on the left. Mr. Brewin, on reaching the topmost floor, made a leap, at imminent danger to himself, from a window overlooking a gully about three feet wide into the third storey of the gaming-house. The Superintendent made his way to the staircase, followed by another officer; but a trap-door on the landing barred further progress. He burst this open, however, as well as another door further on, and almost before the scared gamblers knew the cause of the disturbance, Mr. Brewin was in their midst. Cards, shells, and money were hurriedly concealed, but a brief search brought them all from their hiding places. The evidence was complete, and thus a most notorious gaming-house was closed, to the great relief of the residents in the locality.

I remember another exciting raid on a gambling-house. A notorious gamester, named Kasu, who was a confirmed opium-eater, and addicted to all sorts of vices, gave great trouble to the police. It was only by careful strategy and manœuvring that they succeeded in gaining an entrance to an adjoining house, from which they made their way by ladders to the roof of the building in which the gambling den was located. When the police suddenly burst the door open, everybody tried to flee, except Kasu, who made no attempt to escape, but calmly threw himself upon the heap of money that was lying on the floor in order to secure as much as possible before he was seized by the police. He was not afraid of being arrested, nor of the police court, for he knew well that in the event of conviction, the fine that would be imposed upon him would not anything like equal the pile of silver on the floor, which, if secured by the police, would have been confiscated. He filled his pockets with silver, and even crammed as much as he could into his mouth.

About seven years back the police made an exciting capture of a notorious gang of gamblers, who kept them at bay for a number of years. They were secured in the same manner as Kasu, but with more exciting results. The police descended on the gaming den from the roof, and surprised the men at play. Instead of fleeing or giving in as Kasu did, the men showed resistance, and a fight ensued, but they were overpowered. Escape by the door was impossible ;

but two of the men, who were determined not to be captured, dashed through a window on the fourth storey, and leaped to the ground. Considering the height from which they had jumped, it was little less than a miracle that they were not killed outright. However, their injuries were of a serious character. One of them had his jaw, an arm, and a leg and several ribs broken. All hopes for his recovery were abandoned; but after a long stay in the hospital he got well. Although he thus regained his freedom, he was disfigured for life. He was also an altered man in another way. He gave up gambling, opened a shop in the bazar, and became a respectable and prosperous tradesman.

Nothing could better illustrate the cunning of gamblers than an incident which occurred about six years ago, and formed a subject of enquiry before Mr. Hamilton, the Second Presidency Magistrate at the Girgaum Police Court. A police officer in disguise obtained entrance to a suspected house, and finding that his surmise as to the place was correct, quietly left. The gamblers smelt the scent of the police. No sooner had the officer gone, than one of them, who had noticed the stranger, declared that the man who had come and suddenly left was a spy. The players were determined to find out whether the police had a watch on the house, and if so, to defeat their aims when they came to the house with a warrant. They secured the door, got out of the rear windows, and in the dark were not observed as they scrambled down the wall. The police, armed with a warrant, and quite confident of their prey, returned to the house, and finding the door barred burst it open. But they were staggered, and disgusted to find instead of a gang of excited gamblers, only a frightened woman, hugging her infant to her bosom. The police, of course, retired, completely beaten this time, and to add to their discomfiture, a charge was brought by the woman against the police officer for criminal trespass, which was, however, dismissed.

CHEATING AND SWINDLING.

DIFFICULT as is the task to suppress gambling, much more so is it to deal with cheating and swindling, which is another non-cognisable offence. About six years back there existed even in Bombay several gangs of cheats who were so clever in their methods of swindling, that they nearly always managed to evade arrest by the police. They were all thoroughly good actors; so smart were they in their trickery, and so naturally did events follow each other in the course of the transaction with the unfortunate dupe, that many shrewd business men in Bombay, would they only come forward and tell their tales of woe to the world, as a warning to others, could relate some extraordinary adventures with Bombay swindlers, and how they had been robbed to the extent of thousands of rupees. The experience of an eminent Bombay Detective, whose identity will at once be detected, related in the subsequent chapters, will be interesting and instructive.

Those cheats do not go about their business in a hurry, but slowly and deliberately, and carefully maturing their plans. Their first plan is to search for a dupe; and as they usually work amongst business men, and men of wealth, people who can stand a heavy drain on their bank accounts, there must be no flaw in the meshes of the net they draw around their victim, for it is the business of merchants to look well into every transaction they have, particularly with strangers, so that it should not turn out a losing concern. Having chosen a subject, and introduced themselves to him, they make the acquaintance of his servants, and gradually, taking care to avoid suspicion, find out all about the master and his habits. Moreover, in looking around for a victim, they generally try to find a man who, they imagine, would not be over-scrupulous for the sake of gain, in acting a little dishonestly himself. Such being the case, many of those swindlers serve the victims very right. The only pity is the police cannot get hold of those artful knaves; but they require a warrant to apprehend and evidence to convict; and the duped, too much ashamed, not only of having been taken in, but of the very shady part they have themselves played in the transaction, prefer to keep the matter quiet, and grin and bear their loss, which may be a very large sum of money, rather than proclaim it to the world, or have their names dragged before the public in such a fashion through a police-court, where they would not themselves pose altogether as paragons of virtue. Even supposing a man whose honesty will not allow him to take part in the transaction proposed by the cheats, informs the police; what then? It does little good; for where is the evidence? It is no use to apply for a warrant, unless sufficient proof is forthcoming to make conviction sure. Those men thoroughly understand their trade; they have studied the law, and know exactly how to work and keep clear of its penalties. They are careful to have the dupe alone present at the proposal of the transaction. The case of a Bombay tradesman who about four years back was taken to a suburban villa, on the pretence of meeting a native prince in the expectation of securing a large order, and there tempted to gamble, though fortunately without serious results, and whose extraordinary adventure was narrated in the papers, was an illustration of how those swindlers go to work; but there are many more artful methods than that, and several of those are explained and illustrated, in the hope that the public may benefit by them, and be put on their guard against the ruses of those clever scoundrels. Cheating at cards is the most common; some wonderful tales can be told of swindling by means of pretended hidden treasure; equally curious are swindles that have been accomplished by notography, and by forged documents; most artful are the cases of cheating which have been carried out by selling stolen property; while the stories of those who employ alchemy to effect their purpose will seem almost incredible.

CHEATING AT CARDS.

THIS method, which is that most commonly practised, must be explained and illustrated first. The cards used are round, one-half having flowers or animals painted on them, the other half of the pack being blank. The game is simple, and yet most attractive. The dupe is always allowed to win at first, the stakes go on increasing, till suddenly the tables are turned, and the unfortunate victim finds that in one game he has lost not only all he has already won, but his own money, which he has brought to carry on the game as well. But first the swindlers have to find their victim. The way they set about it is this. They rent a large bungalow, fill it with the most handsome furniture they can hire, and dress themselves as a native chief or nobleman and his staff. They then bring a tradesman in a good position to the bungalow on the pretence of giving him a large order, as in the case of the raja and the cavalry outfits, treat him well, pay great deference to him, make a confident of him in some matter, win his good graces in turn, and finally invite him to play. If he consents, ruin is bound to follow, or if he declines, the wily scoundrels generally manage to invent some excuse for not giving the proposed order for goods.

THE DOCTOR AND THE SHARPERS.

NOT long ago a Hindu, who from his dress appeared to be the servant of a native prince, called at the bungalow of a Bombay doctor, and betraying evident excitement, asked to see the doctor at once. The doctor was in, at which the man made many expressions of delight at his good fortune, for as he explained it was a most urgent case he required his services for, though, no doubt, he had been on the watch to secure the doctor when he was at home. Being shown immediately into the doctor's presence, the man explained that he wished him to come immediately to see a servant of the raja from up-country, then on a visit to Bombay, who was lying seriously ill. The doctor, deceived by the man's dress, and his apparently excited manner, expressed his readiness to set out at once. His visitor took him to a carriage that stood at the door, and together they drove off to Bhuleshwar. The doctor was taken into a bungalow, which was handsomely furnished, and moving about the rooms he saw a number of gaily liveried servants, which conveyed to him the impression that he was in a house occupied by some nobleman. After a short interval he was taken to a chamber, wherein lay the invalid he had been brought to prescribe for. That man the doctor really found suffering from dropsy. On examining the patient the doctor gravely shook his head, saying the man had evidently been suffering a long time, that medical aid ought to have been sought long before now, and that he was afraid he could not do much for the sufferer. On hearing this alarming piece of news, the man who had brought the doctor thither disappeared, but, returning after a lapse of a few minutes, signed to the doctor to follow him. In another room, reclining on a couch, a man who from his rich dress and sparkling jewels, had all the appearance of a native prince, invited the doctor to come and sit by him.

"I am told by my secretary," he said, speaking in good English, "that my servant is seriously ill. I hope the malady is not dangerous. Tell me what you can do for him."

"Your Highness' servant," replied the doctor, "is undoubtedly in a serious, I might say an alarmingly advanced stage of dropsy, and I fear my services can be of little avail."

On hearing this the raja betrayed evident signs of emotion.

"It grieves me much, doctor," he said, "to hear you say so; but you must save him. He is an old and valued servant. He was a servant of my father before I was born. To lose him now would be a source of much sorrow to me, not only on account of my attachment to him, but because I have, as you tell me, neglected so long to seek medical advice. Doctor, you must do your utmost for the man. I care nothing for the cost; only save his life, and I will pay you well."

The doctor was touched by the apparent concern of the prince for his servant, and though he inwardly felt the malady was beyond his skill, he promised to do his utmost to relieve, if not to save him. The prince was most fervent and profuse in his thanks, and taking a valuable ring from his finger insisted on the doctor accepting it.

The doctor departed, and was at the bungalow again early next morning. After five or six days, to the doctor's own astonishment, and to the raja's delight, the patient seemed to be recovering. His Highness' joy, in fact, was so unbounded that he again made a most valuable present to the doctor. He opened a large cash-box, and displayed rolls and rolls of bank notes. Some of those notes he gave to the doctor, and forced him, much against his will, for they amounted to more than double the fees he would have charged, to accept them.

Another day the doctor came, and this time the scene was changed. He found the raja sitting playing at cards, with a stranger, a man he had not seen in the house on any of his previous visits. His Highness was in a most hilarious mood, and immediately informed the doctor that the reason of his happiness was the servant who so greatly improved that morning that he was then almost out of danger. Then he invited him to sit down and watch the game. The doctor did so. The raja and the stranger were playing at cards, the same sort of round cards as described in introducing the subject, and to his amazement the raja played in a most reckless fashion. Every game he lost, and at the end of every game he took notes from the cash-box by his side, throwing them down, calling out "Double the stake; double it this time," till latterly the doctor saw, to his horror, the raja's opponent lift up notes worth twenty thousand rupees. Then only did the raja seem to recover his senses.

"I will play no more," he called out angrily, scattering the cards about the floor, banging down the lid of his cash-box, and hurriedly leaving the room. The other player only smiled, and walked away complacently with his gains.

"Who is that man?" asked the doctor, speaking to the servant, or secretary, as he was called, whose acquaintance he had first made. "He is not one of your people, is he?"

"No," was the reply; "he is a stranger."

"I thought so," the doctor said, "and I should say he was a sharper. His Highness lost a tremendous amount of money to him in that short time."

"Oh, that is nothing," the servant said smiling.

"He is an inveterate gambler, though he plays so recklessly. But it matters little, for he is very rich, and can afford to lose. Did you not see the notes he had in the cash-box?"

The doctor admitted that he had.

"Now," said the man confidentially to the doctor, "I have something to propose, if you will agree. Why should you not play with his Highness and win some money?"

"I could not afford to play for such heavy stakes," said the doctor, shaking his head.

"You can, and I will help you," the secretary persisted. "I cannot play with my master, but if you play, I will lend you money, and on what you win for me I will give you ten per cent. Bring to-morrow Rs. 1,000, and I will give you Rs. 2,000 to play with. Bring Rs. 10,000, and I will give you Rs. 20,000. If you do not play with his Highness, this man will come again and take away much money; why then should you not win, and help me too? Had I not chosen to come for you, you would not have got this patient, and those presents my master has given you. Play with the raja to-morrow, and I will lend you money to win for me too."

The doctor went home and thought the matter over. It was very true, as the servant had said, if he did not play, the raja would find some one else to gamble with. He had seen sufficient of the game, too, to perceive how simple it was, and how easily the cards were manipulated by the dealer, or shuffler, to win. He thought, therefore, there would be little harm in taking perhaps a thousand rupees with him to try his luck. Next morning he repaired to the bungalow at Bhuleshwar as usual. The first he met was the man who played the secretary.

"Have you brought your money, doctor?" were his first words.

"I may try a few games if opportunity offers itself," said the doctor.

"Yes; how much have you brought?"

"A thousand rupees."

"Ho! that is nothing. Never mind, I was prepared. Here are Rs. 2,000. With that you should win much money. You know the terms?"

Having seen his patient, he was afterwards, as usual, received by the raja, whom he satisfied as to the progress of the sick servant.

"My secretary," the raja finally said, "tells me you were amused with the game you saw me play yesterday, and would have a try with me."

"If your Highness would so honour me," the doctor politely replied.

"Yes; bring the cards," the raja called. "How much do you play for?"

"I cannot play for high stakes, as I am not able to afford it?"

"And I must play high, or I find little excitement in it. However, say Rs. 100 for the first," said the raja.

The play began; the doctor manipulated his cards as he saw the raja's opponent do the day before, and he, of course, won. The trick was so simple; he was amazed that the raja did not see through it. The game proceeded, and as the raja continued to lose, he grew more reckless, insisting on the stakes being increased, till finally he stopped, refusing to play any more, and retired as he had done the day before.

The doctor and the raja's secretary then counted the winnings, which amounted to Rs. 4,800, leaving the doctor, with 10 per cent. on the amount he had won with the secretary's Rs. 2,000, the sum of Rs. 1,920.

"Now, you see how simple it is," said the Hindu. "Bring more money to-morrow, and play for higher stakes. I will double what you bring, as to-day, though it should be Rs. 20,000.

A second day the doctor played, and again he won, the raja finally throwing down his cards, saying in well-assumed disgust, "I will play no more for such small stakes. I cannot take interest in the game, and so I lose. I will play for a lakht not less."

The doctor was now thoroughly infatuated with the game, and was quite prepared for another afternoon's play at larger stakes. If the raja, he thought, was so stupid that he could not perceive, or so reckless that he did not see through the trick, he thoroughly deserved to lose his money. The doctor, therefore, went back, and the game went on as before, the raja losing again, and growing more and more excited as the money was drawn over to the doctor's side of the table, until in an apparent frenzy the raja emptied his cash-box, putting a pile of notes on the table, against which the doctor laid all the money he had brought with him and won as well. This was the crisis, the cards were dealt, the raja having previously shuffled them. There was a shout of triumph as the cards were turned up. *The raja had won.*

"Come on again," he cried, "a lakh of rupees on this game!"

The doctor gave no response. He simply looked on aghast. He had lost Rs. 20,000 of his own money, all he had already won, and Rs. 40,000, belonging to the secretary.

"You do not play?" inquired the raja, as no response came to his challenge.

"I cannot; I have no more money."

"You fool," cried his Highness; "did not I tell you I only played for high stakes? Why did you not bring more money," so saying he gathered up his money and retired. The doctor then began expressing regret to the secretary for having lost his money, and he replied apparently in great concern: "I borrowed it, and it must be returned. You must play again, and win it back. Bring more money to-morrow. I will borrow money to help you."

"But I cannot," said the doctor; "I have no more money to bring."

He left the raja's bungalow disgusted with himself for allowing himself to be carried away by the temptation to gamble. That night, as he was looking at the ring he got from the raja, he noticed a green stain on his finger. He pulled it off, examined it carefully, rushed off and showed it to the nearest jeweller. It was only brass, and the supposed diamond was only a bit of common crystal; then it dawned upon him that he had been swindled, and so it was. When he returned to the bungalow it was empty. The raja, his retinue of gorgeously apparelled servants, the man dying from dropsy, the handsome furniture, all were gone. The raja was only the chief of a clever band of swindlers, and the dropsical patient was a poor man, who had been discovered in some part of the native town, and had hired himself out for the occasion.

CHEATING BY HIDDEN TREASURE.

The tale of the doctor among the sharpers is only one of many that might be told if only those who have been so swindled would come forward and make them public. They may, as they sometimes do, inform the police, but cheating being a non-cognisable offence, requiring a warrant for apprehension of the swindlers, and as it is impossible to gather evidence, owing to the dupe having no witness to bring forward, he has to bear his losses as best he can. It is rather hard no doubt, and it is most irritating to the police and to the public that so much swindling should be so carried on on so extensive a scale, and they should be powerless to prevent it. All that can be done is to warn the public against the wiles of those scoundrels who, as would be seen from the tale related above, are most accomplished actors.

Even more wonderful than the cheating at cards is that accomplished by means of a pretended hidden treasure. This, however, is not so frequently performed, as the cheats must secure, to be successful, a man who has a more than usual belief in the supernatural. This is usually done by a man pretending to be a native priest, who is in league with the King of the Genii, and who has, like Aladdin in the Arabian Nights' tale of the "Wonderful Lamp," one or two genii at his command who can reveal to him enormous wealth that has been hidden away for generations and forgotten. As an instance of this method of swindling we give the following story, which has never yet been made public, but the truth of which can be vouched for, wonderful though it may seem.

THE PIR, THE PARSEE, AND THE GENII.

There once came to Bombay a Mahomedan, who took to himself the name of the Pir, or Saint Syed Magrabi, who, morning and evening, was to be seen down on the sea-shore earnestly praying and bowing to the east. To the same spot and at the same hours there also came to pray a Parsee, who was attracted by the venerable aspect of the supposed Pir, and many a curious glance he cast in his direction. The Pir's quick eye detected the curiosity he had aroused in the Parsee, and scenting a probable victim, he at once proceeded to lay his snare. He set his accomplices, who were well schooled in the trickery he practised, to follow the Parsee, with a view to discovering his profession, if any, the character he bore, and his means. That they accomplished only too well, and the Parsee was found to be a man who would, in all likelihood, not only be readily cheated, but who would yield much gain to the Pir and his swindling crew. They were, however, in no hurry to commence operations. They allowed, in fact, the Parsee to make the first advances. They guessed, and guessed rightly, his curiosity to learn something of the strange man he saw there praying every day would overcome him.

One morning the Parsee accosted a man whom he rightly took to be one of the Pir's associates (one of his accomplices in fact) and said to him :

"Who is this man? He is a stranger, is he not? Where does he come from?"

"Know you not the great Pir Syed Magrabi?" the man queried in return. "Oh, a great man is he? He is a saint, who has given up all connection with worldly affairs. He has control over immense fortunes, but those he devotes to doing good amongst his unfortunate fellow-creatures, living only on charity himself."

"A strange man," said the Parsee; "I would much like to speak to him."

"I am not sure," said the man doubtfully, wishing to rouse the Parsee's curiosity still the more, "if the Pir would converse with you. You are not of his creed. But if you are anxious, follow me slowly;" and he moved in the direction of where the Pir was kneeling.

Just then a man approached the Saint Syed Magrabi from the opposite direction, and kneeling in front of the holy man, bowed low his head to the ground and addressing him, said:

"O great Pir, and most benevolent master, who so bountifully bestowed on me Rs. 10,000, thou hast helped me out of countless difficulties and saved me from ruin. Think not thy miserable servant ungrateful or avaricious that I come to thee again, and bowing low my head before thee crave thy assistance to obtain Rs. 5,000 more; for my daughter must be married in a few days more."

"Come to my dwelling," said the Pir, in reply, "just as before, and the money shall be thine."

The man, salaaming, slowly rose, and murmuring his thanks, went away. The Parsee and his companion were on the point of advancing again, when another stranger approached the Pir and kneeling beside him, as the former had done, said:

"O great Pir of Mahomed, whose works are as mighty as those of the Prophet himself, I have discovered the treasure thou didst send me to find, and have come to thank thee for thy kindness in delivering me from the poverty I and my family have been suffering from."

"Then go," replied the Pir, "and see thou tellest it to no man, and I would warn you further, while thou and thy family will live now in comfort till the end of your lives, spend none of thy new found fortune on the frivolities of this world. Distribute it well in charity, and use it in relieving thy less fortunate fellow-creatures. Go ; and peace be with you."

The Parsee was bewildered at hearing those extraordinary interviews, and thought the Pir one of the most remarkable men he had ever seen, which indeed he would have been had there been an atom of truth in the marvellous things those men who had just appeared before him had confessed to. His wonder he expressed to his Mahomedan companion, who said :

" Yes ; the Pir is a most remarkable man. The King of the Genii, who is his slave, reveals to him hidden treasures, which sometimes amount to inconceivable wealth, and it is by that means the Pir is able to give away such enormous sums of money to the unfortunate."

The Pir then rose from the ground, and moved away ; but as he passed the Parsee he stood, pressed his hand to his forehead, and gazing at him earnestly for a moment, shook his head, and moved on again muttering something to himself.

The Parsee went home marvelling much at what he had seen and heard, and the desire to talk to the Pir grew so strong that he determined to approach him next morning after he had finished his prayers. To the shore at Chowpati next morning he accordingly went, and he succeeded much beyond his expectations, for the reverend Pir had no sooner raised himself from his sacred carpet than, finding the Parsee standing close beside him, he started as he had done the previous day, stood for a moment regarding him in silence, and then said :

"O thou descendant of Noshirvan and Darius ! Thou art the man who has been revealed to me in a vision. It is thou for whom I have been waiting here. It is for thee I have been sent hither by Allah, for thou hast been selected by divine decree to become, through me, a great benefactor to suffering humanity. Thou, O son of the immortal Noshirvan and Darius, art destined to become the possessor of great riches; for thee great treasure, hidden for generations in the bowels of the earth, is reserved. Thou wilt become the possessor of many ships, which in fleetness shall surpass all others that sail upon the sea, and which shall carry pilgrims to and from Mecca, where is the tomb of the great Prophet. Amin! Amin! Amin!"

The Pir then knelt down in front of the bewildered Parsee and bowed three times towards the east. Then rising again, he once more addressed the Parsee, saying:

"Art thou, O most happy, most fortunate, most honoured of mortals, ready to follow me to where fortune awaits thee?"

The Parsee was too much astonished at the remarkable utterances of the strange man to refuse; but whether it was that Pir was not quite ready for so decided a reply, or that he had some preparations to make for the Parsee's visit, he did not take him away with him just then, but said:

"To-night at sunset meet me here again."

The two men then parted, and met again as appointed. The Pir uttered no word, but signed to the Parsee to follow. Over the railway level crossing along Mathew Road, and thence into Breach Candy Road they went, till Grant Road being reached, the Pir entered a bungalow, signing to the Parsee to follow him still. They passed through a room dimly lit into another which was dark but for two tall *samai* or lamp stands on which burned strange yellow lights, which gave to the Pir's face, as he stood between them, a weird, death-like paleness, The Parsee was awe-struck by what he saw, and the scene was rendered the more supernatural by men in dark cloaks that hid their features, moving as silently as spectres through the gloom in which the room was enshrouded. In a voice that sounded strangely hollow in the large empty room, the Pir, speaking for the first time since they had re-met, said :

" Son of Noshirvan, advance no further till thou hast removed thy shoes, for here is sacred ground."

The Parsee tremblingly did as he was bid, and then the Pir handing him a cloth, added :

" Take this carpet and stand upon it, for otherwise the King of the Genii, whom I am about to summon hither to reveal to us the treasure of which I have already spoken, would destroy thee. To all my invocations, also, thou must lowly salaam, and say ' Amin ' continually.

The Pir then unrolled a large square carpet for himself on the space between which stood the two yellow-burning lights, leaving a portion of the unmatted ground between himself and the Parsee.

" Hassan," he then called, " come here and perform thy task."

A man advanced with a basin, and placing it in front of the Pir, who stripped himself of his garments, poured into it, from a phial, a strong scent, which filled the room with a pleasing odour. The Pir having bathed himself in the perfumed water, ordered the man to dig in the ground. Hassan, having himself performed some ablutions in the perfumed water, began to dig. He had only removed a few spadefuls of earth, when he suddenly fell back with a loud cry, and the Parsee saw, to his amazement and horror, blood issuing from the man's mouth.

" There," he cried, pointing upwards with his finger, " is a fearful demon coming, with flames issuing from his mouth, and he bids me stay."

The Pir thereupon began making mysterious passes with his hand, muttering something in Arabic, which the Parsee did not understand, but to which he continually responded "Amin, Amin!" as he had had been commanded by the Pir.

The man Hassan then raised himself from his prostrate position on the ground, saying,

"Ah, there the demon flies away," whereupon the Pir made a mysterious circle with his finger round the place where Hassan had been digging, and bade him proceed.

The man had not removed much more of the earth, when he cried out in a still more terrified voice,

"Ah, my master, there I see more terrible demons flying towards me, whirling huge serpents round their heads. Save me, great Pir, or they will consume me."

The poor Parsee trembled with terror, his knees knocked together; he felt as if he would drop on the ground; and he uttered "Amin, Amin," as rapidly as he could.

The Pir noticing his tremor, spoke encouragingly to him, and bade him fear nothing so long as he remained on the carpet.

"The demons crowd round me," called out Hassan again. "They come in hundreds."

"Heed them not," said the Pir; "they will not harm thee. Go on."

The man, thus encouraged, dug on, until he had made a deep hole, when he fell back once more exhausted, and the Parsee saw, rising out of the ground, apparently by supernatural aid, a large copper vessel. When the pot stood still, the Pir bent over it, and with hands outstretched, muttered a long speech in Arabic, having finished which, he stooped down and removed the lid, when to the Parsee's increased amazement a large cobra rose out of the pot and wriggled about fantastically, opening and shutting its mouth. The Pir, muttering mysterious language, made a circle with his finger in the air three times round the head of the snake, and then dipping his hand into the pot, brought forth five bright gold pieces, which he presented to the Parsee.

"Take these, my son," he said, and examine them carefully. They are gold mohurs, and millions more will be thine if thou wilt only pay heed to, and obey my instructions. The cobra thou seest is a slave of the Genii King; he is able to take any shape, of reptile, or man, as his master commands him. He has taken this snake-like shape to-night as a sign that the time is not yet ripe for carrying away the treasure; but keep thou those gold pieces to thyself in the meantime, for to me who have discarded all worldly goods and riches they are of no use. I will now send a message to the King of the Genii requesting his permission for you to bear away the treasure that is thine."

With these words the Pir wrote with a golden pen and gold ink on a small sheet of perfumed green paper, murmured a charm, and threw the paper into the air. The mysterious paper hovered a moment over the yellow light burning in the *samai*, and disappeared in a flash of fire.

"The reply," he said, "will come in the course of a few minutes."

The bewildered Parsee then fell at the feet of the Pir, saying,

"O great saint! I am prepared to do whatever I am desired."

"O thou son of Noshirvan," replied the Pir, "I have said all this treasure is for thee, for I, who have abandoned worldly affairs, have no need of riches. My life is spent in devotion to Heaven, and in doing good to the people."

He then stretched forward his hand in the direction of the *samai*, and appeared to receive from out the light a green envelope sealed with green wax. Opening this he read some words in Arabic, and then addressing the Parsee said :

" It is the command of the King of the Genii that the mortal, who is to receive this treasure, whom thou art, must, before thou canst become the possessor of the gold, feed twenty-five thousand beggars on the best and richest food the country can afford. He, moreover, dictates that thou shalt provide covers for the tombs of saints which he here names. The cost of all this will be Rs. 20,000, which thou must provide, and till which be forthcoming, his servant whom you see here in the form of a snake will watch over that treasure, which will be safe, as it is invisible to other eyes than thine and mine."

It was, however, very soon proved visible to other mortal eyes, for at this moment the romance ended, and stern, very stern reality took its place. The doors flew open, and in stepped, at the head of some police, Sardar Mir Abdul Ali, Chief of the Bombay Detective Department. He marched up to the Pir, whose turn it was now to show signs of surprise and terror, and showed him a warrant for his arrest. It appears that not long before he had visited a Native State, and swindled a too credulous prince, in the same way as he was now imposing on the Parsee, by pretending to reveal to him some hidden treasure.

The Genii King's slave, otherwise the cobra, was easily disposed of, it being a harmless snake, hired from some snake charmers for the purpose of adding effect to the deception. The copper pot on being emptied, was found to contain a number of pie pieces, gilded over to make them glitter like gold. The mysterious uprising of the pot out of the ground was nothing very wonderful after all. The hole in the ground was found to be full of chunam, and that, together with a small overturned chatti, revealed the secret of the trick. Chunam swells when steeped in water, and it would seem that the man whom the pretended Pir called Hassan had, in digging, turned over the chatti, upsetting the water over the chunam, which swelling gradually raised the pot containing the coins out of the ground. The "blood" that issued from the man's mouth was only the juice of a root which he had been chewing. The only other mysterious performance remaining to be explained was the disappearance of the green tissue paper letter in a flash of fire, and the return of the reply, but that, as many will know, is a common feat of jugglery often practised by conjurors. The yellow flames that gave such weird light were simply produced by salt steeped in methylated spirits.

The Pir and his accomplices were not convicted and punished as they deserved, sufficient evidence to prove the case not being forthcoming, but the police by their prompt intervention had the satisfaction of knowing they saved the Parsee from being robbed of the large sum of Rs. 20,000, which, he admitted, he had been quite prepared to furnish the following day.

THE DUPLICATE CURRENCY NOTES.

It may seem hardly credible that there are to be found people who believe in the possibility of a currency note being made out of another, and being equal to it in value. Yet it is so, and it is through the credulity of people believing in the possibility of such miracles being wrought that they are swindled. It will be noted that in many of the instances of cheating and swindling we propose to quote, in order to illustrate the different methods of cheating, if the swindlers do not represent themselves to be rajas or noblemen, they often pretend to be fakirs, religious mendicants, priests, or holy men of some sort. They know very well that there are many who trust in their priests so implicitly that they will believe in their power to perform the most marvellous feats, such as changing the baser metals into gold and silver, changing one rupee into hundreds, melting a gold mohur down, and causing it to swell out to a huge nugget of the precious metal, or turning a bank note into two. It is this cheating by "notography," or making two out of a currency note, we propose to explain and illustrate here. The duped parties never seem to consider for a moment the absurdity of the transaction, that each note, as it is issued, is differently numbered, and that the number cannot be affixed anywhere but at the Currency office; nor do they stay to think of the dishonesty of manufacturing a currency note. Whatever their priest does must surely be right. The method of cheating by notography, as it is known, is this. Supposing a dupe is found, he is taken to a man dressed up as a fakir who, it is explained to him, possesses the extraordinary power of converting one currency note into two, but that he will only do it for a person in need of money, or for any one whose fortunes have fallen, and who, for the sake of helping a charity, or for any other urgent necessity, requires a large sum of money. The fakir is generally somewhat doubtful at first about beginning, but apparent difficulties or prejudices being surmounted, a note is handed to the fakir, who straightway commences operations on it. He takes his dupe into a darkened room, and making a solution of nitrate of silver, wets a piece of sensitised paper such as is used by photographer in it. This being dried again, it and the note are folded together and put into a case similar to that used in a photographic camera for holding the plates, and placed in the sun for a few minutes. The fakir then opens the case again, and shows the man that the paper which went in blank has now a faint impress of the note upon it. Any fear the dupe may have had for his note now generally disappears, and he grows still more interested and expectant when the fakir says the note has yet to be subjected to some further process. By a simple sleight-of-hand movement he substitutes a genuine note for the sensitised paper, and when the frame is opened once more after a further exposure to the sun the swindled party is delighted when he is presented with a brand new note in addition to his own. He is then told any other time he requires money to bring his note to the fakir. He goes out, changes it finds it is all right, and is satisfied as to the genuineness of the priest's strange art. He of course very soon returns with a note for a larger sum, probably one representing as much money as he is possessed of; and now it is that the poor dupe is thoroughly victimised. The same process is gone through as before, but on the photographer's frame being opened the first time to discover how the printing is progressing, the genuine note is discovered to be all spotted in a peculiar fashion, which the fakir accounts for through the sensitised paper not having been dried in the dark. That, however, he professes to be able to remove. He then secretly substitutes another piece of paper for the genuine note, dips it in a strong acid solution, and puts it in the sun to dry. Immediately, the victim of the transaction is horror-stricken to see what he imagines to be his note begin to smoke, curl up, and go on fire. In a second the paper is reduced to a black ash. The fakir and his confederates express great concern at the failure of the attempt, but ask him to bring another note, when they will be careful to make it good to him.

The movements of the cheated one are carefully watched. If he goes to the police the swindlers decamp, and find other quarters; so that when any inquiries are made for them they are nowhere to be found. The following is an illustration of this "cheating by notography."

A BROKEN OFF ENGAGEMENT.

A Hindu merchant in Bombay had a young daughter, whom he was anxious to see wedded, and who had been asked by a brother merchant as a wife for his son. The match being an advantageous one, the first-named merchant was anxious to accept the offer, only fortune had not been smiling on him of late years, and recently he had lost a large sum of money in speculation. His elder daughters had all been comfortably married; and now the thought that he had not the means to furnish for his youngest and favourite daughter a dowry worthy of her position and of the young man for whom she had been asked made the poor old man sad. Borrow he could not, for what property he had was already heavily mortgaged. His distress he did not keep to himself, but went about informing his friends of his misfortune, none of them, however, did or suggested anything to help him. Now, it was this public display of his grief which wrought his ruin, for his unfortunate predicament became known to a gang of swindlers, who are always on the prowl for a victim.

The Hindu was one day sitting at the gate of a temple, brooding over his inability to find means to prepare for his daughter's wedding, feeling and looking very sad, when he was accosted by a man with whom he had a slight acquaintance.

"You are in distress, my friend," he said to the unfortunate man. "I have heard of it. Would you allow me to help you?"

"You," exclaimed the Hindu. "Can you provide me with Rs. 25,000?"

"I can," said the stranger, "show you how you may provide yourself with more if necessary,—all, indeed, that you may require to relieve yourself from your distress."

"Ah," said the disconsolate Hindu, "you would propose some speculation; but I have had enough of it. No, no! No more speculation for me."

"You are wrong in your conclusion, my friend," replied the stranger. "I am no speculator, and know nothing of that mode of making money. I have something very much simpler to suggest."

"Are you jesting with me?" inquired the other. "Or do you really mean what you say?"

"Come with me, where no one can hear our conversation, and I will explain more fully."

The Hindu, not loath to accompany a man who promised to be a friend in need, rose from the stone on which he sat, and together the two men walked along the street.

"I know a fakir," said the stranger in a low voice, as they moved slowly along, "who has been granted the power from Heaven of finding, even making out of nothing, money for the relief of the poor, and people who are in distress. To him I will take you, and tell him of your misfortune."

"I have heard," said the Hindu, the cloud passing away from his countenance, "of holy men being endowed with so great power, but such an unusual method of getting out of my difficulty never suggested itself to me. If we find this fakir, and he helps me as you say, you will be a friend, stranger though you may be to me, far before any of my acquaintances to whom I have appealed in vain for aid."

A garry being hailed, the two men seated themselves in it, and were driven to a house with a most uninviting entrance, in a small lane off the Kalbadevi Road. Up a narrow, dark, creaking stair they went, and entered a room, the air of which was charged with evil-smelling vapours. There, in a corner, with painted face, matted hair, and naked but for a very dirty loin cloth, sat what appeared to be a holy man or fakir earnesty engaged in devotional exercises. To him the Hindu and his friend lowly salaamed, whereupon he stopped muttering his prayer, and asked the men their errand.

The Hindu, at a sign from his companion, told his tale of distress, and concluded by saying,

"My friend, who has brought me here, informs me that you, most holy man, have the power to aid me. I crave of you to grant me the assistance I ask."

He did not think, in his anxiety and earnestness, of the ridiculous nature of the scene and the absurdity of the demand. This well-dressed Hindu, who lived in a large, well-furnished bungalow, and who, though he had lost much money by unfortunate speculations, had still a good business that provided him with a comfortable income, his only distress being that he had not the ready cash to marry his daughter, was standing in a room, in which there was not an article of furniture, asking a miserable, dirty, naked old mendicant for pecuniary assistance. But the old man was a fakir, a man who, on account of his renunciation of all wordly affairs, was gifted from above with powers beyond ordinary mortals, and in that power of course the Hindu had faith.

"It is my mission here," said the fakir, "to relieve fellow beings in distress, but what I, by the power that has been given me, provide for you, must not be used as a means of securing for yourself any luxuries or of adding to your worldly goods."

"I only want to marry my daughter," said the Hindu; whereupon the fakir entered upon a harangue on the benefit of early marriages, and concluded by saying, "Marriage is a necessity. Your daughter must be married; and knowing the circumstances, it is my duty to assist you. Have you a currency note with you?"

The Hindu quickly took a note for Rs. 10 from his pocket and handed it to the fakir, wondering what he meant to do with it, for, it must be understood, the man who had brought the victim of misfortune thither had not informed him of the nature of the wonders the fakir professed to work.

"This will be of but little service to you," said the fakir, "for with this I can only produce Rs. 10 more. With one note I can only make for you a note like it, and of equal value. If you want Rs. 1,000, or Rs. 10,000, you must show to me a note representing a like amount."

As the Hindu looked puzzled, the fakir continued :

"You do not understand ? This will do for an experiment. I will show you what I mean. Follow me."

The fakir took the Hindu into another room, which was very dimly lit, and which was also unfurnished but for a large cupboard. The doors of this the fakir threw open, disclosing rows of mysterious looking bottles, and phials, and boxes. Selecting a bottle, and removing the stopper, he poured some liquid from it into a small earthenware vessel, and dipped a piece of white paper of the same size as the Rs. 10 note into it. Taking it out again he dried it, and putting it through the process already explained, presented to the Hindu two notes, one of which he recognised as his own, and the other a brand new note. The Hindu examined the new note given to him, and stared at it in amazement.

"I have heard," he said, "but never believed in the power to turn one note into two ; but now I do belive."

"Take it," said the fakir, "it is yours, for I made it for you. It will convince you of my power, and as I am desirous of helping you in your affliction, bring me again to-morrow another note for any sum you like, and, no matter how large the amount, I will reproduce another of like value for you."

The Hindu went away, but still doubting, made a purchase with his new note, and being convinced of its genuineness, became quite joyous at his good fortune. Then he began to consider "I am in need of Rs. 25,000. I can only produce a note for Rs. 5,000, but with that I will be able to get Rs. 5,000 more. Then those two will produce Rs. 10,000, and the same experiment repeated will give me the required amount."

To the fakir next day he returned, taking with him his Rs. 5,000 note, and the same process as before was repeated. The note and the blank paper were placed in the case, which, the window being opened for the purpose, was put in such a position as to allow the sun's rays to play full upon it. On the case being opened again, the original note was found to be very much spotted.

"I am sorry," said the fakir, "that this has happened. The other paper has not been properly dried in the dark, and so those spots have been caused. But no matter, that can soon be remedied. I have a solution here which will remove the spots."

The fakir then dipped what seemed to be the real note into a basin of liquid, and spreading the paper on a plate, put it under the sun to dry. In a second or two it began to smoke; the fakir ran with the apparent intention of seizing it, but before he could rescue it, it had taken fire, and burned up.

"This is unfortunate," said the fakir. "I have made the acid too strong, I never made such a mistake before."

The unfortunate Hindu turned sick with disgust at seeing his note destroyed in that manner, observing which, the fakir remarked:

"Do not be downcast, my friend. It can be remedied. What is the number of the note?"

"Alas !" replied the swindled one, "I know not. I have had it in my possession for months ; I do not remember the day I got it, and never noted the number."

No doubt this reply to a question which was undoubtedly put with the intention of discovering what the Hindu knew about the note, was satisfactory to the fakir, although he pretended to be much concerned.

"That is indeed unfortunate," the scoundrel said, "but do not despair. I will succeed next time ; so bring another, and I shall be more careful with it."

Whether the swindler, with all his pretended concern, betrayed some satisfaction in his look, we cannot say, but the impudent demand to bring more money another day, seemed to open the eyes of the Hindu to the fact that he had been swindled.

"Give you another note," he cried, "to destroy for me, or spirit away by your trickery ? No, though I had a thousand Rs. 5,000 notes, not another would I allow your fingers to touch. But alas, I have no more ; you have robbed me of all the money I had left to me."

He left hurriedly, and in a state of high excitement drove to the nearest police station. To the officer on duty he related his sorrowful tale ; but when a search was made for the pretended fakir and his accomplice, the rooms they had occupied were untenanted, and they had disappeared no one knew whither, in all likelihood to fields and pastures new to look for another dupe. As to the unfortunate Hindu, being unable to provide the necessary funds, his daughter's engagement had to be broken off ; but he is now trying hard by honest and legitimate means to recoup his losses, and be prepared for the next suitor that offers himself.

A DEFAULTING BILL COLLECTOR'S STORY.

Many other instances could be narrated of persons who have been swindled in this manner, through their absurd belief in fakirs having the power to convert one currency note into two. Not long ago a defaulting bill collector was tried in Bombay for embezzlement, and, being found guilty, was sentenced to a long term of imprisonment. The story he told to the police was that he had been addicted to gambling. Having lost all his own money he tried his luck one night in a gaming-house, which was a common resort of his, with some money he had that day collected for the firm in which he was employed, and lost a considerable sum of that as well. He was leaving the house in a very depressed state of mind, wondering how he would account to his master for his deficiency, when he was accosted by a man who sympathised with him, and taking him to a drinking shop treated him to some refreshment. There he confided to him that he knew a fakir who had the marvellous power of converting a currency note into two, and told him so many wonderful tales of services that some holy man appointment to people in distress, that the erring bill-collector services to believe, and fell into the trap. Next day he met him a erring friend by appointment, bringing a note for erring 00 with him. To the fakir they went, and the same prison une befel him as did the credulous Hindu who wanted to raise a dowry for his daughter. Unable to meet his deficiencies, the bill-collector absconded, but he was pursued, arrested, tried, and sent to prison.

CHEATING BY DOCUMENT.

While many of the methods of cheating practised in Indian cities—for these swindlers are not to be found in Bombay alone, as they frequently shift their camp, taking tours all over the country—are ingenious, and so cleverly worked out that the shrewdest of business men are occasionally "taken in and done for." Some of the devices are shallow in the extreme; as, for instance, the case of the rupee notes narrated above. As absurd, and even more dishonest in purpose, is the method known as cheating by document. It is only men who are not overscrupulous in their business transactions, men who care not whether they make money by fair or dishonest means, so long as they find their bank accounts swelling, who can be swindled in this way. Had those men who have been "cheated by document" not been, in fact, blinded by avarice, and a desire for gain, they would have seen through the knavery that was proposed, and if they had been unable to bring conviction home to the swindling gang, they would at least have escaped themselves, and made public the trick that had been attempted to be practised on them, as a warning to others. The manner in which "cheating by document" is carried on is as follows:—One of the swindlers will call upon a tradesman in the city, and ask him to come to a certain house to receive a large order. He goes, and while there, a man pretending to be a landowner enters, and addressing the master of the house and others supposed to be his brothers as old acquaintances, shows to them a *sanad*, or some such document, purporting to confer on him a large tract of land or some villages. He also points out how the document might, by a skilful hand, be altered in such a way as to bring him a still larger amount of land or property. They arrange to get this done for the landowner for a certain sum; then discovering that the stranger, who is no other than the dupe, has heard the whole transaction, they offer him a share in the commission, to keep silent.

A man supposed to be an expert penman is sent for, and he, recognising the nature of the job, asks a very large fee; perhaps several thousand rupees, to be paid down at once. The dupe willingly pays his share, for he expects to receive probably four times this outlay as his portion of the money to be paid by the nobleman or landowner, and he suspects nothing on seeing his confederates, without any hesitation, paying their share. The work being completed, the owner of the *sanad* discovers a grievous mistake, and says it has not been done according to his instructions, but the clerk who had performed the operation in the *sanad* shows his written instructions given to him by one of the brothers who had undertaken to get the work done for him. The fault, therefore, really lies on the side of the middlemen, of whom the dupe is one. A dishonest man himself, he readily falls into the snare laid for him by those swindlers. Out of it he can only come at the cost of a heavy ransom, for which there is no redress, and it undoubtedly serves him very right. How is it that those cheats cannot be caught? That has been explained in foregoing pages; but in "cheating by document," those swindlers are very careful. They make sure of the man whose pocket they propose making a haul out of, before they try him. They go about their work deliberately, and by persevering inquiry find out the character of their man before they approach him. The following illustration will explain more clearly how "cheating by document" is carried on.

THE BROKER AND THE SANAD.

A MAN carrying on business as a stock-broker in Bombay was called upon one day by a clerk, who said his master had a large sum of money he wanted to invest in property or in stocks. The man mentioned the name of a native firm in Walkeshwar which was unknown to the broker, but the man's story was so plausible that he, rather than miss an opportunity of making a good fee, resolved to accompany the clerk. Walkeshwar reached, they stopped in front of a large, clean-looking house. Entering, the broker was taken into a room which was furnished like an office, but the fittings were all of the best. Here he was introduced to two young men, whose dress and courteous manner proclaimed them to be well-bred and educated.

"My father," said one of them to the broker, "wished to consult you about some shares he thought of purchasing, and to transact some business for him. He stays at Nepean Sea Road, and has not come to office yet, but if you take a seat, I do not think he will be many minutes now."

The broker sat down as invited on a chair by the window, while the two young men, seated at desks opposite each other, went on with their writing. Presently another visitor was announced, and in came a man, handsomely attired, and wearing most valuable jewellery. He seemed very familiar with the young men, who in turn expressed great surprise and delight at seeing him. From the conversation it appeared to the broker as if the new-comer had just arrived in Bombay from some Native State in which he held a high position. Greetings having been exchanged, the stranger produced a scroll, and unfolding it, said in a low tone of voice, but loud enough for the broker to hear.

"I have come here for your assistance in a matter which, besides being a service to me, may bring some money to you as well."

At these words both young men put down their pens, and bent earnestly over the document.

"You see here," the man continued, "is a *sanad* conferring on me certain lands and property in the State of B——. Now you read this part here, and you will see by erasing those few words, making '*twenty*' read '*one hundred and twenty*' and make '*east*' read '*north-east*,' I would become the possessor of additional land that would be worth several lakhs of rupees more to me. You will see from this plan what I mean," he added, opening another paper.

"But," said one of the brothers, "how do you expect to get possession of this property? When you claim it, the Chief will know it was never handed over to you."

"I will never claim it," replied the supposed landowner. "I have already told a certain man that I have been presented with this land and property for services rendered to the State, whereas I really own merely this small portion you see on the plan enclosed in the boundary coloured red. I have also told him I wish to go away; he has offered me a certain sum of money, and the sale is to be conducted in private, by a simple transference of the *sanad* to him. So you see without this required alteration in the document I should be unable to secure all this money that has been offered."

"It is dangerous," remarked one of the brothers.

"I admit it is risky, but it is worth the attempt; and if you could get this alteration I want effected on the deed well and neatly, I shall pay you well."

"How much?"

"I would willingly give Rs. 15,000 or Rs. 20,000 to have the job done well; but there must be no mistake, and it must be done according to a copy I will give."

The two young men thought for a few moments, and then one said to the other,

"I think we know who would do the work."

"You mean——?" asked the other brother.

"Yes!"

"But he is such an avaricious thief himself, and so cunning too. When he sees the document he will understand the value of it, and will be sure to demand an exorbitant fee for making the alteration."

"Who else can do it?"

The men remained silent for a short time, and then the brother who had been carrying on the conversation with the stranger before, addressing him once more, said: "I think we can find somebody who will do the job satisfactorily for you. Would you leave the *sanad* with us and come again to-morrow?"

The supposed landowner then asked for a picco of paper, and wrote something on it which, he said, was how he wished the paragraph that was to be altered to read. When he had gone, the two brothers began to talk over the business, saying they must keep it secret from their father who would no doubt be very angry at the swindle they were engaged in. They examined the *sanad* again, and conversed earnestly about it, having, to all appearance, entirely forgotten the presence of the broker, who began to weary at the long time he was detained. At length, determined to attract the attention of the young men, he rose from his chair, saying,

"I am afraid I cannot wait here any longer to-day. I have much business to attend to; but here is my card, and if your father will do me the honour to call on me, I am at his service."

The two young men showed, or pretended to show, some agitation.

"Stay a moment," said one to him confusedly, and then a few words were whispered hurriedly and earnestly between the two brothers.

"No doubt," said one of the young men, "you heard the conversation that took place between our visitor and us a short time ago."

"Well," replied the broker, smiling, "I could not altogether close my ears to what passed between you. A pretty little plan you have concocted between you to swindle the State of B——out of some lakhs of money. Suppose I tell your father what sort of trade you employ yourselves on?"

Those words of the broker only afforded them the opportunity of playing their parts to the greater perfection. They pretended to quake with fear, abusing themselves for their stupidity in allowing him to remain in the office while they had been talking over a matter of such importance.

"Do not, I entreat you," pleaded one of the young men, "inform our father of the conversation you have just heard. It would grieve and make him angry. Besides, it is not we who are the swindlers. We are only endeavouring to undertake a job for which we shall be well paid. Now listen to me. You have heard what has been proposed; and neither my brother nor myself wishes to treat you badly. It is only due to you, and may be some recompense to you for your time and trouble in coming here to-day. We are quite willing to share with you the profits out of this transaction."

The broker chuckled inwardly as he thought, by playing upon the young men's fears, he had forced them to make this offer.

"And so by giving me a share of this money promised to you, you imagine you would stop my mouth?"

"Nay; it is your due."

The broker fell into the well-set trap.

"Very well," he said, consenting to the proposal, "I will join you in this affair; and as I must go now, I will come back to-morrow morning to consult your father about his investment, and also learn how your transaction with the land-owner progresses."

The broker went away, thinking he had made a most excellent stroke of good luck by his journey to Walkeshwar, and was true to his appointment the next morning. He found the two brothers in their room engaged in earnest debate with another man who, the broker soon discovered, had been procured to undertake the necessary alteration in the land-owner's document. The writer had apparently been cunning enough to perceive an enormous sum of money was to be made out of the business, and was levying blackmail accordingly. He first demanded Rs. 5,000, but after much hot debate he agreed to do the work for Rs. 3,000 if paid in advance. To that the brothers agreed, and suggested that they should pay down Rs. 1,000 each, which they immediately produced, asking the broker to contribute a like amount, as he was to share in the money to be paid by the landowner. The broker readily consented, but as he had not the money with him, asked one of the young men to accompany him back to the city, when he would pay him the money. This was done, and the man pocketing the notes, amounting to Rs. 1,000, asked the broker to visit his office at Walkeshwar the next morning to meet the landowner, when the alteration of the deed would, no doubt, be completed, and he would be paid at least Rs. 5,000, as his share of the spoil, which would be a clear profit of Rs. 4,000.

Next morning he found the broker back again at Walkeshwar. The two brothers and the writer were already there, and the broker received a hearty welcome. He was shown how the alteration on the *sanad* had been carried out; and he expressed his admiration of the very neat manner in which it had been done, declaring it would be impossible to detect any erasure. They had not waited long when the landowner himself arrived, and to him the document was submitted for his approval. He looked at it, held it up to the light and frowned.

"How is this?" he asked. "It has not been altered as I directed. Here is a grievous error. You have made it read, '*south*-east' instead of '*north*-east,' which makes the deed absurd."

He also pointed out another serious error, which, he averred, completely spoilt the document.

"It is," said the writer, "according to the written instructions given me."

"That cannot be," said the landowner, indignantly; "show me the paper bearing the instructions I gave you."

"Here it is," said the writer, producing a small scrap of paper.

"What is this?" inquired the landowner. "This is not the paper I wrote."

"No," said one of the brothers, appearing confused; "I mislaid the paper you gave me, and wrote this out myself from memory."

"Ah, that accounts for the blunder," said the landowner, "and see, you have completely spoiled my deed. You must alter it again, and make it right."

"That," said the writer, "I cannot do. The paper is too thin to stand any further erasure."

"It is my mistake," said the young man, who had admitted mislaying the original paper indicating the nature of the required alterations, "and it must be rectified."

The writer on hearing this determined to levy more black-mail.

"I am willing to try, for a further sum of Rs. 2,000," he said.

"And I," said the man, "who had committed the blunder, have no more money of my own to advance. Will you," he said, addressing the landowner, "advance this Rs. 2,000 to help us out of our difficulty?"

"I will pay nothing," was the reply, "till this alteration is completed to my satisfactoin. How do I know that this writer will manage it? He may spoil the document completely; and then what am I to do?"

The broker was next appealed to, and said:

"We must not fail now in this business. I will advance you the money, on condition that I am not asked to bear a share of this additional fee to the writer."

To this both brothers gladly agreed. Again he returned to his office, and paid the Rs. 2,000 to the young man who accompanied him, and was granted an I. O. U. in exchange for it. The young man went away thanking the broker most profusely for his kindness, and inviting him back to Walkeshwar the next morning to receive payment of the money due to him.

The broker did not fail to put in an appearance the next morning, at the appointed time, when to his amazement he found the office closed. On making inquiries he discovered the owner of the bungalow, who explained that he had found the doors standing wide open that morning and the tenants gone, where, he knew not. His sole lament was that the men owed him Rs. 130 for house rent. They had left the furniture behind, but that belonged to a borah from whom it had been hired. Thus the broker was swindled out of Rs. 3,000, and from that day to this he has heard nothing of the men who led him so cleverly into the trap. He went to the police and informed them of the swindle that had been practised on him; but the thieves had got a good start; and he had no evidence but his own extraordinary tale. Besides, had the swindlers been arrested and taken to court, the dishonest part he had himself played would have told very much against him, and probably done much harm to his business. He, therefore, deemed it most prudent to pursue the case no further, and bear his loss as best as he could. His adventure would, however, no doubt teach him a lesson to be honest in his business dealings with people, for had he resisted the temptation in this instance to gain money by swindling, he would not himself have been swindled.

CHEATING WITH STOLEN PROPERTY.

There would seem to be no end to the methods of cheating practised by the professional swindlers who tour through the cities of India. There is, perhaps, no other country in the world where cheating is carried on so systematically and so cleverly as in India. They practise their swindling most daringly, and without much fear of arrest, for they know, before their victim can inform the police, and a warrant can be obtained for their apprehension, they have plenty of time to get out of the way. It is a thousand pities the police cannot, though cheating being a non-cognizable offence, go after and arrest those people at once, without the delay at present entailed in going to a magistrate, stating the case, and asking for a warrant. Another ingenious method of cheating is by means of pretended lost or stolen property which the swindlers sell, but never give up. Finding out a man of means (those fellows always take care to discover a man in good circumstances), he is approached by one of the swindling crew who confides to him in a very insinuating way that in some place up-country, some valuable property, usually of jewellery, or hidden treasure now forgotten, formerly belonging to a certain Native Chief now dead, has been discovered, and the finders are anxious to secretly dispose of it. If he could get it sold for them, they would gladly give him a large percentage on the proceeds. The dupe, taken in by a glowing account of the treasure that had been discovered, and thinking this a golden opportunity to make money, would fall into the trap, and accept an invitation to visit a certain house to see some samples of the property. The bungalow was, in a case of this sort, always situated in some lonely spot in the jungle. There he is shown some very ancient looking specimens of jewellery which convinces the man of the value of the hidden treasure. Then he is told that the property is still up-country, that they are too poor to bring it to Bombay themselves, and the man gives them some money to pay expenses, the swindlers promising to come back and inform him when the jewels, &c., had arrived. In a few days he is visited by one of the gang who tells him the property is all secure in an iron safe which is buried in the ground in the jungle. He goes that night to the same bungalow as before, whence he is taken out to a more dense part of the jungle. There are discovered a number of coolies ready for work. A pit is dug in the ground, a large, old rusty iron safe is dragged out, and lifted on to a cart ready there for the purpose, the poor dupe pays over the money agreed upon, and the cart moves on. Presently some policemen appear, and, suspicious of the movements of the party in so strange a place at such an hour, take charge of the safe, and the man, knowing that stolen property is in his possession, is glad to get away, leaving the safe and all his money behind him. Such, in brief, is the method employed ; but cheating by means of pretended lost or stolen property will be best explained by the following sensational case which actually occurred near Parel some years ago.

THE MYSTERY OF AN IRON SAFE.

One afternoon in the rainy season, some five or six years ago, a wealthy Bombay merchant was sitting in his office, when there was shown into his room a man who, from his dress, was apparently a stranger to Bombay. The man having, in answer to a query, replied that he came on important business, was offered a chair, and he soon had the merchant put in possession of all the facts, first broaching the subject with much fineness for an uneducated countryman as he appeared to be, and skilfully emphasising the points of his tale, so as to create the greatest impression. He told the tale of a certain wealthy nobleman who had died many years ago, leaving much property to his sons. All that property, however, disappeared in a most mysterious manner, and it was given out the house had been robbed. No trace of the stolen property which included rich jewellery and the most costly of precious stones could, however, be found, and suspicions arose that one of the brothers himself was the robber. If he was, he did not live long to enjoy it, for he was poisoned in as unaccountable a way as the property of the dead nobleman had vanished. Only a few weeks ago, had this man himself discovered, by mere accident, the hiding place of the lost property. He had, of course, to keep the matter very secret, if he wanted to make any gain out of it himself, for should the heirs to the property learn of the discovery, very little reward would be his.

"Now," he said, having fully related his tale, and roused to his satisfaction the interest of the merchant, "I and my friend want to dispose of this valuable property to the best advantage and as speedily as we can. We are quite strangers in Bombay, but on inquiry we thought that you, Sahib, would be the best man we could find to help us. Help us to dispose of this property, and we shall allow you a large commission. We will give you twenty-five per cent., even fifty, rather than you should decline to help us in our difficulty."

The merchant considered a little. What, he thought, if this man's tale were true, he had way to dispose of such property, and perhaps in a very profitable manner to himself.

"What," he asked his visitor, "is the value of the property?"

"That I don't know," was the reply. "We have not valued it carefully yet. There are gold belts set with large costly stones, knives with richly chased and jewelled sheaths, neck ornaments studded with diamonds and all kinds of the finest of precious stones, and some hundreds of valuable rings."

"Can you show me some first? Before making any arrangements with you, I should like to see one or two pieces."

"I have not any here, Sahib," replied the visitor. "I did not wish to carry any with me, being afraid that I might lose it; but if you could come to the bungalow at which I and my friends are staying, I could show you enough to satisfy you."

The merchant considered to himself again that the property was evidently of considerable value, and the man did not seem to have much idea as to its worth. He might succeed in making excellent terms for himself. Accordingly he said:

"Yes, if you can call for me later in the day I will go with you."

At the hour appointed the man came back, and the merchant set out with him. They drove to a bungalow situated in the jungle near Parel, and there the merchant was introduced to some other Hindus, also from their dress, apparently travellers from up-country. A box was produced, from which were taken some beautiful pieces of antique looking jewellery, set with brilliant costly stones.

"How much more jewellery of this sort is there?" asked the merchant.

"There is," said the man who first introduced himself, "hidden up-country," naming the place, "a large iron safe filled with property like this."

"Then," responded the merchant, "bring it here, and I have no doubt we will be able to get a fair price for it."

"We will," said the man, "but unfortunately our expenses for travelling and staying here have been so heavy, that we have not now the means to return and bring the safe here. If you can lend us a little money, we will bring the jewellery here at once."

"How much do you require?"

"We will want about Rs. 50."

"Is that all?" said the merchant. "That difficulty is easily got over. There is the money you need," taking from his pocket five notes for Rs. 10 each, and handing them over. "Now, when can you be back with the safe? You will, of course, bring it here to avoid suspicion by taking it through the city."

"Yes, Sahib, you are right. We will have to bring it here, and hide it in the ground till you can come for it. In four days more we will be here with the property all secure."

At the end of the four days the merchant, full of expectation, returned to Parel just at dusk, and as he drove up to the bungalow he saw two or three low caste men who had a very *jungli* appearance about them; and those, he was told by the Hindu who received him at the door, were the men who had been brought from up-country with the safe, for although he had gone to his native place by train, he had to bring the safe back by road, that method of travelling being safer. As those men had to return home, he was likewise informed about Rs. 50 would be required to send them back, which the merchant paid as before. Going in and sitting down in a room, the merchant opened the conversation by very naturally inquiring,

"Where is this safe?"

"Buried underground," was the ready reply. "You could not expect me to keep it exposed in one of those rooms. Anyone seeing it would at once guess, from its appearance, it had been a long time buried in the ground."

"How then are we to have it removed?"

"We must select a dark night for the purpose, and get a cart with two good bullocks."

"The nights are very dark just now," remarked the merchant, "and there is no moon. Suppose we suggest to-morrow night."

"And where will you carry it to?" queried the Hindu.

"I will arrange for that," said the merchant knowingly. "I will take it where the things can be disposed of easily, and without risk."

"Well," said the Hindu, "and what about the terms? If we give you custody of the property we must surely have some security."

"Granted," said the merchant readily, who was quite eager to get the contents of the safe into his own hands, "I will pay you a sum in advance before removing the safe; but you have no idea of the value of the entire amount?"

"Not of the exact value, but it must be worth some lakhs."

"And how much do you expect me to pay you as security?"

"I do not know," said the Hindu, shrugging his shoulders in the manner peculiar to the race, "how much money master can afford to pay; but perhaps a lakh———."

"A lakh of rupees!" cried the merchant in astonishment. "Pay a lakh of rupees in advance for what I have not had an opportunity of examining? Pooh! Ridiculous!"

"But you will have it all in your own possession," said the Hindu mildly.

"Of course; but I cannot give you so much as a lakh of rupees."

"Very well, what Sahib likes." Then after giving the merchant his own choice he naively suggested, "Give me half a lakh."

"Listen to me," said the merchant somewhat excitedly, as he did not want to part with such a large sum of money, nor yet lose the safe of valuable (?) jewellery; "I will pay you down in cash, before receiving charge of the safe, Rs. 10,000. As the goods are disposed of you shall have the remainder."

"Rs. 10,000," replied the man, "is very little for so much valuable jewellery."

"And you are poor men, you say. You should be very glad to get as much as Rs. 10,000, in advance, besides being relieved of all the risk of recovery."

"Very well," said the Hindu, no doubt inwardly pleased at the prospect of the Rs. 10,000, "bring the money, as you propose, to-morrow night after it is dark. I will get a bullock-cart for you, and we will hand over to you the iron safe."

Another night the merchant came to the bungalow, leaving his carriage on the road outside the jungle till his return, and was rather surprised when he arrived to find the house in darkness, not a single light burning at the windows or on the verandah. When he went up to the door, however, and called out, he was joined by one of his Hindu partners in the jewellery business, who said to him,

"We thought it better to keep the place in darkness to-night, so that anybody coming round this way may imagine we have gone away somewhere. We are ready now. The cart is standing on the road yonder, and will be called when wanted."

By this time the man was joined by two of his associates, and three or four other men dressed like labourers carrying pick-axes and spades, one having an unlit lantern. All then set off through the dark jungle which, owing to the rain which had fallen copiously during the day and the previous night, was very wet and muddy. Whether it was that the men who apparently came from the country were accustomed to making their way through jungle on a very dark and cloudy night, or that they were acquainted with the route they were now taking, they cleared their way through the shrubbery without any apparent trouble, while the merchant who had never been in such a place at such a time before stumbled in the dark over the uneven, clayey ground, splashing blindly into pools of water, knocking against tree trunks, and tearing hands and clothes with thorns, all in his anxiety to keep pace with his companions. It was a relief to him when they came to a standstill, and the Hindu who had made the bargain with the merchant, and who was apparently manager of the business, ordered the lamp to be lit. That being done, digging operations commenced, and after about half-an-hour's work the men, with much grunting and groaning, raised out of the ground a large square object which the merchant carefully examined; and sure enough he found it an old iron safe, all muddy and rusty from being to all appearance, long buried in the ground. Satisfied so far, he asked for the bullock-cart, and soon it was heard coming, rumbling through the jungle, the driver cracking his whip, and making so much noise, that the merchant said to his Hindu friend in alarm,

"Stop him coming any further, or tell him to make less noise; otherwise we shall have everybody within hearing down upon us."

"What are we to do?" the Hindu inquired. "We cannot get the safe away from here without a garry, for it is too heavy to carry far."

"Tell the man to come slowly," continued the merchant. "Tell him to be cautious, and stop his howling."

No doubt the noise was all part of the play, as well as the pretended fear that any one might see the bungalow lit up. The cart had just come to a standstill, when another man came upon the scene, calling out,

"Ho! what are you all doing on my land at this hour of night? And what is this you have got here? I will have you all arrested for trespassing."

The Hindu began apologising to the new-comer, saying he was unaware that they were on private ground. That would not, however, satisfy the man, who pretended in fact to become even more enraged.

"Shall I make a compromise?" whispered the Hindu to the merchant. "Shall I ask him how much he will take to leave us alone and keep silence about what he has seen?"

"Yes, yes," replied the merchant, who was in terror of being discovered, "make whatever terms you like; only get him away."

"Then give me your money."

"Make your terms, and I will pay."

The landlord on finding the trespassers were prepared to appease his wrath with a sop in the shape of rupees, dropped his angry tone, and became more conciliatory; though he betrayed great curiosity to know what the iron box contained

It was finally arranged that he should leave them in peace, and tell nobody of what he had seen, for the small consideration of Rs. 5,000. The merchant was horrified to find his money being thrown away in this fashion, but afraid to make any demur, he took the notes from his pocket, counted out Rs. 5,000 by the light of the lamp, and handed them over. When the land proprietor had disappeared, the merchant ordered the safe to be put upon the bullock-cart.

"No, no," said the Hindu. "The money first!" to which the merchant replied by giving over the remaining Rs. 5,000.

"Oh, no," continued the Hindu. "Our agreement was for Rs. 10,000; and you have only given me the half of that."

"But you see how I have been forced to part with Rs. 5,000. Had you told that cart-driver to be silent the proprietor of this land would not have found us out, and you would have had all your money."

"When you produce the Rs. 10,000, and not till then, the safe will be handed over to you," said the Hindu firmly.

"But I cannot get the money now? Take this, and to-morrow you will have the remainder."

"The safe will be all right here till to-morrow at this time, for the land-owner will not trouble you again."

The merchant, finding the Hindoo stubborn, could do nothing but yield. He had already parted with over Rs. 5,000, and the only way to recoup himself for his losses was to get possession of the jewellery in the safe. Accordingly next night he appeared again with the required money, and having paid it over, took charge of the safe on the bullock-cart. But his troubles were not yet over. The outskirts of the jungle were just reached when a policeman appeared, and demanded to know what was in the cart. The merchant, irritated at being so questioned, refused to give any information regarding it. The policeman, who was dressed as a havildar, then said something about a jewel robbery, remarking that he had suspicions the iron box contained the stolen property, and sounded an alarm which was promptly responded to by some sepoys. The merchant on being informed he was arrested on suspicion, resented it, and used his fist to some effect, knocking the sepoys down one after the other. Then he ran off along the road in the direction where his carriage was standing, leaped up, took the reins from his sleepy driver, lashed up his horses, and fled home at full speed. He had lost Rs. 15,000, besides the other small amounts he had paid at the commencement of the transaction; but he preferred to lose that money, large as the sum was, to being accused of having in his possession stolen jewellery, and perhaps figuring in court as well for having assaulted the police.

BREAK-UP OF THE IRON SAFE GANG.

It must not be imagined, from the stories of cheating and swindling that have been narrated in which people have been represented as losing, beyond recovery, money amounting to thousands of rupees, that the police are never able to put their hands on these gangs, and bring them to justice. It was not long after the events narrated in the tale of the iron safe mystery, that the same band of swindlers who robbed the merchant of over Rs. 15,000 was caught and broken up by Sardar Mir Abdul Ali, Khan Bahadur, Chief of the Bombay Detective Department.

One day a Hindu, the same old rascal, no doubt, as called upon the merchant of the iron safe mystery, visited a Brahmin occupying a prominent position in Bombay, and presented to him a letter of introduction, purporting to be from a friend up-country. He then told him a tale of a hidden treasure. The prime-minister of a certain Native Chief, he said, had died, and the deceased minister's relatives, one of whom he (the Hindu) professed to be fearing that his property would be appropriated by the prince, had buried all his moveable effects of value and jewellery in the jungle, while they sought for purchasers.

"Your friend," he said in conclusion, "who gave me this letter of introduction to you, told me he knew of no one in Bombay who would be more pleased, or who was better able to assist me in the disposal of this jewellery."

This was quite right. The Brahmin was, indeed, a man who, though not a jeweller himself, was connected in such a way in his business that nothing would be simpler for him than the disposal of such a property as was mentioned. Accordingly he said to his visitor, after re-perusing his friend's letter :

"Well, if you show me this jewellery, I might try to dispose of it ;" and then, perhaps to impress the Hindu with the idea that it would be a great sacrifice to him to devote his time to it, he added, "Of course, you must know, I am not in this line of business now, and have not the same opportunities as I had formerly, but I know many people in the trade, and I would not like to disappoint my friend who writes to me. I will therefore do what I can."

"You do me too much kindness," exclaimed the Hindu with seeming gratitude, "but I wish to recompense you for your services, so that whatever time you devote to assisting me in what I have come to Bombay for, you will not quite consider it time thrown away. Whatever the property is sold for, I am quite willing to give you 25 per cent. or even more, if you will only help me out of my difficulty."

So the conversation went on, and in the same way as the merchant, the Brahmin was taken to a bungalow, where he was shown some jewellery worth Rs. 5,000 or Rs. 6,000, such as is worn by Native Chiefs and their ladies.

"Is this all the property?" the Brahmin asked, after having examined it carefully and satisfied himself as to its genuineness.

"No," replied the other. "This was only brought here as a sample. The remainder was left behind in the meantime, while we arranged for its sale."

Then the same old tale was told, that they were too poor to go home and bring the old safe with the jewellery to Bombay, and the Brahmin was constrained to pay about Rs. 50 to defray the expenses of removing the valuables to Bombay. Then he left, the Hindu promising to call for him in the course of a week, and arrange for the disposal of the property.

As the Brahmin was returning home, the same idea passed through his brain as occurred to the merchant's mind. He considered how he might get all the jewellery into his own possession, so that he might be able to dispose of it with better advantage to himself. Why might he not have the safe removed under cover of night to his own bungalow ? He never conceived for a moment that by that means he would be playing into the hands of the swindlers, that that, infact, was the proposal they wished to make themselves. Accordingly, at the end of a week, when the Hindu re-appeared, and the Brahmin suggested the removal of the safe to his bungalow, the former made the most extravagant demonstrations of delight, saying,

"Yes, yes ; we are so afraid of being found out by our Chief that we will be very glad to get it out of our hands ; and it will be better with you than where it is."

"Where have you got it now ?"

"Buried in the jungle."

"Can we remove it to-night ?"

"The day is late now, and I would require to go home, inform my brothers that the treasure was to be removed to-night, hire labourers to uncover it and lift it out of the ground, and procure a strong cart with good bullocks."

Wily scoundrel that he was, he had certainly preparations to make, but not those, and it was only to gain time that he proposed the following evening. However, the Brahmin acquiesced, and then it was arranged that for getting the property into is own custody, the Brahmin should pay, immediately on the safe being unearthed and placed on the bullock-cart, Rs. 3,000 as security. It was with much trouble, and after a considerable amount of debate that the Brahmin succeeded in getting the promise of the safe for so small a sum. The Hindu wanted a lakh of rupees to begin with ; but no doubt when he saw, as he fancied, even Rs. 3,000 within his grasp, he thought it too good a chance to throw away, and when the Brahmin showing some heat, said, "You ought to feel very happy, even at the expense of a heavy commission, to find a man ready to undertake so great a risk for you; you should be glad to be relieved of the burden, without demanding any security at all; but as I am to be a participator in the sale, and as I have already seen part of the property, I am willing to pay you all I can afford, namely Rs. 3,000; if you do not agree to these terms, there the transaction must end;" the Hindu gave in.

At dusk the following evening the Hindu re-appeared ready to take his dupe to where the treasure was to be unearthed. They drove out to Matoonga, and descending from the garry, the Brahmin was taken to a lonely spot in the jungle, near the Hindu temple there, where he found a number of men congregated, some standing, some squatting on the ground. In front of him was a dark, deep hole, out of which the men, to all appearance hired labourers, drew an old, rusty, heavy iron safe, at the command of the Hindu. The unearthing of the safe was of course the signal for the landowner to appear as before, but here the story loses all semblance to that related before. The Hindu having managed to soothe the land-proprietor's wrath, offered to pay him Rs. 2,000 to leave them alone, and tell no one of what he had seen. The man agreeing, the Hindu whispered to his intended victim,

"Pay him Rs. 2,000 and let him go."

"No," replied the Brahmin, "with none of my money will I part, until I have the safe secure in my possession. If you have been foolish enough to offer him Rs. 2,000, pay it yourself."

"But I have no money."

"Why then," said the Brahmin again, loud enough for the pretended land-proprietor to hear, "did you tell the fellow you would pay the enormous sum of Rs. 2,000, merely for the sake of getting him to go away and leave us to ourselves, when a mild thrashing with our sticks would have secured the same end?"

"Sh!" hissed the Hindu, pretending to be alarmed at the Brahmin's threatening attitude. "Do not let the man hear you speak like that, or it will be bad for us. You have Rs. 3,000. Better for us to let him have Rs. 2,000 than allow an alarm to be raised by the landlord of this ground and have ourselves arrested for trespassing. The safe would be taken in charge by the police, and we would all be ruined. Pay him the Rs. 2,000 and let him go."

"I do not believe," said the Brahmin, "this man is proprietor of the land at all. He is some impudent jungliwalla who is trying to impose on us. I will show you as effectual a means of getting rid of him as consenting to pay him his black-mail;" and raising a thick stick he carried in his hand, he advanced with the intention of laying it about the pretended landowner's shoulders. Seeing this, the latter turned and fled, calling "police, police," and soon the Brahmin found himself in the grasp of a couple of yellow-turbaned sepoys. He laid about him vigorously, and the blows that fell upon his would-be captors were not at all light, and made them howl lustily. Just when victory rested with the Brahmin, the two sepoys were joined by another couple of their brethren, very much to the Brahmin's surprise, as he wondered how they had come there, such an out-of-the-way place as it was, far from the ordinary haunts of men. Had he looked at them carefully, he would have perceived those men were only sham sepoys, members, indeed, of the swindling gang. But he paid no attention to any defects in their dress, and continued the struggle against the heavy odds, calling upon his Hindu friend to assist him, but he of course would not, pretending to be afraid to attack a police sepoy. In the struggle the notes, which the Brahmin had refused to give up, were stolen from him; but assistance was at hand in a shape that none of them anticipated. Real police suddenly put in an appearance with Sardar Mir Abdul Ali, Khan Bahadur, the Chief of the Detectives, at their head.

There was no fighting with them, for they very soon had all the swindlers handcuffed together. It would appear that one of the gang had fallen out with his confederates regarding some spoil, and determined on revenge, he informed the police of the plot to cheat the Brahmin. Had the swindle been successful, the Brahmin on getting home the safe would have got a surprise, for on being opened it was found to contain nothing but stones and mud. The end was that the swindlers were all committed to the Criminal Sessions and sentenced to long terms of imprisonment.

CHEATING BY ALCHEMY.

There is a common belief amongst Asiatics, Indians especially, that to certain fakirs, viragis, and other recognised holy men, is commuted the power from their gods to change the baser metals into gold and silver, for the purpose of working good amongst unfortunate beings who come to them for help ; and there are certain swindlers, who play the parts of those supposed inspired priests, with the view of getting credulous persons into their toils, and robbing them of large sums of money, which, strange to say, is frequently done. The general belief is that those real fakirs, or viragis as they are termed, use, in transforming copper and quicksilver into gold and silver, the ashes of a certain herb, called *aksir*, and oil of red sulphur ; but the swindlers, to carry out their deception, procure the entrails of a fawn or goat, into which they insert some gold or silver filings, and these entrails being dried in such fashion to resemble tree roots, are passed off by them as the sacred aksir. Having so prepared themselves for business, they, disguised as religious mendicants, repair to a town or village, and take up their abode in some ruined or unfrequented temple, mosque, or shrine. The appearance of strange holy men in their midst creates, as a matter of course, considerable curiosity amongst the villagers or townspeople, who flock in crowds to see the priests and secure their blessings. The impostors then take good care to let their visitors understand that they have not come amongst them for the purpose of begging money of them, but that all they want is a little food sufficient to keep them in existence. Then some of the followers of the chief priest, or to put it more correctly, the head of the gang of swindlers, circulate the astounding report amongst the people, that he, by reason of the holy life he has led, the penances and sufferings he has undergone through his devotion to his holy duties, has been gifted with the wondrous power of changing copper into gold, and baser metals into silver. They bide their time until they secure a man of wealth, or at least a man who, they know, has got a few thousands of rupees he can call his own. To him the fakir promises to teach the wonderful art he knows, and to gain his confidence, he substitutes, while pretending to go through the necessary ceremony, by means of simple sleight-of-hand trickery, a gold coin for a copper piece. After that he usually finds it a simple matter to rob his dupe of a considerable amount of money and disappears. Another method is to mix with cow-dung some gold or silver filings, and pile that over a crucible in which is placed some quicksilver. When a fire is lit and the cowdung fuel is consumed, the gold or silver melts and runs into the crucible from which, by the heat, the quicksilver evaporates, and the credulous dupe, naturally imagining the precious metal has been produced by the power of the fakir, is ready to pay any sum of money to learn the secret. This is known as cheating by alchemy, and it cannot be better or more fully explained than by the narrating of certain cases of this method of swindling which have actually occurred.

THE ADVENTURES OF A FAKIR.

At Khadak, in Bombay, there lived, not long ago, a mulla, or Mahomedan priest and school-master. Being a priest, he was, of course, in regular receipt of alms from people who came to him for his blessing, while his wife went about visiting Mahomedan ladies, who kept her well supplied with cast-off clothes and food. Being a very mean man, the mulla and family were accustomed to live off the food supplied to them in charity; none of the money he got, or made by tuition, would be spent on the necessaries of life. Living so frugally, the mulla in time amassed a considerable fortune, and, at the time the incident we propose narrating occurred, was the possessor of three houses in Bombay, worth about Rs. 20,000, while jewellery and other property he had of about Rs. 5,000 in value. Yet not one pie was he ever known to give away himself in charity. For his avarice he was severely punished. A gang of swindlers found him out, and playing upon his greed for gold, robbed him most unmercifully.

The mulla was in the habit of calling regularly at a certain coffee-house, where, being a priest, he was always entertained to supper by any of his own creed who might be there. One night he was accosted by two munshi brothers in the coffee-house, and invited to partake of supper with them. The mulla accepted of course, and bestowing his blessing on the two munshis, was asked to join them another night. The mulla was treated to such excellent dishes that he went, night after night, to the coffee-house to meet his new-found benefactors; and soon the trio became very good friends. They had known each other about a week, when the munshi brothers invited the priestly-schoolmaster to visit them at the shrine of Saint Mama Hajani, near Worli, and afterwards dine with them. The mulla, who was as gluttonous as he was avaricious, suspecting no evil, eagerly accepted. He met the two men at the shrine as appointed, and after prayers the three went for a walk over the hill.

Suddenly they came upon an aged Mahomedan sage, kneeling upon a deer skin that was spread upon the ground, and earnestly praying while he turned the beads of his rosary. The three drew back so as not to disturb the venerable priest, though the mulla asked,

"Who is this holy man? I have never seen him before."

"No, but you must have heard of him," said one of the munshis. "He is a very great man, and I have been informed he possesses the gift of being able to make gold and silver out of nothing."

"By what name is he called?" asked the mulla eagerly.

"I do not know," was the reply; "but why do you, being yourself a mulla, not speak with him?"

"I have heard," said the priest, "of saints of our race who by reason of their religious lives, have had bestowed on them, by divine power, the secret of converting metals of little value into gold and silver, but never out of nothing."

"No doubt," said one of the cunning munshis, "that is the power this holy man possesses. I may have been mistaken, and exaggerated his power."

"When did he come here, and where does he reside?" asked the mulla.

"I do not know that. He has undoubtedly come on a visit to the Saint Mama Hajani's shrine, and will, I suppose, only remain here a few days."

The sage, having concluded his prayer, looked up, and perceiving his visitors, said,

"Sit down, children;" and entering into a conversation with the men, pretended to be much pleased with the devoutness of the mulla. At length, pointing to a rudely-shaped head of a hookah, which lay on the ground in front of him, he said to the mulla,

"Will you, friend, take up that chilum, and prepare it for me."

The mulla having done as desired, the sage added:

"I had a vision in which the great Prophet Mahomet appeared to me, and told me my days on earth were drawing to a close. He directed me to journey hither, and await, near the shrine of the revered Mama Hajani, the visit of a priest of our creed, to whom he directed me to reveal the wonderful secret I possess. Something within my soul tells me you are that priest for whom I have been waiting; and I am now about to put you to the test. Have you a small copper coin with you?"

The mulla fumbled in his pouch, and drew forth a quarter-anna piece.

"Now," said the aged priest, "take the chilum, and put it in the hole in place of a pebble."

It should here be explained that in smoking a chilum without a pipe, natives are accustomed to partly stop up the hole with a pebble to prevent the tobacco running out. The mulla, therefore, understood what he was asked to do with the pice, and put it in the hole as directed.

"Now," continued the sage, "here is some aksir," handing over a small piece of dirty looking substance like a charred root and tobacco leaf. "This aksir has the power, if properly applied, and if used in a good cause, of converting copper into gold. Press this aksir and tobacco into the chilum on the top of the pice, and then give it to me to smoke."

The mulla again did as he was directed, and the sage smoked on for a time in silence. Then shaking out the ashes from the chilum out dropped a bright gold coin.

"Ah," said the old man, smiling, "I was right. You are the priest ordained by the Great Prophet to succeed me in working much good for the benefit of mankind. The success of this experiment tells me you are the man to whom I am to impart this great secret. But I cannot to-day, for my hour of prayer again approaches. Take this gold coin with you, for I, who have discarded all affairs of this world, and to whom riches are useless, have no need of it. Go now, and come again."

The mulla went home inflated with joy at the thought of the good fortune that was about to come to him. He believed in the power of the supposed holy man he had met; for, had he not seen him, before his very eyes, convert a worthless copper coin into a valuable gold? Yet, doubting, he went to a goldsmith, and had the gold tested, when it was declared to be "one hundred touch," the purest of the precious metal. At that rate, therefore, he sold it, and returned to his dwelling still more rejoiced. He passed a sleepless night, imagining to himself—poor, deluded, foolish man—the maunds of copper he would purchase, which, when possessed of the secret, he would convert into so much gold. In a short time he would become fabulously rich, and be the envy of the world.

Next day he sought out the munshi brothers, and wanted them to accompany him at once on another visit to the old priest by the shrine of Mama Hajani; but in order to work the mulla up to a still greater pitch of excitement, and get him more within their power, they said that was a day on which the sage devoted himself to worship, and could see no one. So they appointed the following day for the second visit, and took with them flowers and sweetmeats as an offering to the old priest. The same trick was repeated, and the mulla carried away with him another gold coin, the priest saying to him before he departed,

"I have had another vision since last you were here, in which our Great Prophet Mahomed appeared to me much pleased with the result of my mission, and himself appointed next Thursday, which is our most sacred day, for me to impart to you the secret I possess."

The three men salaamed lowly to the old sage and departed. On their return to the mulla's house, one of the munshis said to their victim:

"You are, friend, a fortunate man; and we, who have been the means of bringing you to the old priest, will expect to profit by your good fortune."

The avaricious mulla, or school-master, grew somewhat alarmed at this, and tried to evade giving a direct reply by saying,

"I have yet profited nothing by the holy father's secret."

"But he has promised," the wily munshi continued, "on Thursday next to teach you the wonderful art, by which you will be able to convert copper into gold. Surely you will not refuse to us, who have been your benefactors, a share in the riches that will come to you."

The mulla appearing to demur, the munshi added with a show of severity,

"Unless you promise that we shall share equally with you in this transaction, we will tell the sage you are an impostor, and in his alarm he will leave Bombay, and appear to you no more."

This threat had the desired effect on the avaricious mulla, who, rather than risk losing the fortune he thought was near his grasp, agreed to the terms forced on him.

Thursday came, and back they all journeyed to the rude abode of the Mahomedan sage.

"You have returned, my friends," the old man said, "and I wish you well. Unfortunately I find my supply of aksir, which I require for further experiment, is nearly spent. The plant, from which the aksir is made, only grows at the beginning of the monsoon, which luckily is near at hand. Till then, however, I must have a suitable place to dwell in, and I beg, friend mulla, that as it is for your sake I have been so divinely inspired, you will carry me to your own dwelling, and lodge me there till the time comes for the carrying out of my commission."

Now, the taking of a guest to dwell with him meant much expense to the mulla, for he would require to provide his priestly lodger with the best dishes he could procure; yet that, strange to say, did not concern the mulla, miser though he was. He was rather rejoiced at the prospect of entertaining his holy guest; and in an impulse, inspired by the thought of the riches he imagined were in store for him, he begged his munshi friends to come also and make his house their home.

Several days went quietly by, till one afternoon, while the sage was sitting at the door of the house talking with his host and smoking a hookah, an old man resting on the shoulder of a youth passed. The young man stopped and cried out excitedly to the older,

"Look, father, look! Here is the holy fakir we are in quest of," and the old man looking up apparently with much surprise and joy, salaamed, and cried, addressing the sage,

"O great, and good, and holy man! At length I am rewarded in finding you after a weary search. O good benefactor! Extend again to me your divine assistance. The Rs. 4,000 you gave me to provide for the marriage of my daughters are spent, and I am now in much distress, wanting Rs. 2,000 more to marry another son and daughter. Extend to me once more your help and blessing, and to you, O holy father, I will be for ever grateful. I do not know where to go to, and as I have been wandering about for full three months in search of you, I trust you will not send me away disappointed."

Now began the drain on the mulla's store of money.

"Had I but the required quantity of aksir," said the sage to his host, "I would soon procure for this poor man the money he requires, but do you give him this sum of Rs. 2,000 and send him away. It is but a trifle to you, for whom great wealth is in store."

"I have not now so much money by me," said the mulla, with a melancholy look on his face. "To procure it, I will require to dispose of some of my jewellery on which I set much store."

"Then sell them at once," responded the aged priest. "The divine command has been given to me that I must never send away a man of my own creed when he comes to me in distress, nor to you will I ever be able to impart my secret for procuring riches, if you ever hesitate to obey my orders in relieving the distress of the poor. That, friend mulla, as I have before told you, is one of the conditions of the divine contract."

The mulla, fearing to offend his priestly guest, and imagining he would soon become possessed of more gold than he would ever require for his own uses, however luxuriously he might live, went off to find his jewels, which he disposed of for a roll of currency notes, and returning, handed them over to the old man who had come begging from the Mahomedan sage.

Another day the fakir took the mulla back to the shrine of Mama Hajani to worship, and while there an old woman appeared, who, falling down on her face in front of the sage, cried out,

"O holy father, I am rejoiced to see you. My husband and son have died, leaving me in poverty with four little children to support. I have been told of your great name and reputation for relieving the poor and distressed; and I am now before you beseeching your help."

The fakir having questioned the woman as to her requirements turned to his host, the mulla, and said:

"You will, my friend, require to bring to this poor woman Rs. 1,500, and Rs. 200 in addition for road expenses. Until her wants are satisfied I cannot leave this place. Go, I will await your return."

The mulla, afraid, after the money he had already parted with, to lose the fakir, and with him the valuable secret he expected to become the possessor of, hurried home, with all speed, for the required Rs. 1,700, and returning, paid it over to the poor woman. Rs. 3,700, besides the extra expense incurred by keeping three guests in his house had now gone, and the more he paid, strange to say, the more readily he parted with more money, afraid lest he migth offend the fakir, and so lose all chance of recovering the money he had paid in charity for the old priest. By such means the mulla was induced to part with a further some of Rs. 2,000; and then the time they were so anxiously waiting for, the bursting of the monsoon, came, when they were to set off on their journey in quest of that rare plant, from the roots of which the aksir was made, but the wonderful adventures met with on that journey are related in the following chapter:

AN UNHAPPY PILGRIMAGE.

THE clouds that had been looming ominously over the city for several days at length broke; the rain came down in a deluge, and the joy of the mulla knew no bounds, for the bursting of the monsoon marked the time when he, with the Mahomedan sage, and his two munshi friends, were to set out on their pilgrimage in quest of the wonderful plant by which they would be able to convert copper and other baser metals into gold and silver. The day was at length fixed for their daparture, and one morning the four men took train, at the mulla's expense, to Kalyan, whence they started on foot for a hill known as Haji Malang's mountain. Having ascended a little way the sage remarked, looking round about him, "Now we are near the spot where the *aksir* plant is found;" but he had no sooner spoken than the monotonous murmuring sound as of some one reciting or praying fell upon their ears, whereupon the mulla's holy friend gave evidences of alarm. He strode rapidly around a rock which hid the speaker from him, the mulla and the munshi brothers following, and there upon the ground in an attitude of prayer was a venerable looking man with a long flowing white beard. He perceived the four men, who thus broke upon his devotional exercises immediately upon their appearance, and rising with apparent difficulty to his feet, as if he were feeble with age, advanced a few paces towards the fakir with a tottering gait, and casting a severe look upon him said :

"Dog! What do you come here for with followers such as these? Would you betray the secret that has been reposed in you to miserable mortal such as these?"

"Nay, father," replied the fakir bowing reverentially, "you are mistaken in me. I have had it revealed to me in a vision that my days are numbered, and that to this holy man, the mulla here, I am to consign the secret for the good of suffering mankind."

"You lie," said the venerable one still more severely. "Your face, your stammering words betray you. But listen. None of the herb you have come for shall be yours, and as I, through the Prophet Mahomet, gave to you the power of converting metals of little value into rich gold, so do I take it away. In your hands the *aksir* shall henceforth be as useless clay."

The fakir, on hearing this, put off his respectful demeanour and showed a defiant attitude.

"You have no power to do that," he said; "and I shall not leave here without the wherewithal to make *aksir*."

"And I," said the old man, "say that you shall not. I would defend the holy plant from the foul fingers of such as you with my very life. Attempt but to touch one of the herbs that grow about here, and I shall call upon Heaven to send its fire to blast you where you stand;" and as if to accentuate the threat, a distant peal of thunder was heard rumbling amongst the surrounding hills. "Listen; take that warning; depart, and repent before it is too late."

The fakir only laughed derisively as he added:

"You, father, take warning from me. Interfere with me in what I do, and your white hairs shall be no protection to you.

Turning his back, he advanced towards a clump of peculiar looking plants that stood out from the grass, and commenced pulling them up by the roots.

"Heaven give me strenght to punish this man," murmured the white-bearded priest, as he threw his cloak from off his shoulders. The fakir was surprised to see him draw his bent form up to its full height, displaying a figure above the average height, and breadth of chest, and showing arms unwithered by age, but muscular and well developed. Muttering some further words that could not be distinguished, he sprang upon the fakir and seized him round the waist with a clasp so powerful that caused him—to all appearance—considerable surprise. The fakir dropped the leaves he held in his hand, and grappled with his adversary ; but the saintly one was either not so old as he appeared to be, or possessed of strength beyond his years, for the fakir was in his hands almost as a child in the grip of a giant. He half-carried, half-dragged the fakir several yards from the plant he had been uprooting, and throwing him on the ground, sent him rolling down the hill, calling after him that if he again came near the Haji Malang's Mountain, he and his party would be stricken down by thunderbolts, burnt up with fire, or tortured in some other terrible fashion.

The mulla, as may be imagined, lost no time in reaching the side of the fallen fakir, though he was more concerned at the disastrous end of the expedition after his heavy outlay, than for the safety of the fakir as his exclamation showed.

" O good father ! " he cried, " how are we to obtain those precious herbs ?"

"We will think of that hereafter," said the fakir with a groan, as if suffering pain from his overthrow. " Help me to my feet. I am hurt."

" Are we to have no *aksir*," the mulla went on excitedly as he assisted the fakir to his feet, " no gold, after I have spent in charity and in preparation rupees amounting to close on ten thousand ? Why would the old saint not allow you to take away the plant you wanted ?"

" Because, my son, as you saw," was the reply, " the saint came before me, and was already in possession of the plant, and being more powerful than I, he overcame me. But do not fear ; all is not lost. We will return home now, for I am not fit to-day to continue the search."

"Why," said one of the munshis putting on a bold air, " could not our friend the mulla and my brother return and take the plant from the old man by force? But the mulla, who had heard, and could not forget so quickly, the threat of death by thunderbolts and fire, did they dare return, expressed the utmost terror at the mere suggestion, and they all, the unfortunate mulla looking much more dejected than the others, returned to Bombay.

A day or two went past, until the mulla, recovering from his fear, began to grow impatient again for the revealing of the secret. He did not yet begin to doubt the fakir's power, as subsequent events will show, but he begrudged his guests their food and lodging. He accordingly renewed the subject one morning to the sage, who naturally expecting inquiries from his host about the matter, and being accordingly prepared with a reply, said:

"The time is near when I must go on a pilgrimage to the shrine at Dhatar in Kathiawar; but before I depart I will make, or show you how you may make, one hundred maunds of gold in the meantime, and next year when the proper time comes, we will go to another mountain where the *aksir* herb is to be found. In the meantime do you go into the bazar and search for copper of Damascus; bring as much as you can get or can afford to buy away with you, and I will show you something that will make you wonder."

The mulla, still unsuspecting, incredible though it may seem, set out with the two munshis in search of the wonderful copper of Damascus, the mulla taking with him the last of the money left out of the sum he had obtained from the safe of one of his houses, which it should have been mentioned before, he had to dispose off in addition to the jewellery, to meet the heavy expenditure.

All day they wandered through the streets of Bombay, searching without success for Damascus copper. At last they entered the shop of a smith, who appeared remarkably startled when he heard that valuable copper inquired for.

"Why do you want it? What do you mean to do with it? Do you know its value?"

"We are," said one of the munshis, "aware of nothing concerning the copper, nor its value. It is not for ourselves we desire to procure it," and he added hesitatingly, "but for a friend."

"Strange, very strange!" said the smith, continuing to eye his customers curiously. "For over fifty years has this copper of Damascus been in the possession of our family, and no one has ever asked for it. No one would buy it, unless he knew how to use it, for it is of greater value than gold."

"Then," said the mulla eagerly, "what is your price? Show the copper, assure me of its genuineness, and let us strike a bargain."

"No," said the smith, "until you tell me for whom you want it, I will not part with it."

The mulla was about to add something, when a sign from the munshi brothers warned him to confess nothing, and he was silent, upon which the smith waxing more eager, exclaimed,

"Show me the wonderful man who knows the power of this copper of Damascus, who knows to what use to put it, and who discovered it was in my possession. Take me to him, and you shall have as much of the copper as you want for nothing." "No?" he inquired, as the men still hesitated. "Then I shall require to charge you at the very least the same price per tola as gold, for though I do not myself know the secret, yet I do know that by it gold can be made."

For a long time the mulla and the smith argued about the price, but not by one pie would the latter reduce the sum he asked, and the mulla, angry and disappointed, turn away and went home. When the sage heard what the smith had said, and that he had betrayed such anxiety to discover who knew the secret of the Damascus copper's power, he called out in apparent alarm,

" Do not, in name of the Prophet Mohamed and all his saints, allow that man to come here. He would spread my name throughout the city, and I would require to flee. Rather pay him the price he asks, and bring the copper home yourself."

" But he demands the same price for it as if it were gold," said the mulla. Why should I buy his copper, when for the same sum I could buy the same amount of gold without all the trouble of making it?"

" Ah, my son," said the fakir, " you do not understand. Did not the smith say it was more valuable than gold? He said true; for with that copper, and a solution made from a small quantity of gold can convert any baser metal into pure gold."

A large quantity of copper was accordinly bought by the credulous mulla at a most extravagant price, which, when the fakir observed, he said:

" Now we have only to get a plant—not the one from which the *aksir* is made, but another—the juice of which is required to make the lotion I spoke of. I have told you of my pilgrimage to Dhatar. It is there that the plant is to be found; you shall accompany me, and we will bring it back together. There shall be no troublesome brother to interfere with us there."

The mulla, afraid to show any sign of disquietude at the fakir's departure on a long journey, loath at the same time to lose sight of him for so long a time as a journey into Kathiawar on a pilgrimage and back would entail, readily agreed to accompany the fakir thither. Fearing that the mulla might be beginning to lose confidence in him through all this delay, he produced, the night before his journey, a piece of *aksir*, and said to the mulla,

"You see this? This is the last piece of *aksir* I have. I kept it because I did not wish to be without at least a small piece. In two days, however, we shall have it in our possession a valuable plant, the juice of which, when distilled, will be even more wonderful in its results than the *aksir*. Now with this I mean to produce as much gold as will provide the expenses of our journey."

He was as good as his word. He borrowed some quarter-anna pieces from the mulla as he did when first they met by Mama Hajani's shrine, and putting them into his chilum began smoking, after which he produced, by the same sleight-of-hand trickery as before, several genuine gold pieces, which restored the mulla's confidence in the fakir, convincing him that he had not yet lost his power, and the poor, credulous dupe was more elated than ever, and ready, when an old man visited the fakir shortly after, entreating help in his distress to pay him the sum he wanted—Rs. 4,000. At length they reached Dhatar, and of course a series of similar performances took place there, many poor people coming to the fakir for help, and the mulla having to find the money, till he had parted with the last of the Rs. 5,000 he had carried with him. Such credulousness, such absurd stupidity in a man, can hardly be believed, but worse was to follow. They took a walk into a jungle one morning, and there the fakir, muttering prayers and incantations as he moved about, gathered a large quantity of leaves which, he said, were of the wonderful plant from which was distilled the magic lotion.

Returning to Bombay, the actions of the fakir became very mysterious. He ordered the windows of his room to be darkened, and shut himself up therein for a whole day and night. The morning after their return, he called the mulla to him and said :

" Now, for the last time, you are required to lay out a large sum of money. I have the plant distilled successfully, and now, to work in conjunction with the copper you bought, we must have one hundred tolas of pure gold."

" One hundred tolas ! " exclaimed the mulla in amazement. " I have not so much money in my possession, I have already sold two houses, and one only remains."

" Foolish man," said the holy man sternly, " would you ruin all when fortune is within your grasp, when you will soon be in possession of that which could purchase for you whole villages, that which will make you a great benefactor of mankind, sought after and blessed by all ? Go ; sell your remaining house with all speed, and bring the hundred tolas of gold. "

Only day sufficed to get the house disposed of, because the mulla, afraid to offend the fakir by making him wait, offered his house at a cheap price, sold it much under its value, but got sufficient to buy the required quantity of gold, which he bought and placed before the fakir in his darkened room, a single cocoanut oil *buttee* giving all the light there was.

Then began the ridiculous part of the swindle. The gold was ground into dust, and put into a mortar, a yellow liquid, which the fakir said he had extracted from the plants they had brought from Kathiawar, being poured upon it.

" Now," said the sage, beginning to stir up the mixture with what appeared to be a steel bar, " we have rather a tedious operation before us. Seven days does it take to make this solution, and for those seven days we must contiuue stirring, and never stop, else will the spell be broken. We will all take our turns, and relieve each other at the work. I will go on now for four hours, at the end of which one of you will relieve me.

The mulla and the munshi brothers departed, leaving the old fakir stirring as for dear life. One of the munshis volunteered next, and then came the mulla's turn. He went in, and placing the little clock in front of him so as to watch how time progressed, began to stir. It was eight o'clock; at midnight he would be relieved. He seized the piston and stirred vigorously, determined that if the spell did not work it should not be for want of stirring. But he was surprised how soon he began to feel tired. Before half-an-hour had passed he found himself changing from hand to hand, and in an hour both arms were aching severely. At the end of the second hour he felt sick and almost exhausted, but still he toiled on. In another hour his stirring was very feeble, and yet he dared not stop. As it drew near the time for his being relieved, he felt as if inspired with fresh strength. He thought if he could only get this turn strough successfully, he would propose they should each take an hour at a time, which would not be so great a labour. The hour was approaching, his breath came quick with expectation. How he had got through that awful four hours he knew not, but his relief was nigh. The handles of the little clock pointed to XII., he could hear a distant bell chiming the midnight hour. He listened, but as the last stroke died away, all was silent. He strained his ears; but there was not a sound. He had struggled through his four hours at the piston heroically; the time had come for his relief, but no fakir or munshi appeared. They must have fallen asleep. How long they would remain slumbering, unconscious of the agony he was suffering, he knew not. How could he find them out and rouse them? He could not stop his stirring, for ruin was the penalty. He called out; there was no reply. He called again louder, the result was the same. One o'clock! His arms were limp and almost useless, his cramped fingers were closed upon the piston and would not open; his agony was intense, and was increasing every moment; a cold, numb sensation crept up his limbs, he felt sick; once more he tried to call, but his tongue was silent; the piston slipped from his fingers, firmly as they held it, and——

He awoke to find the munshi brothers shaking him, and bathing his forehead with vinegar. When he had sufficiently recovered to remember what had happened, he struggled to his feet and looked for the mortar. There it stood; no one stirring it.

"Where is the priest?" he called.

"I do not know," said one of the munshis. "When he found you asleep here, he grew very angry, and went away. You may never expect to see him again."

The mulla, on hearing this awful piece of news, was like one distracted. He seized the bowl, poured out the contents, and found that brass had been substituted for the gold filings, whereupon the munshi brothers pretended to be as concerned as the mulla himself, and swore by all the saints whose names they could call to memory at the time, to find the fakir and make him suffer for the ruin he had wrought on the poor mulla.

Day after day they searched for the runaway fakir but nowhere could he be found, and at last the poor school-master priest, or mulla, as we have been calling him, robbed of all his jewellery, houses, and all the property he possessed, was reduced to the lowest depths of poverty. One day one of the munshi brothers, in pretended pity, gave the mulla a few rupees to go out and purchase provisions for them all.

He went to the bazar, not noticing that he was closely followed by the scoundrel who had given him the money. He had no sooner entered a shop, than the munshi accosted a man who was also on the point of entering the same place, and pointing to the mulla in the shop said :

" See that man ; he is a counterfeit coiner. Go and warn the shopman." Then he disappeared into a gully to watch the result. The mulla was accused, very much to his astonishment, he was still more astounded when the coin was found to be really bad. The police were called and poor mulla was taken off to chowkey, where, on being searched, several more counterfeit rupees were found in his possession. His house was searched, and appliances used in the coining of counterfeit money were found in one of the rooms. He was tried, and sentenced to a long term of imprisonment. He suffered for his folly, while the swindlers escaped, and were never found. It was after his release that he made public his sorrowful tale, but it was too late then to do anything.

There was no doubt that all the mendicants who came begging from the fakir, the old saint on Haji Malang's mountain who threw his brother down the hill, and even the smith in the bazar who sold the copper of Damascus, were all accomplices ; and there was no doubt either that it was the munshi brothers who put the coining apparatus in the mulla's house, so as to have guilt thrown upon him, while they had time to escape. The mulla was foolish, but he suffered severely for his folly.

A PRINCE AMONG THIEVES.

It may be seldom that a dupe's ruin is so thoroughly effected as was of the avaricious mulla, who was robbed of all he possessed, and thrown into prison to suffer for an offence he never committed; but cheating by alchemy, as it is termed, is commonly practised. It is, too, often successful, and that is due to the implicit trust reposed in saints and fakirs, so that when an impostor appears, if he plays his part well, he generally concludes the game a winner. But it sometimes happens that those swindlers overreach themselves by attempting too much, and fall on the other side. An instance of that, while it will also illustrate another method of cheating by alchemy, we propose to give in the tale of "A Prince among Thieves."

A Mahomedan, pretending to be a saint of the name of Piala Shah, once came to the capital of a Chief of Gujarat, and took up his abode in a rudely-constructed hut, situated in the suburbs of the city. He was accompanied by a few followers, who, of course, soon noised the fame of the Saint Piala Shah abroad, and he, as a consequence, had many visitors. Ill-clad and poor, though to all appearance he was, he distributed much money among the destitute who came to him for aid, and to the weak he gave juices of certain herbs that he distilled himself, which, strange to say, seemed to have a remarkable power of curing many diseases. Alms from his more rich visitors he would not take, but lived on the proceeds of certain caps that he employed himself in manufacturing, when not engaged in devotional exercises.

To the Chief's ears came the news of this stranger's appearance on the outskirts of the city, through some merchants with whom he dealt, who told him of the saint's seemingly endless store of wealth, which he did not use for himself, but for the benefit of the poor, and of his marvellous power in curing diseases. The Chief's curiosity was naturally roused to learn more of this stranger, and he resolved to go and visit him. He could not command the saint to come to him, for it is a rule that is seldom or never broken, that even Chiefs and Princes shall go and pay their respects to saints and fakirs, not summoning them to their presence, as they would do others of their subjects, no matter how high their rank.

He saw the saint, and had an interview with him, and while he stood outside the saint's hut, several poor people came and received small sums of money as alms from the saint, while others came running and leaping, and falling down before him, worshipped and praised him for the marvellous cures he had wrought in them. The Chief was convinced of the power of the saint, and it became a familiar sight to see that princely personage, undecked with jewels, and clad in the plainest of garments, holding converse with the holy man, Piala Shah.

The Prince on every visit he paid to the saint, saw him give away sums of money, and marvelled at it, for he could not conceive how he became possessed of so much riches. At last, one day, burning with curiosity to learn the secret, he said to Piala Shah :

"O wonderful man, how do you, who refuse to receive charity from me or any other person, and whose only apparent source of income is the making of those caps, which can hardly bring in sufficient to keep you alive, manage to give away large sums of money daily to the poor? Have you discovered some hidden treasure that you are distributing thus for the benefit of suffering humanity? I have heard of such things being done. Or were you once rich and prosperous merchant yourself, who, retiring into seclusion, prefer, in the goodness of your heart, to let your fellow-creatures benefit from your toil, than live at ease and in luxury yourself?"

"No, great Chief!" replied Piala Shah. "Neither of your surmises is correct. No hidden treasure have I discovered ;

nor did I ever engage in trade more than as a humble maker of caps. When a child of only five years our great Prophet Mahomed appeared to me in a vision, and told me he had selected me to be one of his fakirs to work for the diffusion of the Mahomedan doctrine through India. From my infancy, therefore, I have been labouring amongst the people, praying with them, and teaching them from the holy Koran through the divine inspiration sent me from above. It has pleased my Master to bestow on me a power beyond many who are looked upon as saints. I am an alchemist, and by the power I possess I can transform mercury into find gold, selling which, I have always at my command much money to give away to the poor and needy, and to all who come to me in distress."

"Your words," said the Prince, who had listened intently to the harangue of the saint, "have only served to rouse my curiosity further. Can you not show me how you perform such a miracle?"

The saint, gratified at the success of his plan so far, he having succeeded in making the Prince believe in his power, replied,

"You asked me, Sir, what I was on the point of myself proposing. My duties call me to other parts of India, where the people are not so well favoured as are your subjects. I must go on travelling continually from city to city, from village to village, from shrine to shrine, till age prevents me moving further. My time in your city, O Chief, is almost spent; but before I depart, I will reveal to you the great secret I possess, on certain conditions."

The Chief delighted beyond measure at the idea of having it in his power to work so remarkable a miracle as Piala Shah had just confessed to him, said,

"Name the conditions; I promise to observe them faithfully."

"Swear first," said the holy man, "never to reveal to any man the secret I am about to put you in possession of, nor to breath to any living soul a word of what I shall say to you."

"I swear," said the Prince, kneeling in front of the saint and folding his arms across his breast.

"Swear," continued the fakir, "that you will not use the power that I will give you to add to your own riches; that only in cases of emergency, to provide yourself with necessaries in case of war, or to stay threatening disaster to your State, to buy food for your people in case of famine, to relieve the distressed as you have seen me do, will you resort to the secret means, to be revealed to you, to provide yourself with gold."

"I swear," said the awe-struck Chief again.

"To none but to your successor will you betray this divine secret, and only to him should he be worthy of it by constant devotion to religious observances. To all these conditions do you swear?"

"I swear."

"That is enough. To-morrow night meet me here again when the moon first appears from behind the hill, and we will begin our preparations."

"That," said the Chief, "will be about eight o'clock. And must I come alone?"

"Alone," returned Piala Shah; "for no one must observe us, or even guess what we are doing. And you must bring with you a large wicker basket, for we will have a load to carry."

"I to carry a basket, and a load?" inquired the Chief in amazement.

"Your Highness," said the saint, "is unaccustomed to labour, I know; but for the sake of the secret you are to learn, and for the good of your people you must, on this occasion, drop your dignity as Chief, and come to me dressed in even plainer raiment than you now wear, so that should you be seen, you may not be recognised."

"And wherefore is this basket?" asked the Chief again.

"We must go into the jungle yonder and collect the dung of the wild cow, which we will require in the experiment we are to try together. You, Chief, must gather it yourself as I point it out to you."

The Chief said no more. He no doubt did not relish the idea of that moonlight expedition with the Saint Piala Shah; but if he wanted to learn the secret, he would require to go. His Highness accordingly promised to meet his saintly (?) friend the following evening exactly at moonrise.

That same evening Piala Shah called at the bungalow of a merchant in the city, and on being shown into his presence, was greeted with the question, "What success?"

"The best," said the saint, with a self-satisfied smile. "His Highness has fallen into our trap, right simply. He believes in the power of my alchemy most implicitly, and to-morrow night has promised to go with me to the jungle to collect the dung of the wild cow for our experiment. But where are your friends? You must call them here to consult further about the business. We need all their help."

The merchant, delighted with the success of their plan, at once sent for his brother-merchants who were partners in the plot, and on their arrival further proceedings were discussed.

"I must," said the saintly one, "have one maund of gold filings ready to-morrow, early, to mix with cow-dung that will be laid in an unfrequented part of the jungle, and there I will take His Highness to gather it himself; and you know what will follow."

The merchants demurred a little at first at having to provide such a large quantity of gold: but Piala Shah impressed upon them the necessity of making a good show to begin with, so that the Chief might be all the more impressed. So the merchants agreed to provide the required gold filings, all but one, who said,

"I am not rich enough to give my share of such a large quantity of gold, on the mere chance of getting the Chief to give up a large sum of money. How do we know that he will not, on getting possession of this gold, that we are to provide, dismiss our friend the fakir, imagining he has learned the secret, and so put an end to further transactions?"

"Leave that to me," said Piala Shah. "You are too timorous. In a game of this sort we must be prepared to make some outlay to begin with."

"Leave it to you?" queried the dissenter. "Let you work the business all by yourself? You are a stranger to us. How do we know you are sincere? Had you asked for a smaller amount, I might have agreed; but a maund of gold is enormous. Besides, I have not got the required quantity I am expected to contribute."

The dispute ended by this man rising and washing his hands of any part in the transaction, at which the others did not feel any regret, imagining that in the end a larger share of the proceeds would fall to each of them. Could they have guessed, however, the treachery that was formulating itself in the deserter's brain, it is questionable if they would have felt so comfortable.

Arrangements for the following day completed, the party separated in good spirits, fully expecting a successful termination to their adventure. It was agreed that the cow-dung should be carefully mixed with the gold filings, and deposited in a convenient place, and that it should be watched by the merchants themselves, who should at the same time exercise sufficient caution that they might not be observed by the Chief when he was escorted to the jungle by Piala Shah.

The moon had just made her appearance in the heavens the following evening, when the Prince, attired like one of the commonest of his subjects, and carrying a large wicker basket, made his appearance before the hut of the pretended saint. Courtesies having been exchanged, Piala Shah also armed himself with a basket similar to that carried by the Chief, and together they set off for the jungle, where, by the light of the moon, they were able to collect the dung that lay scattered about.

The Chief was beginning to stagger under his load, when Piala Shah said :

"Now, I think, your Highness, we will return. We have sufficient for our purpose. Have you a room in your palace where you could keep this safely under lock and key for a day or perhaps two? It is valuable, and must not be tampered with."

The Chief was a little alarmed at this proposition, as his words showed.

"Can you not," he asked, "keep the baskets safely in your dwelling? I have had trouble enough already escaping observation in leaving the palace in this dress, and when I return I will have to steal in again like a thief. What, then, would any of my servants think, did they see me returning in your company carrying on our backs heavy loads of this ill-smelling matter? What gossip it would cause! What a tale it would be to circulate through the city!"

"Were any explanation needed," replied the saint, "you need only say you had certain religious rites to perform, and as I am now well known and respected among all your subjects, my presence will satisfy them."

The Chief unwillingly agreed to Piala Shah's proposal, and took him to the palace, which they succeeded in entering by a side-door unobserved, and gaining a room which His Highness thought would suit the saint's purpose.

"Now," said the saint, when they had each deposited their loads, "keep this door securely fastened, and let no one enter till I return. This deposit of the wild cow that we have collected is most valuable, being the best fuel that can be used in making gold. Procure, before to-morrow night, one maund weight of mercury or quicksilver, and I will show you how it may be transformed into the finest of gold."

So saying he went away, only, however, to return the following day, bringing with him a crucible which he said was required for the experiment. They shut themselves up in the room, whither the Chief brought a large vessel containing the quicksilver he had been told by the saint to procure. The crucible being placed on the centre of the floor, which, fortunately for the requirements of the experiment, was of stone, the mercury was poured into it. Then the Chief was told to bring the basket he had filled in the jungle, and taking the material therein pile it over the crucible, which he did; Piala Shah at the same time packing the fuel from his basket underneath and around the crucible. To that he put lights, and as the fire began to burn he muttered strange incantations which were unintelligible, and therefore sounded mysterious to the Prince.

Now it must be explained that the dung which the Chief had collected, and which had been pointed out to him by the supposed saint, was only that which contained the gold filings, while that which Piala Shah himself had gathered, was old, dry material that would burn readily as fuel. Only that collected by the Chief was packed over the crucible, so that as it grew red-hot the gold melted and ran into the crucible, from which the mercury, by the heat, evaporated. Therefore, when the fakir saw the whole a glowing red mass, he knew the work was complete; but to mystify his victim still further, he produced a box, from which he drew a dark-coloured dry root, which, he said, was a piece of *aksir*, and the power of which he explained. Over this he muttered another incantation, accompanied by mysterious gesticulations, and dropped it into the fire. Then he ceased adding any more fuel, allowing the fire to gradually die out. Then clearing away the ashes, he revealed to the astonished gaze of His Highnes the crucible almost filled with a mass of pure gold. Had the Chief any doubt before, he was now convinced of the saint Piala Shah's wonderful power as an alchemist.

The saint left His Highness to ponder over the result, test and examine the gold as he pleased, and did not appear again till next morning, when addressing the Chief, he said :

"We cannot contiuue our experiments to-day, nor can I remain any longer in your city in the meantime, as my supply of *aksir*, which is indispensable, is finished. I used the last I had in turning your quicksilver into gold last night. Without *aksir*, I can do nothing in ministering to the wants of the poor; and I must go to the mountains in search of the plant from which I make the *aksir*. I will also, before I return, complete the pilgrimage I am now on; and then, laden with this precious plant, I will come back, and we will make crores and crores worth of gold, by which your Highness will be able to build such institutions, and so improve the condition of your people, that beggars will disappear, everybody will live in confort, and your State will be the happiest and most prosperous in all India."

"O wonderful; O most mighty saint!" exclaimed the Chief in an ecstasy of delight. "How ever shall I reward you for——?"

"My reward," said Piala Shah, interrupting him, "is not on this earth. But if you are desirous of showing your gratitude to the Great Prophet, from whom this power comes, by helping me in my work, while I have not the means myself of continuing my relief of the distressed, who come to me in expectation of help, you have now an opportunity?"

"If you want money," said the Chief unhesitatingly, "say how much you want, and it shall be given you instantly."

"You saw," continued the fakir insinuatingly feeling his way cautiously before making any proposal, "that I gave away daily very large sums of money, all of which I made by the secret I know of converting quicksilver into gold?"

He was a most accomplished cheat. He had indeed given away enormous sums of money in full view of His Highness; but the apparently distressed people were not poor at all, but accomplices.

"When I have been hard pressed by misfortune," he went on, "I have known occasions upon which I have given away in one day lakhs upon lakhs of rupees. I may be absent now about two months, and I may require a few lakhs of rupees."

Before the Chief could express either surprise at the impudence of the demand, or readiness to accede to it, the curtains at the entrance to the room parted, and a servant appeared saying,

"Your Highness, the merchant Hoosein Ali has come."

"Tell him to wait till I am disengaged. I am busy now."

"He is in a great hurry, and much excited; and wants to see you on a matter of great importance, which concerns your Highness alone."

"Ah, that is a different matter," said His Highness, "I will come now."

The name of Hoosein Ali rather startled the good Saint Piala Shah. Hoosein Ali was the man who had disputed with the other merchants about the required gold filings. What could he want with the Chief? Could he mean to betray the swindle? He must see.

He accordingly, putting off his sandals, stealthily followed the Chief out of the room, and stood at the door of another which His Highness entered. He listened. It was the Hoosein Ali he knew. He could recognise his voice. He spoke quickly and excitedly. He was denouncing the Saint Piala Shah as an impostor. He was relating the secret of the converting of the quicksilver into gold. The game was lost; so was the gold, and the lakhs of rupees.

The Saint Piala Shah disappeared as mysteriously as he came. As for the dishonest merchants, they thought it best, on receiving a quiet hint from the Chief that it would be dangerous to remain in the city any longer, to take their departure also, leaving behind them their precious gold.

THE SEALED PACKETS.

Of all the different methods of swinding, none could be meaner, and at the same time smarter, than that which is practised, most commonly on jewellers and dealers in precious stones, and as it is a trick by which any man might readily be deceived, it deserves minute description and illustration. The usual way of those swindlers who cheat their victims by means of sealed packets, is, that one of the men belonging to the gang, dressed to represent a servant of some one occupying a high possition, enters the shop of a jeweller, and asking for the proprietor, tells him of a certain lady of rank who wants to dispose of some valuable jewellery. Would he come and value them? He does so, and probably offers a certain amount of money; or it may be the lady may only want to put them in pledge with the jeweller, in which case an agreement is drawn out and signed by both parties, the jeweller lending so much money on the valuables, and the lady granting power to the jeweller, in the event of her not redeeming them within a certain period, to dispose of them in any way he chooses. The case containing the jewellery is sealed up in presence of, or by the jeweller himself with the lady's own seal, but while the document is being signed, or the jeweller's attention is diverted for a moment, another box, exactly resembling that which had just been sealed, is substituted and the jeweller marches off with it. The three, or six months, or whatever term agreed upon in the signed contract, elapse, and the jeweller, thinking the articles are not to be redeemed, smiles to himself, imagining he will, by the selling of them, make an enormous profit. He breaks the seals, opens the case, and finds, not the jewels he had seen placed therein, but stones and mud. The swindlers may go still further. They may, we will suppose, get Rs. 5,000 advanced on jewellery, which the expert himself recognises is worth Rs. 10,000. If they imagine their dupe has a good current account at the bank, they will, before the term stated in the agreement expires, make their appearance at the jeweller's shop, pay down the Rs. 5,000, with required interest, and demand the case of jewellery. They get it, look suspiciously at the seals, perhaps making a remark that they fear the box has been tampered with, open it hurriedly, and empty on the floor, to the jeweller's astonishment, stones and mud. Then they charge the poor, innocent jeweller with breach of trust, and threaten to call the police, and the falsely-charged man, in his bewilderment and terror, yields to the demands of the cheats, and pays them the money demanded.

THE LADY AND THE MARWAREE.

A Marwaree was sitting one afternoon in his shop in the bazar, when a landau, drawn by a pair of well-caparisoned horses, stopped at his door. From the carriage descended a Hindu lady, who, from her rich dress and the servants who accompanied her, appeared to be connected in some way with the house of a Native Chief. She looked round the shop, admiring the various pieces of jewellery, asking the prices of various things, and making small purchases. She expressed herself well satisfied, and said she would come again, which she did, making *bona-fide* purchases, and paying prices which quite satisfied the jeweller.

One day she appeared at the shop of the Marwaree all alone, and taking him aside put on a very concerned look, and said,

"Will you help me out of my difficulty? I have run short of money, and want some immediately."

Now, the lady was well made, and her large black eyes looked so pleadingly into those of the Marwaree that he, close-fisted though he was, felt his heart melt towards the woman, and he replied,

"How much do you want? If your demand is not beyond my means, I will try to give you what you want."

"I require Rs. 10,000, and at once."

This rather staggered the Marwaree. The lady was beautiful, very beautiful, and to oblige her would be a pleasure, but she was a stranger to him, and Rs. 10,000 was a deal of money.

"I do not think," he said cautiously and hesitatingly, "I have so much ready cash, at present; but if you could find security for the money, I have no doubt I could raise it for you."

"Oh," said the lady, "that is easily settled. I have my jewels, and they are worth Rs. 50,000 at least. If I give you some of them in trust, and pay you so much interest on the loan of Rs. 10,000, for a few months, will you not lend me the money I want?"

The Marwaree was ready on such terms to do anything the lady wished. Her point gained so far, she began to take the Marwaree into her confidence. "I have now," she said, "been in Bombay a few months, and like it so well, that I have determined to purchase a house, for I shall be a frequent visitor to this city now, and would rather have a house of my own to live in than lodge with a friend. Well, I have seen and chosen a house; but I canot get it for less than Rs. 25,000. I have only Rs. 15,000 available at present, and the proprietor says unless I complete the transaction to-night, he will sell the house to another, who is ready at once to pay the same sum. What am I, therefore, to do? You are the only man I have had any transaction with in Bombay, and it was only you I could think of to help me. Will you come and see my jewels?"

The Marwree promised faithfully to be with her within an hour, and the lady left.

Within the hour, the Marwaree presented himself at the house, the address of which had been given by the woman, and was immediately ushered into her presence.

"You are punctual," said the lady, smiling to him. "Have you brought the money with you?"

"I have," answered the Marwaree, "the sum you want which, on your satisfying me of the value of your jewels, I will hand over to you."

The lady ordered a case to be produced. It was opened, and was found to contain numerous little tied bundles of muslin, which the lady undid herself, disclosing to the Marwaree's eyes quantities of really valuable jewellery. He tested the gold, examined the precious stones, and found them altogether worth more than Rs. 50,000, as the lady herself had stated.

"With those jewels in my possession," he said, "I am quite willing to advance Rs. 10,000.

"Very good," the lady said, "at what interest? You will not make it heavy, considering the jewels are so good security, being worth fully five times the money you lend for them?" she inquired; as if she cared whether the Marwaree asked large or small interest.

"No," replied the man, "from you I could not ask too much. But how long will you require the money? When do you expect to redeem your property?"

"Oh," the woman said carelessly, "I shall not require it longer than three months, perhaps less."

"Then," said the Marwaree, "let us make out an agreement for three months at five per cent."

"Five per cent. for three months!" the lady exclaimed, pretending amazement. "That would be Rs. 500; or should I require it for a year, Rs. 2,000. An enormous sum to pay for the use of Rs. 10,000 for such a short time!"

"Not heavy, I assure you," said the Marwaree; "Rs. 10,000 is a large sum of money, and more than I possess myself. To procure it for you I have had to pay heavy interest myself. To others my rates are much higher. To some of those English Sahibs who come to me for money, I will perhaps lend Rs. 1,000 for three months, getting 25 per cent. interest, so that in a year I get back my Rs. 1,000, and Sahib is still Rs. 1,000 in my debt."

"But those men give you no security beyond their names; and they sometimes escape up-country or to England, and you are a loser. But with me you are safe."

"And so," said the Marwaree, "I give it to you for five per cent. for three months."

"Very well," said the lady, pretending to be resigned to her fate; "let it be so. I must have the money, and your rates are perhaps lower than many other Marwarees."

The jewels being returned to the case, the woman called for cords and bound it tightly up with her own hands, after which she took a stick of sealing-wax in her hand and ordered her servant to bring a taper.

"Why," queried the Marwaree, "would you seal the box?"

"For your satisfaction as well as mine; so that both you and I may know, by merely glancing at it, that the jewels are safe."

The seals being fixed, a man who appeared to be a lawyer's clerk, and who seemed to have been in waiting, was called in. A document was drawn up, in which the Marwaree agreed to advance Rs. 10,000 for three months at five per cent., holding as security the jewellery in the sealed case, while the lady agreed that at the end of three months, did she not redeem her jewels, they should become the property of the Marwaree, who should be at liberty to break the seals and sell the jewellery for whatever he might get.

Both parties having signed the deed, the lawyer's clerk took the paper away, and the Marwaree having handed over the Rs. 10,000 in notes, also departed, carrying with him the case which he supposed contained the jewellery.

One day the Marwaree was sitting in his shop talking with a friend who had looked in from over the way for an hour's gossip, when the Marwaree began telling his companion of the excellent speculation he had made; but his laughing and chuckling ceased when he noted the serious, inquiring look in his friend's face.

"I saw," he said, "the woman came to your shop, and meant to warn you; but I thought perhaps you knew her well."

"Warn me?" inquired the Marwaree anxiously; "what is it you mean?"

"Is it possible that you can have lent that woman so much money? She is not the lady of a Sirdar, or noble of any kind, but a notorious woman in the city known as Amba."

"You must be mistaken; at any rate, I have the jewels safe."

"Are you quite sure? Let us see."

The Marwaree went and fetched the case, and explained how it had been sealed up in his presence.

"You are quite sure all the jewellery you speak of is there?"

"I saw it put in myself."

"She is a clever, deceitful woman," said the Marwaree's friend calmly. "I know how she has tricked others before. I would not, were I in your place, allow the three months to expire before breaking the seals. I would satisfy myself now."

The Marwaree became so alarmed that he broke the seals, cut the cords, and opening the box found stones certainly, but not at all precious—common bits of road metal set in dried mud.

The Marwaree hurried to his solicitor, a warrant was obtained for the woman's apprehension; she was arrested, and brought before the Magistrate; but what a tale did she tell him.

That Marwaree, she said, was the impostor and not she. She admitted her name was Amba, she had never tried to conceal it, and denied she had ever personated a lady of rank. The Marwaree came to her house one day, and she refused him admission, for which she supposed he had concocted this case against her. She was only defended by Mr. Inverarity.

There being no evidence, the case was dismissed, and the Marwaree, if his story was true, and there is little reason to doubt it, saw no more of his Rs. 10,000.

THE PAREL SWINDLING GANG.

A CASHIER ROBBED OF Rs. 15,000.

THE city of Bombay seemed to be overrun with gangs of swindlers, considering the number of cases of cheating which came to the notice of the police in the year 1891. About thirty-five gangs of swindlers, it would seem, were then visiting Bombay, and they had succeeded in cheating many over-credulous people. They had swindled rich and poor alike with impunity, and the police, as we have already remarked, owing to the want of a necessary provision in the Penal Code, had no power to prosecute them. It seems that on one Saturday, the very day the public were warned in the columns of the *Gazette* against the swindlers, a cashier of a certain firm of Marwarees was swindled by some of those cheats out of Rs. 15,000, and on account of his unfortunate adventure, he was charged before the Magistrate as a criminal himself. It appears that a man went to this cashier and told him that one of his friends had got certain jewellery belonging to a Chief of enormous wealth at Kolahpur, but owing to some untoward circumstance, the Chief found himself short of money and wanted to dispose of the jewellery at a very cheap rate. The man therefore asked the cashier to assist him in disposing of the property. This was temptation enough for the cashier, who fell blindly into the snare, expecting to make a good bargain. He made up his mind to buy the jewellery either for himself or his master's firm. The jewellery was accordingly shown to the cashier, who promised to buy the same at Rs. 15,000. On Saturday evening, as previously arranged, he went to a bungalow at Parel, taking with him Rs. 15,000 belonging to his master's firm. He was there welcomed by the man who had first offered him the ornaments for sale, and then he was introduced to another man, who, it was explained, had brought the Chief's jewellery for sale. A servant was brought, who dug under the floor in the room and brought out a box containing the jewellery, which was handed over to the cashier, who paid the Rs. 15,000, and left the bungalow under the impression that he had driven a lucky bargain and was a gainer in the transaction. His satisfaction was of short duration, however, because he had only gone a few paces from the bungalow when somebody shouted out "Thief! Thief! *Puckro! Puckro!*" Owing to sudden alarm the cashier became frightened, and throwing away the box, which it was afterwards ascertained contained only false jewellery, he foolishly ran away to evade arrest. Next morning he went to the bungalow which, to his surprise, he found empty. The unfortunate man told the strange story to his manager, who took out a warrant against him on a charge of criminal breach of trust and criminal misappropriation of Rs. 15,000. This story should be an additional warning to the public to be on their guard, as those swindlers would seem to have all manner of ingenious tricks for the swindling of the unwary.

THE "NAWAB" AND THE MONEY-CHANGER.

There would seem to be no end to the ruses by which those professional swindlers who infest Bombay cheat their victims out of large sums of money. Their daring is something to marvel at. They will carry out their plans in broad daylight, and risk large sums themselves in gaining their object. A curious instance came to light only in February 1891, which for cleverness and daring equals, if it does not surpass, any of the tales told in the foregoing pages. A man personating a 'Nawab' goes to a shop in Bombay, carries on a large business transaction with a merchant and so gains his confidence, that throwing him off his guard, he manages to get away with between Rs. 8,000 and Rs. 9,000.

The unfortunate man who lost this money and appealed to the police for help was one Harridas Lakhmichand, a money-changer, who once carried on business in the Esplanade Hotel, and occupied a shop opposite there.

One fine morning, about half-past eleven o'clock, a splendid landau, drawn by a pair of beautiful horses, with coachman and footmen dressed in yellow and black livery, stopped at the door of Harrida's shop. From this carriage descended a friend and brother in trade of Harrida's, named Rustomjee Nusserwanjee, a man carrying on business in Church Gate Street, and with whom Harridas has had many business transactions during the last two years. After him came from the carriage a man who, from his dress, had all the appearance of a rich Nawab from a Native State. On Harridas coming out to meet his visitors, according to custom, Rustomji said,

"The Nawab Sahib wants some English and Italian money;" whereupon Harridas said,

"Then will you ask the Nawab to come in.,"

The princely looking personage, called the Nawab, accepting the invitation, the two money-changers paid him great deference, and saw him comfortably seated in a chair before coming to business, and Harridas took a chair opposite him. Taking a paper from his pocket, the Nawab studied it carefully for a time, and addressing Harridas said,

"I want to change Rs. 4,350 into English gold and notes. I have Rs. 4,100 that I want changed for Italian gold and notes, and Rs. 250 that I wish Italian and English silver for. Can you do that business for me ?"

Such a large order, involving as it did Rs. 8,700, so cooly given, rather staggered Harridas, and he concluded that his friend had brought him this rich customer as he had been unable himself to meet the demand; but such an enormous amount for foreign money, the money-changer was not in the habit of keeping by him in his shop. He accordingly said to the 'Nawab' in reply,

"I have not the money ready now; but in half-an-hour I could get it for you."

"That is quite satisfactory," said the pretended nobleman; "I will go and see my friend Sirdar Abdul Huq, and return in an hour. That will give you plenty of time to get the money for me."

The Nawab and Rustomjee then left, whereupon Harridas set about getting the English and Italian money asked for. He succeeded in the time he said he would, and was waiting for his visitors when they returned between twelve and one o'clock.

"Have you got the whole of the money ready ?" was Rustomjee's first question, to which Harridas readily replied in the affirmative.

"Then," said the other money-changer, "we will drive in the Nawab's carriage to his bungalow, and there he will give us the money."

The Nawab invited Harridas to enter the carriage, and all three drove off. During the drive, his Pretended Highness made himself very affable, and the poor money-changer was quite won by his noble (?) customer's smooth tongue.

"Why did you leave the Esplanade Hotel?" was one of the questions asked by the Nawab. "I am sure that was a better place for business than where you now are?"

"Yes," admitted Harridas, "but I could not afford it: the rent was too high. When I went there first I only paid Rs. 25 a month. Then it was raised to Rs. 50, and latterly I was asked to pay Rs. 100, which was too much for me; so I came away."

"Ah," said the Nawab, "I can sympathise with you; but I know the Sirdar well, and will speak to him for you. I know he will give you your place at a moderate rent if I ask him."

The poor money-changer was more charmed with his princely patron than ever, and was ready to exchange as much as he wanted into English and Italian money at the rate of Rs. 15 to the sovereign.

The carriage drove on till Clerke Road was reached, and stopped at a large, stately, two-storeyed bungalow, near Mahalaxmi station. The Nawab took the two men into a handsomely-furnished room, and asked them to be seated. The apartment, which was large, had pictures hung round on the walls, and a massive chandelier hung down from the centre. The furniture consisted of handsomely upholstered couches and chairs, richly carved tables, with flower epergnes set upon them, while the floor was laid with a thick, soft, brightly coloured carpet; truly a chamber fit for a prince to receive his guest in.

"Now," said the Nawab, "let us come to business. What have you brought with you?"

Harridas immediately began counting out the money he had brought with him. He counted out and gave to his friend Rustomjee, calculating at the rate of Rs. 15 to the £, and 25 francs to the £240 sovereigns, who re-counted them, and handed them over to the Nawab. He also gave ten Bank of England notes for £5 each, Italian notes amounting to 5,000 francs, and 1,050 francs in ten-franc pieces. The whole amounted in value to exactly Rs. 8,440. The Nawab, having got the money, and satisfied himself that it was all right, called a mehta or clerk who was sitting in the room, and addressing him said,

"Pay this man from my cash-box the sum of Rs. 8,440 for this money I have just got from him, and obtain his receipt." Then turning to Harridas and Rustumjee he said, "You will excuse me while I go and take my meal. My mehta will pay you the money," and, bowing slightly, he departed. When he had gone, Rustomjee said to his companion,

"But I was forgetting; I gave the Nawab fifty sovereigns yesterday; you might include that in your account."

"Very well," said Harridas, "that will make the total Rs. 9,190 in all."

"But," said the mehta, "my master only instructed me to pay Rs, 8,440. I will go and ask him, and bring the key of the safe at the same time," with which words he departed also.

The time went by; but the mehta did not reappear. When over half-an-hour had passed, Harridas said to Rustomjee,

"I am beginning to grow alarmed. Why does that man not come back?"

"Do not fear," said Rustomjee calmly, "he is a rich man. Only yesterday I sold him coins and jewellery worth Rs. 500, and received Rs. 10 commission on the transaction as well;" and the unconcerned tone in which he spoke at once allayed the fears of Harridas for a time. But as the house remained quiet, and neither the 'Nawab' nor his mehta gave any sign of their returning, Harridas grew more nervous about his money, and his alarm increased, notwithstanding all Rustomjee's endeavours to allay his fears. He bore the suspense for nearly two hours, and then, unable to control his excitement any longer, he determined to search for the Nawab himself. Followed by Rustomjee, he passed from one room into another, and stood amazed. It was empty. He ran to another. Not an article of furniture even was there. Through the whole bungalow, upstairs and downstairs, they ran, but not a soul could they find. From there they ran to the police-station. On Inspector Jones coming in answer to the inquiry for him, Harridas called out,

"I have been cheated of Rs. 8,440. I knew there was a band of swindlers working in Bombay, and was determined they should not cheat me, and now I have lost all this money. What is to be done?"

Inspector Jones did all he could under the circumstances. He examined Harridas, took down his statement in writing as it has been narrated above, and communicated with the Chief of the Detective Department, Sardar Mir Abdul Ali, Khan Bahadur, who did all that can be done to secure this scoundrel pretending to be a Nawab, who belonged to the same gang, but he had made himself scarce. A warrant was issued for his apprehension. He was captured, but was let off in the absence of sufficient evidence by Mr. Hamilton. It was just another warning to people in the city to be on their guard against such visitors. Trust no stranger, how ever rich and high in rank he may to all outward appearance be, until his name and thorough guarantee of good faith are obtained, and all the details of the bargain are satisfactorily completed.

LIFE SENTENCE ON ONE OF THE "GOLDEN GANG."

A COUPLE of notorious swindlers, and members of the combination, known as the "Golden Gang," were brought to book at Hubli, in Dharwar, and one who had given both police and public a vast amount of trouble was removed from harm's way for the remainder of his existence. The pair referred to are the well known Cooverjee Shapoorjee *alias* Cooverjee Sorabjee, and his comrade Purshotam Thackersey, who finding some time ago that Bombay had become too hot to hold them, transferred their operations to Hubli, in the Dharwar Collectorate. At this latter place they were not long in finding what is known as a "plant," and they were successful in relieving a Mysore Brahmin of valuable ornaments. The system adopted by the swindlers was to present themselves as agents of a Native Prince, who are empowered to purchase jewellery for the State. In the present case the men represented that they had a gold neck ornament, valued at Rs. 600, for sale, but which they would agree to exchange for one the Brahmin was at that time wearing. Without making any enquiries as to whether the ornament was what it was represented to be, the Brahmin gave his neck-chain away in exchange, but was not long in discovering that he had been duped, and that the ornament he had become possessed of was a worthless piece of brass. The transaction was immediately reported to the Hubli Police, who smartly laid the pair of rascals by the heel. Communication was at once opened with Sardar Abdul Ali of the Bombay Detective Department, and Mr. Gell, officiating Commissioner of Police, despatched a detective officer to identify the men and detail a few of their exploits in Bombay. Cooverjee and Purshotam were placed before the local Magistrate and committed to the Criminal Sessions, when Mr. T. S. Hamilton, C.S., Sesssions Judge, heard the case. They were found guilty of cheating, and Mr. Hamilton, in sentencing Cooverjee, remarked that the world, Bombay, and Hubli in particular, had had enough of him, and a sojourn in the Andamans for the remainder of his existence was absolutely necessary. He, therefore, sentenced him to penal servitude for life. Cooverjee was greatly surprised at the sentence, and left the dock in tears. Purshotam has also a bad record, but it was decided only to give him three years' rigorous imprisonment, during which the Judge trusted he would acquire something like a rudimentary knowledge of the rights of property.

Cooverjee's history in crime is an extraordinary one, and proves that for cunning knavery he could hold his own with the most notorious members of his profession. There was no form of fraud or cheating which he was not good for, and his last misfortune robbed the "Golden Gang" of one of its brightest ornaments. Cooverjee Shapoorjee was about forty years of age, and considering that he had spent the greater portion of his life in exercising his talent for cheating, he had had a fair immunity from imprisonment. He had generally been too clever to allow the police to obtain incriminating evidence against him, and it was only when he descended to the vulgar practices of his profession that he found himself in the clutches of the law. On one of these later occasions he was smartly detected uttering false coin by Inspector Cobb, and this indiscretion robbed him of two years of his liberty. The only other occasion on which he had been convicted was some few years ago when he bungled over a well-conceived piece of cheating, and paid the penalty of imprisonment for one year. One of his smartest performances was in playing on the ignorant cupidity of persons who desired to become possessed of ill-gotten gain. He, in company with Purshotam and three others, went to Hubli, the scene of their last exploit, and persuaded a young Hindu that they had discovered means for splitting one-thousand rupee notes in such a manner that both parts could be exchanged for Rs. 1,000. The man produced a note which the gang proceeded to deal with. They first substituted, unknown to the Hindu, a counterfeit note for the good one, and placed the bad note in an elaborated piece of machinery made of glass. The false note was then treated with acid and burnt to a cinder. The sharpers then professed to be very much astonished at the result of the experiment, but undertook to put matters straight if the Hindu would bring a second note for treatment. The Hindu was eventually persuaded to bring another note for Rs. 1,000 which was again substiuted for a bad note, and the latter treated in the same manner as the first with a like result. In this way the Hindu was robbed of Rs. 2,000. The gang returned to Bombay, but the proverbial honour amongst thieves being wanting, Cooverjee and Purshotam who had failed to obtain their share of the proceeds of the swindle, informed the police of what had taken place. The remaining three were immediately arrested, but owing to the fact that the Hindu, who was connected with some large business house, could not be got to appear in Court, the men got off on that count, but received three months' imprisonment each for being in possession of money, of which they could give no satisfactory account. The money was confiscated by Government. Purshotum, who was a man of about forty, had in the main led a quieter life than his illustrious *confrere*. He commenced life ostensibly as a goldsmith, and under cover of this trade managed to practise petty villanies so neatly that he generally kept well clear of the police. On one or two occasions he had been caught red-handed, but had never undergone a sentence of the same period as that which he was this time doomed to work out.

A CLEVER GANG OF SHARPERS.

WARNING TO WHOLESALE TRADERS.

Merchants in Bombay and managers of large firms were more than once surprised by a party of clever swindlers who had taken up their abode in a large bungalow at Fergusson Road. They had already received warning from the experiences of the representative of a large firm in Bombay who ran a narrow escape from falling into their clutches. The mode in which these thieves—for they were nothing else—carried on their work was undoubtedly smart, although their plan was not a new one. We have heard before of men being inveigled away to a house, induced to gamble, and robbed of all they possessed. That was apparently the method of those dangerous visitors residing at Fergusson Road; but their method of "fleecing" unwary victims will best be understood by one instance related below which may serve as a warning to others whom they may try to swindle. A man, described as a stout, well dressed Hindu, entered a certain wholesale establishment in Bombay. The Hindu explained that he was the agent for a certain Raja at present on a visit to Bombay, and he wished, he said, to leave an order for four hundred cavalry outfits. Mr. A. was naturally delighted at the prospect of obtaining so large an order for his firm, and expressed his willingness to undertake the contract. The Hindu said the Raja stayed in a bunglow at Malabar Hill, but he came to another bungalow at Fergusson Road every morning to transact business. Would Mr. A. then come to Fergusson Road next morning and have an interview with the Raja? This was agreed upon, and the fat Hindu returned the following morning for Mr. A., whom he drove to Fergusson Road. At the door of a certain bungalow they stopped, and Mr. A. was invited to enter. Mr. A. did so, and soon found himself being profoundly salaamed by a crowd of well-dressed natives, who appeared to be the servants of the Chief. The room he was in, too, was, if not, extravagantly at least handsomely furnished. But there was no Raja there—only, on a carpet, a man lying, apparently very sick. He saluted his visitor, apologised for being in that state, and said he was very unwell. He pretended to be the Raja's *pucca* agent, the fat Hindu being apparently only a sub-agent or superior sort of servant. The sick man was sorry the Raja was not there, but he began to question Mr. A. about his terms for four hundred cavalry outfits. The latter said they would cost Rs. 212-8-0 each, upon which the sick agent asked him if he secured the order for him, how much commission he would give him. To that Mr. A. replied he would be contented with the Rs. 200, which would mean Rs. 80,000 for the four hundred, and allowing the agent the extra Rs. 12-8, that would mean Rs. 5,000 as commission to him. The agent seemed to think this a very good bargain, and shaking hands with Mr. A., promised he would use his influence with the Raja, and if he came back again on the morrow he would no doubt get the order. Accordingly at ten o'clock the following morning the fat Hindu came again to Mr. A.'s warehouse in Bombay, and drove him out once more to Fergusson Road. There he was saluted by the same servants, and after waiting a short time the Raja himself appeared. He was dressed like a Hyderabad nobleman in handsomely embroidered clothes, and was literally covered with diamonds and other costly jewels. There was one curious feature about him, and that was that his face was almost unrecognisable by reason of a large pair of "goggles," which he wore across his eyes, completely hiding whatever expression he may have had. To the Raja Mr. A. was introduced, and after some conversation about the outfits, the price, &c., his Highness expressed himself satisfied, but said he only wanted one hundred outfits for himself, and that the other three hundred were for a noble friend of his up-country to whom he had written.

Would Mr. A. kindly come back next day, when he (the Raja) would no doubt have received the reply he wanted, and a settlement would be come to about the contract? Mr. A. was beginning to feel worried by this time with his repeated visits to Fergusson Road, but anxious not to lose the large order he did go back.

The second act of the comedy now began. While waiting for the goggle-eyed Raja, a man whom Mr. A. had not been seen before appeared. He looked like a Parsee, was well-dressed, and wore a Persian cap. Addressing the fat Hindu first referred to, he began telling him of his wonderful manipulations of cards, and how he had won an almost fabulous amount from a certain person in Poona but a few days ago. The stout one began to grow interested. The Parsee took from his pocket a pack of round cards, some of which had horses upon them, and began explaining how he manipulated them, so that he was bound to win every time he dealt them out.

"Now," said the Parsee, "you try and get the Raja to play with me. He has lakhs and lakhs of rupees. It will not matter if I win a lot of money from him. I am a poor man, and I want to get my daughter married."

The fat Hindu would not listen to this at first, but the Parsee persisting, the former said:

"Then look here, if I get his Highness to play with you, how much of your winnings will you give me?"

"I will give you," said the sharper, "six annas out of every rupee I win."

The Hindu laughed at the idea, and insisted on share and share alike, which after much debate was agreed upon between the two. Mr. A. hearing all this conversation felt rather annoyed that he should be a party, though only a spectator, to such a swindling transaction as was about to be attempted, but determined to wait and see how things went before interfering.

Presently his spectacled Highness appeared, and after saluting Mr. A. he asked who the Parsee stranger was, when it was explained to the goggle-eyed Chief that he was a sort of conjurer who could show him a number of card tricks. "His Highness" was delighted, and after some time was prevailed upon to play. Every time the cards were dealt the stakes were doubled, and each time the Raja lost, till in a few minutes he had been "fleeced" to the extent of Rs. 2,400. Mr. A. then thought it was time to interfere. He told the spectacled Raja he was being swindled, and advised him to stop playing, which advice the Raja took. He produced a cash-box, and taking therefrom a large roll of notes paid the Parsee the money he had won, and retired to his private room. A dispute then took place between the sharper and the fat Hindu. The latter demanded his share of the winnings, whereupon the Parsee turned on him and said, "Not a pie! You promised not to interfere with the play, but when this gentleman," pointing to Mr. A., "called me a swindler, you backed him up and advised his Highness to stop playing. I will give you nothing." Then as the fat Hindu began to wax wroth, he continued coolly, "Look here if you do not let me go away quietly, I will call the Raja and confess to him that you were my accomplice in swindling him."

That silenced the stout one, and the swindler was allowed to go in peace. He had no sooner gone than Mr. A. discovered he had left his playing cards behind him, and picking them up put them in his pocket. This action seemed to alarm the others in the room, and the fat Hindu begged the cards so earnestly that A.'s suspicions began to be aroused for the first time.

And now we come to the third act of this curious play. A sudden idea seemed to strike the Hindu.

"Did you see," he said to Mr. A., "how the man performed with the card?"

"Yes," he said.

"Do you think you could do it?" asked the Hindu.

Mr. A. said it was simple enough, that the man who handled the cards could not but win every time.

"Very well, then," said the Hindu. "Listen, and I will tell you how we will do. The Raja is worth lakhs, and has more money than he knows what to do with. It will do him no harm to lose a few thousands, but it will be a good thing for us. I will tell him you can play that game; you will win, and we will share the money."

Mr. A. was averse to this: but before he could say much the spectacled one returned, and to him the stout Hindu said Mr. A. would play for small stakes for love. The Raja appeared delighted, and Mr. A. to please him played for small stakes and won. The cards were dealt again, three to tho Raja and three to Mr. A.

"Now," said his Highness, "I propose we put Rs. 5,000 on each card."

Mr. A. pleaded that he was a poor man, and had not the money. "Never mind," said the Raja, "I can trust you;" but still Mr. A. declined.

The Raja then turned over the cards, and showed that while he himself possessed three blank cards Mr. A. had three horses.

"What a fool you are," exclaimed Prince Goggle Eyes; "if you had put on the money you would have won Rs. 15,000."

Mr. A. was astonished, but changing the subject inquired about the order for the cavalry outfits he had come about. Again the Raja put him off, saying he had not yet received the communication he expected from up-country, and Mr. A. unwillingly consented to call again the following morning. Before he went, however, the Hindu agent took him aside and told him he should bring plenty of money with him next day, that he would himself lend him Rs. 2,000 of his own money, and if he would only play with the Raja for high stakes, they would win a lot of money. Mr. A. could not understand what all this anxiety to get him to gamble meant. He was beginning to think he had got amongst a gang of swindlers, for all the servants, as well as the fat Hindu, were now pressing him to play; and on the other hand he thought the Raja had simply got a lot of dishonest servants around him, who considered it their duty to cheat their master as much as they could. Thinking, too, that the agent had, as he seemed, a deal of influence over the Raja, he consented when he came next day about the order to bring plenty of money with him. He did return next morning, and he was at once asked by the fat Hindu how much money he had brought. Mr. A. said he had Rs. 5,000, although in reality he had nothing, but he was determined to get a final interview with the Raja as to the order for the cavalry outfits. His Highness appeared once more, and beckoning to his agent the fat Hindu, Mr. A. heard him whisper in Hindustani:

"Has he got the money?"

"Yes," replied the agent also in a whisper.

"How much?" inquired the Raja.

"Rs. 5,000!"

"That is good," muttered his Highness, and he approached Mr. A. and asked him politely if he meant to play. But Mr. A.'s suspicions were now thoroughly roused. He had no longer any doubt but that he was being imposed upon by a gang of swindlers, and he promptly replied that he had not come there to gamble but on business. Did his Highness want those cavalry outfits or not ? This sharp retort the Raja received very calmly and said :

"Well, I am sorry I have not yet heard from my friend, but you can go on with the hundred outfits for myself."

Mr. A. was not, however, to be put off with that, and said that before he could go on making the outfits, he would require a substantial sum in advance. As was to be expected, the Raja would not pay the sum named. He merely said he would have to satisfy himself as to the genuineness of Mr. A.'s firm. He would, however, call on him at his office the following morning, and if Mr. A. satisfied him as to his ability to carry out the contract properly, he should have the order and the money at once.

As may be imagined, neither the Raja nor his agent have been seen by Mr. A. from that day to this, the police being informed of the matter, it would seem, from inquiries that have been made, that more than one has been swindled by the same gang in the same manner as they tried to trick Mr. A. ; but rather than admit how they have been done, they prefer to suffer their losses in silence than lay a charge against the swindlers. Until a charge is made, the police are powerless to act.

AN ALCHEMIST AND A CHUNAM-DEALER.

Sardar Abdul Ali remembers another interesting and extraordinary tale of a chunam-dealer being duped by a native alchemist, who was known by the name of Bengalee Bawa, who passed off as a saint, and apparently lived in a respectable manner. He always dressed himself in an old shawl robe, faded turban, and wore round his neck several strings of beads. His white beard, and the fact that he belonged to the priestly class, gave him the appearance of a holy man. In December 1865 Dwarkadas Dayabhoy, a shroff, called up one Pandoo Ratanj and told him that the holy man was possessed of marvellous power, which he would be willing to communicate to his disciple, who might choose to learn alchemy. Pandoo showed his desire to learn alchemy which might at once bring him wealth. Dwarkadas then took him to the alchemist's house, and told the Bawa (saint) that he had brought Pandoo to learn alchemy. The Bawa told him to go away then and to call on the following day, and bring with him Rs. 600. They then left the presence of the holy man, and the next day returned again, bringing with them another man named Ananta, and also Rs. 600 in a canvas bag. The man of science was at home when they came in, and immediately commenced to burn incense and muttered some Cabalastic words; this was continued for about an hour. He then produced a box, and told Pandoo to give him the money (Rs. 600) and take away the box. As he said this, he managed to throw a mystic light into the box, which made it appear to be filled with glittering gold coins. Pandoo therefore gave him the bag with the Rs. 600 in it. As soon as the holy man got possession of the money, he said to Pandoo, that as it was past 9 o'clock at night, he had better not take away the box till the following morning, as the police would be sure to stop him. Accordingly he left with his friend Ananta, and returned on the following morning at 7 o'clock, but could not find the Bawa. They were kept going backward and forward to the house successively for three days before they could see the alchemist again. On the third day they were fortunate enough to fall in with the object of their search, but when he was asked for the box of sovereigns he told them he had no box, and that he did not know what they meant, and that he would have nothing to do with them. Upon this Pandoo prostrated himself before the man of science, and saying (imploringly), "Bawa, I am a poor man, don't ruin me." The Bawa replied, "Don't tease me in this manner, go away, and come to-morrow." They accordingly left his presence and returned on the morrow, when the alchemist told Pandoo to go away again and fetch an eight-anna stamped paper. Pandoo told him that he had not got eight annas, whereupon the Bawa magnanimously handed him a rupee, and bade him go and procure the paper. Ananta, thereupon, went out and obtained the paper, when the old man told his dupe that he might then go away and come in the evening. On returning in the evening they found Dwarkadas there; he had written something on the paper. There were also four or five other men present, when the Bawa insisted upon Pandoo signing the paper, and when he had done so, the Bawa handed him over twenty-six bright yellow coins, saying, "Now go away, I owe you nothing." Previous to that, on the first occasion of his going there, the Bawa gave him a golden sovereign, which he found to be a genuine coin, valued at Rs. 10 in the bazar, but the twenty-six coins which he received were all found to be worthless when examined. The matter was reported to the police, and the Bawa was arrested under a warrant issued by the Senior Magistrate at the instance of Pandoo. The case was committed to the Sessions for trial. The Bawa declared that when he gave the coins to Pandoo they were all examined by the shroff, but the complainant averred that they were examined by Dwarkadas, who was a confiderate of the prisoner. Prisoner said that he claimed to have his guineas returned to him by virtue of the paper signed by the prosecutor, and that he was determined to sue him for the same in the Small Causes Court.

The complainant's story was indeed painful. He had lost all his earnings. He told the Court that Rs. 600 were the proceeds of the sale of chunam during the Dewali, when he sold some Rs. 1,500 worth, as a great deal was used at that time for white-washing houses. It was Dwarkadas who told him that the Bawa could transmute metals, and it was at his suggestion that he became a student in alchemy. After some other evidence had been taken, the stamped paper, which was found in the prisoner's house, was produced and translated; it purported to be a receipt for twenty-six sovereigns lent to Pandoo by the prisoner, which was to be paid in nine days' time, and was signed by the prosecutor and attested by a number of signatures. So far everything was done in a complete manner to outwit the complaint.

His Lordship afterwards asked a witness how he knew whether the guineas were good or bad ? He admitted that he took one of them up in his hand and examined it, but did not look at the others.

The prisoner here indignantly asked the witness if he was going to join the other persons against him, but the witness replied what he said was the truth.

When called upon for his defence, the prisoner frankly admitted that he was not versed in law, and said he had come from the seaport of Karachi, and was a holy man. He assured the jury that he had lent the prosecutor the twenty-six guineas, and was to have been repaid in nine days, but before three had elapsed, they got up this plot against him, and he was a victim of a deep-laid conspiracy, which was planned in order to cheat him out of his money. He had not summoned any witness, as he was told to reserve them for his action in the Small Causes Court when he sued the prosecutor. His Lordship was about to sum up, when the foreman of the jury said that they had agreed to their verdict and found the prisoner guilty, but recommended him to mercy on account of his age.

His Lordship then sentenced him to six months' rigorous imprisonment.

A BHATHIA IN SEARCH OF A WIFE "SOLD."

About the same time as the Bawa was convicted, professional poisoners abounded, not only in Bombay, but in all parts of India. It was believed that in the no less form than poisoning secret murders of men were encompassed in those days. Against the burglar, the garotter, and even the thug a man may at least struggle for his life, and in some instances successfully, but against the secret poisoner there can be no resistance. In 1861 Dr. James Irving, Civil Surgeon at Allahbad, in describing the modes of operation of the professional poisoners in other parts of India, said that the poisoner makes up to a traveller, finds out where he is going, professes that he is going to some place in the same direction, and asks to be allowed to accompany him. Either on the road, at the halting-ground, or in the *serai* the poisoner watches for and obtains his opportunity, and administers the poison. This he effects in various ways, and one of the most common is to give it mixed in flour from which the bread is made, or in the bread itself, and great address is often shown in the manner in which the poisoner manages this. From a confession made to the worthy Doctor by a female poisoner, it appears that she was one of a gang of men and women who obtained a living by drugging travellers and others, and stealing from them such valuables as they possessed. The members of the band have a chief who employs, and to whom they make over the property stolen, and who gives them a half of all they earn. When they receive the order from the master of the gang, they start on their several expeditions; one man generally accompanies each girl, and very often an old woman joins them. When a traveller, who seems likely to have money, is discovered, the girl, who is provided with a few jewels and is generally well-dressed, manages to attract his notice, and pretends she has lost her husband and his party. The traveller, beguiled by this or some other specious story, or ensnared by her blandishments, commences an acquaintance, and permits the woman to accompany him. She chooses her opportunity to mix poison with his food, and while he is in a state of insensibility, she purloins his valuables, and again joins her party, which, though not immediately in sight, has never been very far from the girl and her victim.

In many instances the poison is mixed with sweetmeats. The poison generally employed by these people is the common *datoora*, which grows so plentifully in most parts of Western India. The seeds, having been ground, are mixed, as above said, with flour or bread, and being almost tasteless, are not easily detected. Sometimes a decoction, made from one or other part of the plant, is used; at others, *datoora* is mixed with arsenic, or oleander, or arsenic is administered alone. It is very difficult to trace the culprits, owing to the fact that their victims are left in a state of stupefaction, and seldom recover till the criminals have placed miles between them in unknown directions. The persons, also, by whom the drug is administered are generally in such disguises, that they could scarcely be recognized. It was pointed out that the greatest difficulty attending such matters was that, "in nine cases out of ten of robbery by means of deleterious drugs, it is only when death has been the result, that the police have become aware of the crime having been committed, as, in the generality of cases, persons when awakened to their senses have been too glad to have escaped with their lives, to care to make any complaint of having been robbed." Moreover, the effect of the *datoora* poison is generally very speedy, so much so that persons who have been drugged with it state they have little or no recollection of anything that occurred after partaking of the poison. A curious case illustrative of the above remarks came to light in July 1866. There was a certain gang of swindlers then in Bombay, who made it their business to live on ill-gotten gains, and in their nefarious business they were assisted by two or three pretty-looking girls, who were their kept mistresses, and who allured people to their dens, told them they were spinsters belonging to a respectable family, and were desirous of marrying some suitable persons. Enchanted by their beauty and captivated by their artful flirtations young men fell into their snares and married them; but only to find next morning that the brides and their so-called relations (accomplices) had disappeared with the property and jewellery after administering dhatura to the bridegrooms. In this manner a man named Moorar Topee was cheated by the gang and four persons. Chappa Wasson, Dayal Soonderjee, Purshotam Kessowjee, Dayee woman, and Jaswadda woman were together charged with abetment of conspiracy, cheating, and abetment, by which they dishonestly induced Moorar Topee to deliver to them money and ornaments to the value of Rs. 7,405. It was brought out in evidence that the prosecutor was a Bhathia by caste and a broker. Some time prior to his misadventure he had the misfortune to lose his wife; and left with two children, naturally wished to obtain another wife to look after them. Of course, being a Hindoo, it was necessary that the wife should be a member of the same caste, and also according to the custom of the caste that she should be an unmarried person, and a virgin, as no widows are allowed to marry again in the Bhathia caste. It seemed that Dayee, as a member of that caste, had been for some time negotiating marriages between different members of the caste; and she, becoming aware that prosecutor was looking out for a wife, went to him and told him that she could provide him with a wife. She stated that a girl of eighteen had just come down to Bombay from her native country, that she was a nice girl, and in every way suited to make him a desirable wife. The prosecutor, considering this to be a desirable connection, expressed his willingness to enter into arrangements for marrying the girl. Dayee then started that he would require to pay a considerable sum of money. Prosecutor mentioned Rs. 7,000 in cash and Rs. 1,200 worth of ornaments; but Dayee said he would require to pay Rs. 8,000 in cash and Rs. 2,000 worth of ornaments, as also Rs. 1,000 to her as a fee. Dayee then brought Chappa and Dayal, and represented them to be the girl's uncles. Eventually it was agreed that Moorarjee should pay Rs. 7,500, and present ornaments to the value of Rs. 1,200, and that he should give Dayee Rs. 1,000 for her fee. It was then arranged that the parties were to meet on 8th July for the purpose of going on with the ceremony, and on that day Moorarjee sent his brother with the Rs. 1,000. Prosecutor and his friends then went to a place called Hajee Moosa's Oart near Parel, where they met Dayee, Chappa, and Dayal. When they had met, these three prisoners told Moorarjee that his intended wife was a nice girl, and that she had a younger sister prettier than herself; and prosecutor then arranged that as his nephew, being unmarried, might marry the sister. Prosecutor remained at Parel, and on Wednesday a shigram arrived with Chappa, Dayal, Dayee, and his intended bride Jaswadda, whose face, according to custom, was thickly covered with a veil. Moorarjee then handed over Rs. 7,400 and the ornaments. The intended bride retired to another room to have the ornaments put on, and then came out again, still covered with her veil. The marriage ceremony was then performed, and the parties afterwards came to Moorarjee's house in Bombay. Of course, according to the custom of their caste, they could not pass the night of their marriage together; and when prosecutor went into Jaswadda's room next morning, found that she had gone, taking with her all the ornaments, a saree, and several other articles he had presented to her. Information was then given to the police, and the prisoners were apprehended. It was then discovered that Juswadda was of another caste altogether, and had been in the "keeping" of Purshotam Kessowjee.

The prisoners were found guilty by the jury, and his Lordship in passing sentence upon them remarked that this was not the first time that the girl had gone through a sham marriage and robbed respectable persons, who were unwilling to come forward and expose the gang because they were afraid of loosing their respect. His Lordship sentenced each of the four prisoners to four years' imprisonment, with hard labour.

Thus a clever gang of swindlers was broken up.